WAR'S DESOLATING
SCOURGE

Joseph W. Danielson

War's Desolating Scourge

THE UNION'S OCCUPATION OF NORTH ALABAMA

 University Press of Kansas

Published by the University Press of Kansas (Lawrence, Kansas 66045), which was organized by the Kansas Board of Regents and is operated and funded by Emporia State University, Fort Hays State University, Kansas State University, Pittsburg State University, the University of Kansas, and Wichita State University

Library of Congress Cataloging-in-Publication Data

Danielson, Joseph Wesley.

War's desolating scourge : the Union's occupation of north Alabama / Joseph W. Danielson.

p. cm. — (Modern war studies)

Includes bibliographical references and index.

ISBN 978-0-7006-1844-6 (cloth : alk. paper)

1. Alabama—History—Civil War, 1861–1865—Social aspects. 2. Military occupation—Social aspects—Alabama—History—19th century.

3. Civil-military relations—Alabama—History—19th century. 4. United States—History—Civil War, 1861–1865—Occupied territories. I. Title.

E551.D36 2012

976.1'05—dc23

2012007158

British Library Cataloguing-in-Publication Data is available.

Printed in the United States of America

10 9 8 7 6 5 4 3 2 1

For my wife and best friend, Lauren Gill Danielson

and

In memory of Neal M. Hughes

Contents

Acknowledgments

This manuscript, and the dissertation and thesis that preceded it, could not have been completed without the hard work, advice, and support of archivists and librarians from across the South and Midwest. When I first started this project, Ranée Pruitt, archivist at the Huntsville/Madison County Public Library, was an immense help and offered several suggestions about where else I needed to go. More recently, she supplied me with a few photographs to use in the manuscript. Toni Carter, a reference librarian at Auburn University's Ralph Brown Draughon Library, tracked down the page number of an important source that I had lost during the final stages of writing. I additionally want to thank all the archivists, librarians, and staff from the following institutions for their expertise and encouragement: the Abraham Lincoln Presidential Library, State Historical Society of Iowa, Indianapolis Historical Society, Robert W. Woodruff Library at Emory University, Alabama Department of Archives and History, W. S. Hoole Special Collections Library at the University of Alabama, Southern Historical Collection, and Duke University's William R. Perkins Library. I also wish to thank those who have made primary sources more accessible through the Internet.

Working with the staff at the University Press of Kansas has been a delight. Michael Briggs, the editor in chief, has been enthusiastic about my topic from the beginning. He was patient as I worked through numerous revisions and motivated me to meet the final deadline. Mike also made sure that the manuscript that I initially submitted, which was an unrevised version of my dissertation, was sent to reviewers who understood that it was a work in progress. The constructive criticisms and suggestions made by Stephen D. Engle and Margaret M. Storey were invaluable to the creation of a final product that I am proud of. Mike also put me in touch with George Skoch, who created the maps for the manuscript. These maps far exceeded my expectations. Susan Schott and Larisa Martin have also been wonderful to work with. They regularly updated me on issues related to marketing and production, respectively, and promptly responded to my questions with a sense of cheerfulness. Kathryn Rogers served as my copyeditor and saved me from what would have been several embarrassing errors.

I have been fortunate to have had a number of remarkable teachers and mentors during my thirty-year career as a student. In the fall of 1997, I enrolled in a composition class taught by Dale Norris at Des Moines Area Community College (DMACC). Over the course of the semester, Dale changed my attitude toward education and inspired me to never settle for being an average student. At the University of Northern Iowa, I found myself in several courses taught by energetic and gifted historians. John Baskerville gave me my first in-depth introduction to African American history. Thomas Connors heightened my interest in Irish history and helped me secure a sizable research grant that sent me to Ireland for nearly two weeks in search of old gravestones and local pubs. As interested as I became in Irish history, Wallace Hettle made the American Civil War too enticing to pass up; he also gave me a list of graduate schools to apply to. One of them was the University of Alabama. During my first semester in Tuscaloosa, I emailed Wally for advice on potential research topics. He emailed back and discussed at length how each prospective historian needs to find his or her own research topics. After elaborating this point, he closed with the suggestion that I look at what was going on in North Alabama during the Civil War. I am really glad I took his advice. At Alabama, I was again surrounded by outstanding historians. Kari Frederickson, Lisa Lindquist-Dorr, and Joshua D. Rothman furthered my burgeoning interest in southern history, while John Beeler, Harold Selesky, and Howard Jones did the same for military history. George C. Rable, who co-directed my dissertation, played a crucial role in helping me turn the dissertation into a publishable manuscript. His meticulous read of the manuscript and honest feedback strengthened many of my arguments and tightened up my prose. One of my few regrets about my time at Alabama was that I did not take more of Dr. Rable's courses. In the spring of 2002, I took a seminar course taught by Tony A. Freyer. Over the next several years, he helped me develop what I readily admit was a very rough paper on the 1862 Union occupation into a M. A. thesis, a dissertation, and finally this manuscript. Our meetings on Friday afternoons motivated me to stay on task and were quite entertaining when we delved into topics unrelated to the occupations. During these years, I got to know his wife, Marjorie, quite well. Tony also deserves credit for telling Mike Briggs about my research and urging me to send Mike a copy of the dissertation. By the time I graduated from Alabama, Tony had become a mentor and a friend.

In the spring of 2010, Rick Dawson hired me as an adjunct to teach western civilization at DMACC's West Campus. Several months later, I accepted a full-time position to teach American history at DMACC's Ankeny campus, the very campus I had attended back in the mid- to late-1990s. I could not ask for a better group of administrators, colleagues, and staff. Many had important roles in the completion of the manuscript. The conversations I had with Bradley Dyke strengthened my argument on the early stages of Reconstruction in North Alabama. He also introduced me to the Des Moines Civil War Roundtable. Lisa Ossian graciously offered advice on writing a book and the importance of meeting deadlines. Katherine Dowdell-Hommerding has been an exceptional mentor. Jim Stick (also a former teacher), Kari Hensen, Dale Norris, Charles Lauritsen, Glenda Johnson, Joanne Dudgeon, Ronn Newby, Barb Schmidt, Hollie Coon, Kate Halverson, Shirley Sandoval, Randy Jedele, Paul Byrd, Judy Hauser, Bonne Doron, David Hauser (another former teacher), Rudy Harris, Rosena Bakari, Maura Nelson, Maria Cochran, Michael "Miggs" Hubbard, Darwin Pagnac, Mary West, Will Zhang, Dennis Kellogg, John Liepa, and Judy Vogel welcomed me to DMACC with open arms and have offered encouraging words as I finished the revisions. I also want to thank my students for their support and for making my job so much fun.

I would not be where I am today without my friends and family. Ryan Cerveny has been a lifelong friend, though our friendship has meant putting up with his favorite sports teams. While writing the manuscript, Heather Hutt Kearney and I spent several hours over coffee or via email discussing my research and the extent to which it might apply to present-day affairs. During my first semester at Alabama, Neal Hughes, the most gregarious person I ever met, befriended me and urged me to start attending a weekly Friday social gathering of history geeks. For the next few years, a core group consisting of Neal, John Beeler, Rob Riser, Amy Crowson, Chuck Clark, Christian McWhirter, Kevin Windham, Mike Mansfield, and I met over cheap beer (or at least John and I drank cheap beer) and decent food. We had a good time at the graduate/faculty gatherings at Boone Lodge as well. Still, nothing beat taking a break from researching and writing like college football in Tuscaloosa. On these Saturdays, Glenn Brasher, Kevin, Michael and Heather Hoekstra, Christian and Corrin McWhirter, Justin and Brooke Turner, John Hooks, Jimmy Burford, Craig Burt, Jeremy and Heather Pressgrove, Kris Teters, Stephen McCullough, Westley Keiser, and Lauren and I made lifelong memories cheering on the Crimson Tide. Rob, Christian, Glenn, Kris, Matthew Downs, and Ryan Floyd either read parts of what turned into the manuscript or told me of sources I needed to consult. So, too, did Neal. He went on a number of research trips with me and let me stay at his place when he moved back to North Alabama. Even in his final stages of cancer, Neal selflessly took it upon himself to scour the Internet for resources that might benefit me. He was also responsible for getting me to adopt an abandoned flat-coated retriever puppy. For several years, Chester faithfully took me on walks to clear my mind and lay beside me as I worked on my research. Like many graduate students, I sometimes questioned whether graduate school was right for me. At one point in the summer of 2006, I considered taking a break. Ryan Floyd and Stephanie Bain persuaded me to stay, and I am infinitely better off for heeding their advice. Soon thereafter, I began dating my now-wife, Lauren Gill.

My parents, John and Beverly Danielson, instilled in me a love of history, and their integrity, compassion, and work ethic continue to serve as a model for the type of person, husband, parent, and historian I aspire to be. I proudly count myself among those whose interest in American history was encouraged at an early age by parents who stopped at countless rest areas to read historical markers to their children. As my interest in the Civil War grew, they took me on spring break and summer trips from our home in Indianola, Iowa, to destinations like Appomattox, Fredericksburg, Ft. Sumter, Andersonville, Gettysburg, and both of Thomas "Stonewall" Jackson's gravesites. I also appreciated Mom and Dad's timely financial support while I was in graduate school. My older siblings, John, Jean, Jennifer, and Jason (yes, all J's), have been a constant source of support. Jean in particular played a pivotal role in helping me hone my writing and analytical skills. The bulk of revisions to the manuscript took place after Lauren and I returned to my hometown in 2009. During this process, we took periodic respites from the manuscript to go fishing or engage in other outdoor activities with Jason, my sister-in-law Jessica, and their two children, Drew and Lauren. My aunt P. K. routinely inquired about the progress of the manuscript during our regular phone calls. I am saddened that P. K.'s husband, Donnell "Mo" Moran, did not live to see the completion of the manuscript. The summers I spent in Omaha, where Mo would put me to work in his backyard, are among my most cherished memories. While dating, Lauren and I made several trips from Tuscaloosa to her home in Marietta, Georgia. While there, Terry and Charlotte Gill, my father- and mother-in-law, kindly let me use their office to work. Whenever I achieved a milestone in the various stages of the dissertation, manuscript, and life in general, I could always expect a phone call or email from

Terry or Charlotte. The same is true of Erin Gill Scott and Caitlin Gill Kimberlin, my sisters-in-law. Words cannot adequately express what Lauren has meant to my life. She has enthusiastically supported my academic pursuits and never complained about the untold hours I spent examining sources or writing. At both the dissertation and manuscript stage, she repeatedly read and reread chapters as they evolved. Lauren saved me from an untold number of grammatical mistakes and offered insightful suggestions for strengthening my arguments. This was especially the case with the introduction. Her unfailing encouragement and faith in me made completing the manuscript possible. With this project ending, I eagerly look forward to being able to spend more time with the woman who has bettered my life in every possible way.

While dozens of individuals contributed to the success of this manuscript, I alone am responsible for any errors.

Introduction

       Abraham Lincoln was convinced that the majority of white southerners did not support disunion. Aside from South Carolina, the president claimed that "there is much reason to believe that the Union men are the majority in many, if not in every other one, of the so-called seceded States. The contrary has not been demonstrated in any one of them."[1] The president's appraisal of the strength of Union sentiment in the South was in line with the views of many Republicans who believed that a relatively small number of influential proslavery advocates had tricked their fellow white southerners into supporting secession. To awaken secessionists' dormant fidelity to the Union, Lincoln did his best to reassure them that the federal government had no intention of violating their rights. On the issue of slavery, Lincoln admitted that he had no authority to "directly or indirectly . . . interfere with the institution . . . in the States where it exists."[2] Given the president's previous support for the controversial Fugitive Slave Act of 1850 and a proposed constitutional amendment protecting the peculiar institution in the South, he likely meant what he said. By taking a conciliatory tone toward Confederate civilians, Lincoln anticipated the restoration of federal authority in the South with minimal conflict and bloodshed.[3]

Union soldiers would play an important role in extending this olive branch to wayward southerners. As the bluecoats marched south, they were told to respect Confederate civilians' property rights and civil liberties in the expectation that it would convince the prodigal sons and daughters of the South to return to the government of their forefathers. In the western theater, General Don Carlos Buell, commander of the Army of the Ohio, served as Lincoln's chief proponent of conciliation. Throughout his involvement in the war, this 1841 West Point graduate and one-time slave owner was committed to achieving Union victory while not disrupting the southern social order. To further this objective, he gave those under his command explicit instructions to safeguard the rights of Confederate civilians.[4] Soldiers who disobeyed his orders faced potential court-martial. With a conservative-minded general in charge of thousands of Union troops, Lincoln had reason to expect that federal authority would be restored to that region.

Northern proponents of conciliation underestimated white southerners' support for secession. Unionism did exist in the seceded states, but not nearly to the extent conciliationists assumed. As Federal troops entered the Confederacy and came into contact with Confederate civilians, they soon realized that these men and women did not desire an amicable return to the Union; they were determined to achieve independence. Over the preceding years, if not generations, white southerners had come to view themselves as culturally and politically distinct. While the North became more industrialized and market oriented, the South remained agrarian and paternalistic. The inability of the two sections to make lasting compromises over slavery lay at the heart of the sectional discord. As America grew in population and expanded westward, the divisive issue over slavery in the national territories and future states deepened the divide between the North and South and led to acts of violence stretching from the territory of Kansas to the floor of the United States Senate to the arsenal at Harpers Ferry. The growth of antislavery sentiment in the North and the creation of a political party openly hostile to the expansion of the peculiar institution pushed southerners to the precipice of disunion. The election of a Republican president in 1860 proved to many white southerners that they could no longer remain part of the Union. To protect themselves from northern assaults on their rights as white Americans, they began calling for secession conventions.[5]

North Alabama—encompassing both the Tennessee Valley and the Hill counties regions—is not often thought of as a bastion of southern or Confederate nationalism, even though there were more supporters of the Confederacy in the area than unionists or those claiming to be neutral.[6] As the Confederacy took form in early 1861, a large portion of the white inhabitants of North Alabama became fervent Confederates; men of fighting age flocked to recruiting stations, while those who remained behind awaited the return of their loved ones and a future free from northern tyranny. At the outset of war, Rebels in North Alabama—like those from across the Confederacy—were nourished by a set of core beliefs in the continuation of Herrenvolk democracy, the heritage of the American Revolution, divine guidance, and southern military gallantry. White southerners' expectation that Lincoln, and Republicans in general, intended to inflict irreparable damage to the institution of slavery led white southerners into secession. Even though a majority of white southerners did not own slaves, nonslaveholders supported Confederate independence in part to ensure the perpetuation of a racial hierarchy where a white person, regardless of his or her station in life, was still inherently better than an African American. Secessionists claimed that northerners' interference, or perceived interference, in matters related to slavery violated their constitutional rights and dishonored the sacrifices southerners had made in the American Revolution. Disunion, Confederates argued, had become necessary to protect the legacy of their Revolutionary era ancestors and the ideals of the Founding Fathers. In their upcoming fight against northerners, Confederates were certain that an independent South was part of God's plan. Through the Lord's guidance and protection, secessionists believed that they would soon be free from an immoral and corrupt North. Imbued with patriotic and religious fervor, Confederate civilians looked to their menfolk in the armies to vanquish the enemy and secure a victory that had been ordained by providence. In their fight for independence, North Alabama Confederates would rely on these fundamental values to sustain them when Federal troops arrived on their doorstep determined to return the region to the Union, even if it meant discarding the policy of conciliation.[7]

"I AM FOR ALABAMA UNDER ANY
AND ALL CIRCUMSTANCES"

After decades of threatening to secede from the United States to protect the institution of slavery, pro-secession southerners finally made their move when northerners elected a president whose Republican platform was heretical to the South. Secessionists in Alabama followed in the footsteps of South Carolina, Mississippi, and Florida to make their state the fourth to secede. Initial support for immediate secession in Alabama was far from unanimous. In North Alabama, issues specific to the region led citizens to send cooperationist delegates to the secession convention. Cooperationists, like immediate secessionists, agreed in the legitimacy of secession and were uneasy that a Republican was in the White House, but they did not want to rush into disunion. The North Alabama delegation diligently worked to delay matters, but it was not enough to stop the momentum of immediate secessionists. Even though cooperationists and their constituents could not prevent immediate secession from happening, they did not abandon their state. Instead, they rejoiced alongside immediate secessionists that they were now free from northern oppression. Within a month of Alabama's break from the Union, seven southern states came together to form the Confederate States of America and draft a constitution that explicitly guaranteed the right to own African American slaves. Throughout this crisis, Abraham Lincoln and a number of high-ranking Republicans were convinced that most southerners did not really want to secede, much less desire armed conflict. The president and his Republican cohorts were mistaken in assuming that a large unionist block existed in the South; southerners were committed to achieving Confederate independence. After Lincoln called for 75,000 ninety-day recruits in response to the Confederates' capture of Fort Sumter, four more slave states left the Union. In North Alabama, Confederate men and women started mobilizing for war with every confidence of winning southern independence.[1]

In the years preceding the 1860 election, the discord between northern and southern whites over issues related to slavery and the fundamental differences between the free North and slave South led to the creation of a southern identity that was ideologically distinct from the North.[2] In Alabama, southern nationalists took one of two approaches toward their place within the United States after Lincoln's election. Immediate secessionists, who were most heavily concentrated in the central and southern counties, viewed the election as a triumph of "Black Republicanism" and a dire threat to the rights of white southerners. They argued that too much was at stake for white Alabamians to remain in the Union; to protect the rights of slaveholders and ensure that the sanctity of whiteness was upheld, Alabama must be taken out of the Union. William Lowndes Yancey was the leader, and most zealous proponent, of immediate secession in Alabama. For over a decade, he had been agitating for southern independence and intended to use the 1860 election to make his dream a reality. As a delegate to the 1860 Democratic National Convention in Charleston, South Carolina, his opposition to frontrunner Stephen A. Douglas of Illinois and Douglas's policy of popular sovereignty fractured the Democratic Party, which substantially increased the chances of a Republican winning the presidency. Spurred on by Yancey's agitation, immediate secessionists would comprise a majority of delegates at Alabama's secession convention.

While there were immediate secessionists in North Alabama, the region was dominated by cooperationists who were also committed to maintaining Herrenvolk democracy in the South and who believed in the legitimacy of secession. There was no uniform cooperationist stance in North Alabama. Some cooperationists demanded that northerners pass an irrevocable constitutional amendment protecting southerners' rights as slave owners. Under this option, southerners could maintain their distinctiveness as part of the United States and never again fear federal encroachment on their peculiar institution. If northerners rejected this demand, these cooperationists would support secession. Other cooperationists embraced a wait-and-see approach toward Lincoln's actions as president. Any egregious assault by the Republican president on southerners' constitutional right to own, transport, or recover runaway slaves would result in secession. Another strain of cooperationists called for collective southern secession to increase their chances of creating lasting independence. What brought these various types of cooperationism together was a shared belief that immediate secession was not in southerners' best interest. Even though North Alabama cooperationists acknowledged the legitimacy of secession and were prepared to secede if necessary, their hesitation during a time of heightened emotion appeared to some as a sign of weak commitment to defending the rights of white southerners or that they were more closely aligned with unionists. A Milwaukee newspaper editor went as far as to state that North Alabamians were "almost *unanimously* opposed to secession."[3] Cooperationists were by and large pragmatic southern nationalists who advocated caution during a moment of intense uncertainty. When the time came for secession delegates to meet in Montgomery to debate potential disunion, North Alabama cooperationists sought delay above all else.

The secession crisis placed cooperationists in a precarious situation. They shared immediate secessionists' belief in the doctrine of secession and agreed that a Republican president posed a serious threat to slavery, but they were unwilling to support immediate secession or separate acts of disunion. Cooperationists' opposition to immediate secession stemmed in part from their concern that a hurried secession could negatively impact their region's economy or lead to an invasion by Federal soldiers. Collectively, the region had stronger economic ties to markets outside Alabama than to markets in the central and southern portions of the state. With no railroads connecting North Alabama to central Alabama and with the mountains in North Alabama making overland transportation prohibitively expensive, civilians were dependent upon the Tennessee River and regional railroads to transport their goods and livestock out of state. By the time secession delegates met in Montgomery, Mississippi had already seceded, and it appeared Georgia would follow suit, but there was no indication whether Tennessee would leave the Union. If Alabama seceded and Tennessee did not, North Alabamians could find themselves cut off from important markets in southern and central Tennessee and be threatened with invasion.[4]

Between 1850 and 1860, North Alabama's economy had done quite well. The number of farms in North Alabama had grown steadily over the decade, increasing from 12,137 in 1850 to 14,416 by 1860. The growth in the number of farms was particularly pronounced in the Hill counties.[5] Over the course of the 1850s, North Alabamians brought an additional 400,000 acres of farmland into cultivation. The total cash value of North Alabama farms increased dramatically during these years. In 1850, they were collectively worth roughly $17.1 million; by the end of the decade, the value had more than doubled to about $36.6 million.[6] The most valuable and fertile farms were those along the northern and southern banks of the Tennessee River with access to both the river and railroad lines.[7] As the value of North Alabama farms increased during the 1850s, so did North Alabamians' investment in farming implements and machinery. Such investments increased by 25 percent (from $1.2 million to $1.6 million) between 1850 and 1860.[8] Less fertile land, fewer slaves, and bringing additional acres of land into cultivation might be the reasons farmers in the Hill counties had to devote more capital to farming implements and machinery than their Tennessee Valley counterparts. Still, the overall prosperity residents of the Hill counties were experiencing made them an important part of the regional economy and undoubtedly influenced their cooperationist stance during the secession crisis. The raising and selling of livestock was one of many business ventures that might be adversely affected by immediate secession or Tennessee remaining in the Union. North Alabamians who participated in the livestock trade saw the value of their livestock increase from about $5.2 million in 1850 to over $9.4 million by the end of the decade.[9] Those people living in the Tennessee Valley who could transport their product by river or rail reaped the largest payoffs. By 1860, 65.5 percent of livestock (based on the total value of all livestock) and 63.3 percent of slaughtered livestock in North Alabama came from the Tennessee Valley. For North Alabamians engaged in any trade dependent on markets or partnerships that lay outside the state, there was no guarantee that these crucial components of their economic livelihood would remain open if Alabama independently left the Union. The efforts by immediate secessionists to get their state out of the Union as soon as possible threatened the economic prosperity North Alabamians had experienced during the 1850s. Moreover, if immediate secession occurred and Tennessee chose to remain in the Union, North Alabama residents might find themselves on a hostile border subject to military invasion. North Alabama cooperationists saw the need to protect their state from a potentially oppressive Republican regime, but if secession was the only option, it needed to be done in a manner that did not bring disaster to their region.[10]

While many cooperationists worked to remain in the Union, they were gravely concerned about having a Republican president. As with their white brethren in central and southern Alabama, they wholeheartedly supported slavery and would not tolerate any federal interference with the institution. J. W. Clay noticed a growth in North Alabamians' support for some type of secession soon after Lincoln's election. Clay, who was editor of the *Huntsville Democrat*, the son of a former Alabama governor, and the brother of a sitting U.S. senator, remarked that the "secession sentiment seems to be growing rapidly in this section of the State . . . and is making favorable progress in other counties of the Tennessee Valley."[11] Jeremiah Clemens, a resident of Huntsville who would become the cooperationists' undeclared leader at Alabama's secession convention, considered the "mere election of Lincoln . . . upon a platform hostile to our institutions . . . an outrage." Still, Clemens and his cooperationist colleagues hoped to stave off immediate secession when the convention met in early January.[12]

Cooperationists' resistance to immediate secession and the relatively low number of slaves in the region has contributed to the mistaken perception that white North Alabamians were not as "intimately involved" with the peculiar institution as other regions in the state.[13] Out of the nearly 435,100 slaves that lived in Alabama in 1860, only 63,500 (roughly 14.6 percent) resided in North Alabama. In 1860, over 10,000 slaves and nearly 2,000 slave owners resided in the nine Hill counties of North Alabama. On average, each county had a slave population of 10.5 percent of the total population. The counties of Cherokee and St. Clair had the highest percentage of slaves, with 16.35 percent and 16.05 percent, respectively. Marshall County followed with a slave population just below 16 percent of the total population. The percentage of slaves in the remaining Hill counties ranged from 13.25 percent in Fayette down to 3.4 percent in Winston.[14] Of the 1,955 slaveholders—which equated to 2.26 percent of the total white population in the Hill counties—498 lived in Cherokee County. The majority of these slaveholders owned between 1 and 10 slaves. Only 27 would have been considered planters—those who owned twenty or more slaves. Aside from Winston County's 14 slaveholders, the number of slave owners in the other Hill counties varied from 102 in Walker County to 257 in St. Clair. Although the number of slaveholders in the Hill counties was quite low, the region's white inhabitants were still tied to the institution of slavery. Individuals who did not own slaves

Map 1. Counties of Alabama, special designation of the Tennessee Valley and Hill counties

could borrow or rent them from their slave-owning relatives or neighbors; some yeoman farmers would have aspired to own slaves of their own one day. Even if a white person was too poor to rent a slave, the color of his or her skin kept them in a social status above that of a black person.

The number of slaves and masters was much larger in the seven counties that form the Tennessee Valley. As of 1860, there were about 51,800 slaves and over 4,000 slave owners living within these counties. Collectively, slaves accounted for roughly 42.6 percent of the total Tennessee Valley population in 1860.[15] Aside from Jackson County, where 18.7 percent of the inhabitants were slaves, each of the remaining counties had a slave population of at least 32 percent of the total population. Two of these counties, Limestone and Madison, had a larger slave population than white population. Slaves accounted for 53 percent (8,085 to 7,215) of the population in Limestone County, while in Madison County they represented 55.5 percent (14,573 to 11,685) of the total population.[16] Whites in Lawrence County narrowly outnumbered slaves 7,173 to 6,788 (48.6 percent). Of the more than 4,000 slave owners in North Alabama in 1860, 1,117 resided in Madison County, which ranked the sixth largest in number of slaveholders in the state. The remaining six Tennessee Valley counties all ranked in the top 37.[17] While the majority of slaveholders in the Tennessee Valley owned fewer than ten slaves, planters were well represented. In Madison County, nearly 20 percent of all slave owners were planters. Ten masters owned over 100 slaves each. The percentage of planters among the slaveholding population was even higher in Franklin County (23.5 percent) and Lawrence County (30 percent). Eight planters in Lawrence reported owning more than 100 slaves each. Only in Morgan and Jackson counties did planters comprise less than 15 percent of the slave-owning population. Aside from these two counties, the percentage of planters in each of the remaining Tennessee Valley counties is comparable to the percentage in several of the counties located along Alabama's Black Belt, where support for immediate secession was quite strong.[18] Despite the smaller number of slaves in North Alabama, compared to the rest of the state, the region's white population was clearly interested in safeguarding their investments and racial hegemony from outside interference. Their initial caution during the secession crisis was not a sign of their lack of commitment to southern independence or to the institution of slavery. Yet, until Lincoln committed some overt act that threatened slavery, cooperationists continued to promote approaches to the secession crisis—simultaneous secession or at least delaying immediate secession—that best fit their particular needs.[19]

Alabama Governor Andrew B. Moore rejected cooperationists' call for patience. In early December, he called for the election of delegates who would travel to Montgomery to debate the merits of secession. The results of the December 24 election indicated a clear separation between the strength of immediatists and cooperationists. Aside from Conecuh County, voters from central and southern Alabama overwhelmingly voted for immediate secessionists to represent them in Montgomery. In northern Alabama, cooperationists carried the day in every county. When the convention convened on January 7, 1861, immediate secessionists held a 53 to 47 majority. As the minority party, cooperationists hoped to convince immediate secessionists that there were better alternatives to the crisis at hand than a hasty secession.[20]

Among the North Alabama contingent, Jeremiah Clemens was arguably the most accomplished, albeit controversial, statesman. In his youth, Clemens attended La Grange College in Florence and the University of Alabama before studying law in Kentucky. In the late 1830s, President Martin Van Buren made Clemens U.S. Attorney for the District of Northern Alabama. By 1840 the Democrat had been elected to the state legislature. Twice during this decade Clemens temporarily left politics and Alabama to fight against Mexican encroachment into Texas. During the Mexican-American War, he attained the rank of colonel. When U.S. Senator Dixon Hall Lewis died in late 1849, Alabama's state legislators picked Clemens as his replacement. After arriving in Washington, Clemens came under fire over his vacillating stance on the sectional crisis that had engulfed the nation. Initially, Clemens opposed elements of what became the 1850 Compromise, but changed his mind to please his constituents. Clemens was subsequently labeled an opportunist by his detractors in Congress and back home. This cloud of controversy hung over Clemens long enough that he was not elected to another term. After leaving public office in March 1853, Clemens moved to Memphis, Tennessee, where he became editor of the *Memphis Eagle and Enquirer*. During this time, he tried his hand at writing novels, though he never attained the same level of success as his second cousin Samuel Clemens. By the eve of the secession crisis, Clemens and his wife Mary had returned to Huntsville.[21]

A few weeks before Clemens was elected as a secession delegate, he wrote a letter to S. A. M. Wood, a fellow North Alabamian and a future Confederate officer, defending his cooperationist stance. Clemens was aware that his call for patience had been "denounced throughout the southern States" and that some southerners were even calling him a "submissionist." These verbal attacks did not bother the former U.S. senator, as he felt he was working in the best interest of all white southerners. Clemens told Wood that "the election of Lincoln is in itself no cause for disunion," but that, rather, the sectional conflicts related to slavery that preceded the election were. He urged immediate secessionists and cooperationists to "unite . . . in common demand" and lay bare to northerners the conditions under which they would remain in the Union. If northerners agreed to southerners' demands and took the necessary steps to assure compliance, "harmony will again be restored to the land." Failure by northerners to protect white southerners' constitutional rights would prove beyond a shadow of a doubt that secession was the only choice. To bridge the ideological divide between immediatists and cooperationists as well as to demonstrate to northerners the seriousness of the situation, Clemens advised that immediate secessionists tone down their fiery rhetoric. Clemens considered such talk a hindrance to collective action and might be construed by northerners as being similar to previous instances where southerners cried wolf but did not follow through with secession. Clemens, as did other cooperationists, held out hope that the creation of a united front might be enough to exact permanent concessions from northerners. If southerners were unsuccessful in such an effort, he felt secession would be unavoidable and justified.[22]

Clemens characterized immediate disunion as an impetuous move. Northerners would not allow southerners to secede from the Union without a fight despite immediate secessionists' claims to the contrary. Clemens commented to Wood that "Everyday we hear [immediate secessionists] talking of the Secession of Alabama as lightly as if it were a thing which a mere paper resolution could accomplish." He became equally frustrated when immediatists suggested that one southerner could "whip three Yankees" and come out unscathed. Upon both scores, Clemens suggested, "they are wretchedly deceived." Alabama's lack of military readiness caused Clemens immense concern. Even though he felt Alabamians had the right to secede, he also felt that they were unprepared to fight, much less win a war. After all, the industrialized North could manufacture the weapons necessary for war at a significantly quicker pace than the agrarian South. "We may assert the right [of secession] as loudly as we please," Clemens warned, "but it will be respected only when we have arms in our hands." If immediate secessionists took Alabama out of the Union before the state was sufficiently defended or received word that Tennessee would follow Alabama into disunion, Clemens asserted that "a well disciplined regiment" would have no trouble marching "from the Mississippi to the Georgia line, &

Jeremiah Clemens (Library of Congress)

never meet a force that was able to stand against them." In Clemens' opinion, immediate secessionists' dismissive attitude toward cooperationists' pragmatic approach could lead to economic, social, and political chaos in North Alabama: the "act of plunging into revolution before we are half ready is simply to invite desolation to our homes, and erect gibbets for our most prominent citizens."[23] Patience and military preparation, Clemens argued, would give Alabamians, and white southerners in general, a stronger foundation from which they could potentially fight a war of independence. He reminded Wood that the "object of the Southern people ought to be to obtain security—not to plunge into revolution for the sake of revolution—we have nothing to lose by the delay of a few months."[24] As North Alabama's most distinguished statesman, Jeremiah Clemens arrived in Montgomery, alongside his fellow cooperationists, intent on convincing immediatists that taking additional time to seek redress from the North while simultaneously preparing for war would prove more beneficial to southern nationalists than immediate secession.

Alabama was already on the road toward disunion before North Alabama cooperationists even had an opportunity to plead their case. In the days leading up to the convention, Governor Moore ordered Alabama volunteer soldiers into action. By the time the secession convention opened on January 7, the federal arsenal at Mount Vernon, along with Fort Morgan and Fort Gaines—both located in Mobile Bay—were in the hands of Alabama military personnel. When news of the capture of Fort Morgan reached Montgomery, Thomas J. McClellan stated "one hundred guns [were] fired" to commemorate the event. The decision to confiscate federal property on the eve of the secession convention outraged McClellan, a cooperationist delegate from Limestone County who was also a planter and involved in the livestock trade. In his estimation, the governor's action "exceeds in usurpation of power any thing [sic] that has yet been done even in South Carolina." When the doors of the convention opened, Clemens, McClellan, and other cooperationists received further confirmation of their worst fears. Immediate secessionists would not even allow a statewide referendum to take place if a secession ordinance was passed. According to McClellan, "From the indications here, [immediate secessionists] intend to carry every thing [sic] their way if they have the power, without giving the people a voice in the matter."[25] Despite the daunting challenges cooperationists faced in Montgomery, they still called for delay or collective state action. James S. Clark, who represented the people of Lawrence County, maintained that immediate secession would result in a bloody conflict and that it was counterproductive to white Alabamians' needs. In an effort to stop immediate secessionists from leading Alabama to war, he reminded them of the comments made by the eminent American statesman Daniel Webster when southerners threatened secession in 1850: "There can be no such thing as peaceable secession. Peaceable secession is an utter impossibility." Clark asked secessionists what they had to gain by immediate disunion: "Will it repeal the personal liberty bills of the North? Will it return a single fugitive slave . . . or the suppression of the inter-State slave trade?" With immediate disunion posing more of a direct threat to the security of North Alabamians than any of the other regions in the state, Clark implored immediate secessionists to "yield something, for once to the de-

mand of North Alabama—to your brothers who have the same common cause."
Separate state action, Clark warned immediatists, threatened the North Alabama economy since a "large part of the produce of North Alabama finds a market in Tennessee, or passes through that State on its way to" market. If Tennessee did not join Alabama in secession, Clark envisioned a situation where
North Alabama farmers and merchants would be forced to "run the gauntlet of
passports, custom houses, and the other machinery of a foreign government as
they go to market."[26] Clark, along with the other cooperationists, begged for
more time to possibly avert war or better protect the people of North Alabama if
war was indeed necessary.

To stop immediate secession from taking place, leading cooperationists presented a series of measures. Authored in part by Jeremiah Clemens, this "Minority Report" called for the United States Congress and northern state legisla-
tures to ratify an unamendable constitutional amendment protecting slavery
and the right of slaveholders to track down runaway slaves hiding in northern
states.[27] Given that a similar amendment proposed by United States Senator
John Crittenden of Kentucky had already failed to get out of committee, the
chance of Congress acting on this measure was slim.[28] If northern congress-
men and state legislators refused to do what was necessary to protect southerners' constitutional rights, cooperationists called for a convention to be held in
Nashville where delegates representing the slaveholding states would discuss
joint action. The authors of the Minority Report likely knew that immediate secessionists had no intention of waiting for northern politicians to reply to their
ultimatum or for another convention. Therefore, cooperationists stated that if
disunionists pressed on and passed an ordinance of secession, it would have to
be ratified by the people of Alabama. Thomas J. McClellan was "heartily in favor" of a popular referendum because he was certain eligible voters would
choose to keep their state in the Union for the time being.[29] Immediate secessionists were quick to condemn the idea, arguing that their election to the secession convention gave them the authority to act on behalf of white Alabamians. The debate over a statewide referendum became particularly heated
between Nicholas Davis, a Madison County delegate, and Yancey. When Davis
told Yancey and the rest of the immediate secessionists that the people of North
Alabama would not submit to secession unless there was a vote, Yancey responded by referring to North Alabamians as "tories [and] traitors" who "ought
to be coerced into . . . submission." Davis became irate over Yancey's disparag-
ing comments and talk of coercing his constituents into submission. He stated

that any such attempt would be met with armed resistance by North Alabami-ans.[30] The argument caused enough of an uproar that there were fears the North Alabama delegation might leave the convention. William Henry Mitchell, an immediate-secession supporter and preacher from Florence who was in Montgomery during the secession convention, reported that "considerable ap-prehension prevails lest the North Alabama delegation should secede from the convention, [but] I don't think they will."[31] Eventually, the quarrel subsided enough that delegates could vote on the Minority Report. In a 54–45 vote, im-mediate secessionists rejected the cooperationists' proposals.[32] There were def-initely grumblings among cooperationists over the absence of a referendum and immediate secessionists' resistance to compromise. Some delegates, along with their supporters, openly discussed seceding from Alabama and joining Tennessee, though nothing came of this.[33] Since the start of the convention, every attempt by North Alabama cooperationists to persuade immediate seces-sionists not to take their state out of the Union had failed. All that remained was the vote on an ordinance of secession.

On January 11, 1861, the day delegates cast their vote on secession, John W. Inzer remarked that "the capitol building was filled from top to bottom with peo-ple anxiously awaiting the results." According to Inzer, a cooperationist dele-gate from St. Clair County, the frenzied atmosphere and the growing number of people seeking entrance into the capital were too much for the "vendors of re-freshments and the peanut dealers in the rotunda. They were forced to beat a hasty retreat for the safety of themselves and their valuables."[34] William Henry Mitchell battled the crowds and vendors entering the capitol to await news of "the birth of our Republic."[35] The lawn surrounding the capitol was crowded with citizens showing great interest in the results.[36] The final outcome was never in doubt. By a vote of 61 to 39, Alabama became the fourth southern state to leave the Union.[37] As soon as the delegates learned that "Alabama was a free, sovereign and independent State," Inzer stated that "the doors of the hall were at once thrown open to the public and men, women and children rushed into the hall amid scenes of the wildest excitement."[38]

Initially, Jeremiah Clemens was the lone North Alabama cooperationist to side with immediate secessionists; but four other cooperationists changed their vote immediately after secession became official.[39] For all of Clemens' dire warnings, he voted for immediate secession, though not before making a few poignant comments. Clemens voted for disunion in an effort to create greater unity between immediate secessionists and cooperationists and out of fidelity to his native state. He solemnly told those in attendance that "I shall vote for this Ordinance, but frankness and fairness requires me to say that I would not vote for it, if its passage depended upon that vote." Clemens directed his next comment at immediate secessionists: "The act you are about to commit, is, to my apprehension, treason, and subjects you, if unsuccessful, to all the pains and penalties pronounced against that highest political crime." Before he took his seat, Clemens promised immediatists to "walk with you into revolution. Be its perils—be its privations—be its sufferings what they may, I share them with you."[40] In return for his support, the former colonel was commissioned Major General of the Army of Alabama. Clemens' transformation rankled some North Alabamians. Lawrence Ripley Davis, a planter and onetime state representative from Limestone County, stated "Jere Clemens has damned himself in the estimation of his friends."[41] Had Clemens waited until after the official vote before switching sides as his colleagues did, his attempt to heal the discord between cooperationists and immediate secessionists would not have seemed so politically motivated. After spending the previous few days trying to convince immediatists to hold off on disunion, the die had been cast in favor of secession with no concessions being given to the people of North Alabama.

Although cooperationists were keenly aware that immediate secession left northern Alabama vulnerable to economic hardships and military invasion, they moved quickly to demonstrate their support for disunion. Cooperationists might not have liked the method of secession, but they were still southern nationalists who had no intention of abandoning their state.[42] With the backing of their constituents, several more North Alabama cooperationists changed their vote on the secession ordinance. Thirty-three cooperationists signed an "Address to the People of Alabama," in which they indicated their support for secession and pledged unending loyalty to the state of Alabama.[43] Cooperationist delegates confidently asserted that the people they represented would stand side by side with immediate secessionists in defending their state and rights from all forms of northern aggression. According to Henry Cox Jones, a cooperationist delegate from Lauderdale County, the voters who elected him "have solemnly and unanimously declared, time and again, that they would not submit to Black Republican rule on the principles enunciated by that party." Jones told immediate secessionists that if the Lincoln administration attempted to force Alabama and the other seceded states back into the Union, the people of North Alabama would not shirk their duties. "Although cautious in council, North Alabama, when the conflict comes, will lead your army to victory and to glory," Jones stated.[44] John W. Inzer concurred with his colleague and stated that he "told the people of St. Clair, while canvassing the county, that I was in favor of co-operation; but said, if Alabama should secede . . . I will go with her and stand by her in every peril, even to the cannon's mouth." Southern nationalists throughout the state would have agreed with Inzer's declaration that "I am for Alabama under any and all circumstances."[45] Within a relatively short period of time from the passage of the ordinance of secession, the dissension that had existed between cooperationists and immediate secessionists was replaced by increased unity and purpose to protect, at all costs, white Alabamians' rights from Republican interference.

Even though cooperationists had accepted the necessity of breaking away from the United States, some still mourned the decision. Thomas J. McClellan deplored any celebration: "We might be justifiable in dissolving our connection with the Federal Government, [but] we ought to show more respect for that glorious old banner which we have lived [under] so long and so happy." McClellan told his wife that they must be careful to not display too much outward sorrow over leaving the United States, or people might think that they supported "the black republican party."[46] Lawrence Ripley Davis, like McClellan, intended to defend Alabama, but he was nonetheless frustrated that immediate secessionists had taken Alabama out of the Union with no clear plan for the future. A few days after the secession vote, Ripley lamented that "The *deed is done.* That old banner under which our revolutionary fathers marched has been ruthlessly torn from its moorings and again we are adrift without chart or compass to guide us through the deep which now surrounds [us]."[47] Disunion was particularly taxing for residents who had strong familial and community ties to both North Alabama and areas in the North. An anonymous letter by a North Alabama woman to the editor of a Wellsboro, Pennsylvania, newspaper epitomizes this struggle. This woman wished there could be peace, but intuitively knew northerners would not allow Alabama and the other seceded states to leave without a fight. For this woman, the likelihood of a civil war where brother would be "warring against brother—is enough to make the blood run cold." This transplanted northerner, who did not condemn Alabama delegates for seceding, was distraught over the impending war. All but one of her relatives, whom she loved "dearly and devoutly," resided in the North, while North Alabamians had "endeared themselves to me by acts of kindness and love, *never to be forgotten.*" To make matters worse, the woman stated, her deceased husband was buried in the North, but "in a Southern graveyard lies my only child."

She insinuated that if "the true-hearted people of the North and South could understand each other as I understand them," it might have been possible to avoid war.[48] For these North Alabamians, and their like-minded cohorts, seceding from the Union was no simple matter; secession entailed reconciling lingering attachments to the United States with a newfound independence and the possibility of war.

Although there were cooperationists who still felt a connection to the United States, secession had broad support in North Alabama.[49] Some cooperationists had changed their stance on secession even before the secession convention had met. A few days before delegates met in Montgomery, A. G. Dimmock, editor of the *Coshocton County Democrat* (Ohio) traveled through the town of Tuscumbia in northwest Alabama and had numerous conversations with the townspeople. According to Dimmock, the "large number with whom I have conversed were for co-operation at first but are now for secession and have no desire for a reunion thereafter."[50] Support for disunion continued to grow as news filtered back to the region that their state was independent. Catherine Fennell, an eighteen-year-old woman who lived with her family several miles to the east of Huntsville, was ecstatic when she learned that her state no longer considered itself to be under the control of the federal government. Fennell, whose family owned numerous slaves, penned "WE ARE NOW FREE!" in her diary.[51] By the end of January, reports were circulating in northern newspapers that "there had been a great reaction in . . . favor [of disunion] in North Alabama."[52] Support for secession in North Alabama received an additional boost in early February when six of the seven states that had seceded established the Confederate States of America with its capital in Montgomery; Texas joined soon thereafter.[53] This act at least partially addressed cooperationists' push for collective state action, though Tennessee still remained in the Union. By the time Lincoln took office and delivered his inaugural address, his promise to not interfere with slavery in the South failed to weaken support for secession in North Alabama. The opportunity for reconciliation had long since passed; southern nationalists in North Alabama had no intention of abandoning their state or the newly formed Confederate government.[54]

When the president responded to southerners' bombardment and capture of Fort Sumter in mid-April by calling for 75,000 ninety-day recruits to put down the rebellion, white North Alabamians were committed to defending the Confederacy. The *Columbus Daily Enquirer* (Ga.) reported that "the mountains" of

North Alabama were "on fire" with intense pro-Confederate enthusiasm after civilians learned Lincoln was raising an army. This war feeling was not localized, but was "spreading and becoming more intensified every day in all the Northern counties." Rallies were held throughout the region to drum up support for the Confederacy and to "receive volunteers for war against Lincoln and his Abolitionists."[55] In the northeast county of Jackson, yeoman farmers of varying ages left their families in droves "to go forth to defend their rights and their government." The *Enquirer* stated that three fourths of the eligible fighting-age men in the town of Bellefonte, the county seat of Jackson, had "tendered their services" to the Confederacy "to repel the mercenary ruffians" sent by Lincoln to "invade and pollute our soil."[56] Catherine Fennell wrote of a large gathering of men in the Marshall County town of Guntersville to organize a company of Confederate soldiers. She commented, "Nearly all of the gentlemen of my acquaintance joined," including her brother William and her brother-in-law Sam Henry.[57] Fennell told William that she intended to make a flag for his company to take with them, but she gives no indication if the flag was completed.[58] About a month and a half later, the teenager returned to Guntersville to see William, Sam, and a few hundred Confederate soldiers leave for war. As the soldiers said good-bye to their families and well-wishers, potentially for the last time, Fennell commented that the "ladies were not alone in shedding tears."[59] Confederate recruits from southern Alabama traveling through the northern counties on their way to military camps in outlying states were impressed with North Alabamians' fervent Confederate nationalism. Thomas R. Lightfoot of Henry County remarked that "the people of North Alabama . . . are the most warlike people I have ever seen. Women cheer us, and the men go along with us."[60] The collective response of North Alabama Confederates upon learning that Lincoln intended to use force to bring the seceded states back to the Union was decisive and unequivocal: they would do their part to help defend the Confederacy and create lasting independence. Catherine Fennell admitted that she did not know how long this would take, but she was certain that a higher power would grant them victory over an inferior foe: "*If God is with us, who can be against us?*"[61]

Protecting their economy and themselves from the enemy were two prominent concerns for North Alabamians as they headed toward war. Part of their unease was addressed with the creation of the Confederate States of America. When Tennessee—along with three other slave states—joined the Confederacy after Fort Sumter, North Alabamians undoubtedly felt more secure. Established business relations would continue and Tennessee would presumably act as a buffer for the northern counties. However, scant military resources and relatively few Confederate soldiers were sent to the region. The limited funds Governor Moore and his successor, John Gill Shorter, had available were spent fortifying the Gulf Coast between the Florida Panhandle and Mobile. Shorter told Confederate Secretary of War George Randolph that he considered "the maintenance of the possession of Pensacola a matter of such prime importance not only to Alabama and Florida, but also to the cause at large."[62] In retrospect, the decision not to devise a strategy for North Alabama proved costly. The region contained an abundant supply of livestock and grains, while the Memphis and Charleston Railroad, which cut across the region, was one of the Confederacy's most important transportation arteries. Any disruption in this line would force Confederate authorities to use less time-efficient routes to transport troops and supplies. Even when Moore viewed the arrival of Union soldiers at Columbus, Kentucky, in late November as a potential threat to the northern counties, he called on North Alabama citizens to protect themselves. In one of his final acts as governor, Moore told them that "Your households and your hearths are in danger," and he asked all available men to defend the region. He promised to pay slaveholders if their slaves built defensive fortifications, but the governor made no mention of whether Confederate soldiers would be sent to offer additional protection. Moore urged that there "be no holding back—safety and success is in speedy actions—danger and defeat in delay."[63] In this instance, Union soldiers did not invade the region.

Throughout the initial stages of the secession crisis, cooperationists from North Alabama followed a conservative approach. They were committed to defending the institution of slavery, but regional concerns led them to push for a solution short of immediate secession. While some cooperationists sought a constitutional amendment explicitly protecting slavery in the South and in the territories, others pushed for joint action by southern states to better protect their region and to increase the likelihood of achieving independence. Their efforts to delay secession proved futile. After the convention voted Alabama out of the Union, onetime cooperationists in the northern counties stood beside immediate secessionists and supported disunion even though none of their primary concerns about the protection of their region had been addressed. Several months later, when the governor perceived a threat to North Alabama, he called on Confederate civilians to protect themselves. Given the number of men from the region already enrolled in the Confederate army, this was hardly practical. North Alabama civilians were surely thankful that this threat late in 1861 passed, but as Union soldiers continued to work their way south in early 1862, the possibility of having enemy soldiers on their soil remained very real.

2

"LINCOLN'S HORDES"

North Alabamians' fears that Union forces might reach their borders in late 1861 did not materialize, though within six months they would get their first glimpse of the enemy. The invasion of North Alabama by General Ormsby MacKnight Mitchel and the 7,000 soldiers comprising the Third Division, Army of the Ohio in April 1862, was part of a larger Union offensive in the western theater. Once Mitchel's soldiers accomplished their goal of gaining possession of the Memphis and Charleston Railroad, the division commander anticipated they would be sent elsewhere. When this failed to happen, Mitchel found himself overseeing a military occupation. As Union soldiers transitioned from an invasion to an occupation force, they were expected to implement a conciliatory civil-military policy advocated by Lincoln and General Don Carlos Buell, commanding general of the Army of the Ohio and Mitchel's superior. Conciliation was based on the assumption that most Confederate civilians had been lukewarm secessionists and could be persuaded back into the Union. After Confederate civilians recovered from the initial shock of the invasion, they made it clear to their occupiers that they had no desire to return to the United States.[1]

The impetus for Union soldiers' arrival in North Alabama in April dates back several months to when Buell replaced General William Tecumseh Sherman as the commanding officer of Union forces stationed at Louisville, Kentucky. After Buell assumed command in November 1861, Lincoln made the liberation of unionists in East Tennessee a top priority.[2] Buell, however, insisted his men take Nashville first.[3] When General Ulysses S. Grant and the Army of the Tennessee captured Fort Henry (February 6) and Fort Donelson (February 16), Buell used the victories as a pretext to disregard Lincoln's original wishes about East Tennessee and maintain his focus on Nashville, which now appeared ripe for the taking. Buell subsequently sent Mitchel and his Third Division out ahead of the rest of the Army of the Ohio to take possession of the state capital. On February 23, Mitchel and his men arrived at the northern bank of the Cumberland River across from Nashville. The following day, the mayor of Nashville surrendered the city.[4]

With Union forces in control of Nashville, Buell and General Henry W. Halleck, whom Lincoln had recently named commander of all Union forces in the western theater, discussed invading North Alabama. Both generals understood the area's strategic importance. If the Union controlled the Memphis and Charleston Railroad, which ran across the northern counties, Confederates would have to use less efficient routes to transport supplies and men between the western and eastern theaters. From North Alabama, Union soldiers could move on Chattanooga and liberate East Tennessee, or they could turn west and reinforce Grant's and Buell's forces that would be somewhere in the vicinity of Corinth, Mississippi. While Halleck and Buell agreed that Mitchel should take possession of the railroad depot at Huntsville, they disagreed on the route the Third Division would take. In the end, Buell's desire to send the Third Division overland through southern Tennessee and into North Alabama prevailed over Halleck's plan to send Mitchel into the region via the Tennessee River.[5]

As Union officers and soldiers made their final preparations for the North Alabama campaign, General Leroy Pope Walker, who was in charge of Confederate forces in northern Alabama, voiced his concern over the region's vulnerability. The former Confederate secretary of war was not pleased that General Albert Sidney Johnston's men had been sent to Corinth, which left the "Memphis and Charleston Railroad from Stevenson to Big Bear Creek . . . exposed to the enemy." With only a battalion of "badly armed" troops from Arkansas, the region could not be adequately defended. To protect North Alabama west of Decatur, Walker asked for "three regiments of infantry, one of cavalry, and two efficient field batteries" to be placed under his command. He also requested that he be allowed to use slaves to build defensive fortifications along the Tennessee River. For this Huntsville native, there was more at stake than losing the Memphis and Charleston Railroad. Failure to reinforce the area would give Confederate civilians the impression that the "entire section is to be abandoned to the enemy," which would do irreparable damage to "the cause of enlistment."[6] By the end of March, there remained only a paltry number of Confederate soldiers in the region. Around this same time, Walker resigned his commission and returned to Huntsville. Without a strong Confederate force to repulse the enemy, Confederate civilians in North Alabama were largely left to fend for themselves.

After marching unopposed through southern Tennessee, the Third Division reached the Alabama line in early April and soon entered the state. Once Mitchel had taken Huntsville on April 11, he commented that Confederates in the city were "completely taken by surprise, no one considering the march practical."[7] Among the stunned inhabitants of the city were Confederate soldiers who had been wounded at the Battle of Shiloh and soldiers who were waiting for a train to transport them east.[8] In addition to capturing "200 prisoners," Mitchel proudly reported that his men took possession of "15 locomotives and a large number of cars."[9] To protect the Third Division from counterattacks, the division commander established a defensive perimeter. He travelled with Colonel Joshua Sill and the Ninth Brigade to secure the Memphis and Charleston line all the way to Stevenson in northeast Alabama. According to a correspondent for the *Louisville Daily Journal*, "Stevenson is one of the most important points [to control] in this part of the country."[10] When Union soldiers encountered Confederate cavalrymen there, a minor skirmish ensued. Eventually, the Confederates retreated to Chattanooga. Soon thereafter, Mitchel returned to his headquarters in Huntsville. As Colonel Sill held the eastern leg of the rail line, Colonel John Basil Turchin—a Russian expatriate who had served as a colonel in the Russian Imperial Army—took his Eighth Brigade as far as Tuscumbia in Franklin County, though he eventually pulled back to Decatur.[11] With well over one hundred miles of railroad track freed from Rebel control, Mitchel claimed that "the great artery of railway intercommunications between the Southern States" had been cut.[12] Over the span of a few days, the Third Division had achieved unparalleled success by penetrating farther south than any other organized group of Union soldiers.[13]

Mitchel garnered considerable praise for overseeing this campaign. Officials in Washington were so impressed with the former astronomer that they

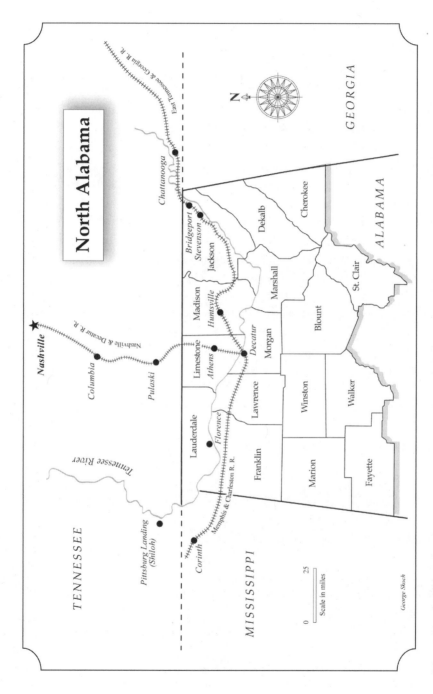

Map 2. North Alabama and southern Tennessee, with special designation of the Memphis and Charleston Railroad and the Tennessee River

promoted him to the rank of major general for his "gallant and meritious [*sic*] conduct on the capture of Huntsville, Alabama."[14] Corporal Robert H. Caldwell of the Twenty-First Ohio felt the promotion was well deserved and considered it as a sign that he and his fellow soldiers' "services are being appreciated."[15] Colonel John Beatty of the Third Ohio offered lofty praise for his commander's military acumen: "No other man with so few troops has ventured so far into the enemy's country, and accomplished so much."[16] While other Union generals, such as Buell and George B. McClellan, were derided for being slow and hesitating, Mitchel garnered plaudits for his efficiency in bringing portions of North Alabama under Federal control. According to one observer, Mitchel was "the only man in command in the West who [has] shown any great ability in handling a small and mobile force." The same individual even suggested that Mitchel had shown Napoleon Bonaparte's gift for performing quick and decisive military maneuvers against his enemies.[17] The accolades Mitchel received were well deserved. With few Union casualties, he had taken control of an important Confederate railroad route and placed the Third Division in position to move on Chattanooga or Corinth.

The invasion of North Alabama and the capture of the Memphis and Charleston Railroad had an immediate effect on the Confederate war effort. Illinois volunteer Charles Dahlmer thought the Federals "have [dealt] the [Confederacy] a severe blow. . . . We captured 17 locomotives and about 45 or 50 passenger cars and freight cars." The bluecoats also corralled roughly three-hundred Rebel soldiers en route for Virginia.[18] Corporal Caldwell commented that the Third Division had cut the "jugular vein of the Confederate States."[19] The people of New Orleans were among those adversely affected. According to General Mansfield Lovell, commander of Confederate forces there, the Federal incursion into North Alabama was partially responsible for the "scarcity of provisions" in the Crescent City.[20] A northern newspaper claimed that without the Memphis and Charleston Railroad "all direct communication between the rebel armies in Virginia and the South-west" came to a halt.[21] With Buell and Halleck laying siege to Corinth and McClellan marching—albeit cautiously—on Richmond, the Confederacy could ill afford costly communication and transportation delays. Edward Norphlet Brown, Sr. of the Forty-Fifth Alabama and his cohorts encamped at Auburn were among those who had to find alternative transportation. They had intended to use the "Charleston & Memphis Road" to reinforce General P. G. T. Beauregard's Army of Mississippi at Corinth, but now they had to find another path.[22] The Union's arrival in North

Alabama also threatened the Confederate economy. With Huntsville serving as the nexus for the regional cotton trade, Union personnel now had access to large stores of the South's most important cash crop.[23] The Union's capture of the Memphis and Charleston Railroad was undoubtedly a blow to the Confederacy and had the potential to play a crucial role in Union and Confederate military strategies in the coming months.

Confederate civilians in North Alabama were stunned by the sudden appearance of Union troops.[24] Seventeen-year-old Sarah Lowe of Huntsville became despondent after the enemy entered Huntsville. According to Lowe, "My heart stops beating at the [mere] thought that '*my* home' is a captured city." This teenager had no idea how long the "despot's heal [*sic*]" would be "on our shore," but she ominously declared, "Nothing but gloom seems to hover over our future."[25] Joshua Burns Moore of Lauderdale County appeared inconsolable. The slave owner concluded, "We will get no mail now. All communication is cut off—so much for the revolution."[26] North Alabamians outside the invasion zone found it nearly impossible to contact loved ones. C. C. Clay, Jr., a former U.S. senator from Huntsville who was serving in the Confederate Congress, remarked that "God only knows when [I will learn] the fate of my father, brother & other relatives [and] property."[27] There were attempts to form a Confederate militia, but problems quickly arose when two of Catherine Fennell's cousins realized that there were "not enough men left . . . to make a company."[28] A few even admitted defeat and sought reconciliation. Jeremiah Clemens, who had previously promised immediate secessionists that he would "walk with you into revolution," experienced an upwelling of Union patriotism when the invaders reached Huntsville.[29]

A number of Confederates attempted to flee rather than face an uncertain future under Yankee control. Prominent Confederates who feared persecution were among those who became refugees.[30] Leroy Pope Walker, 1860 presidential candidate John Bell, and *Huntsville Confederate* editor J. W. Clay were among the most noteworthy men who escaped. Clay claimed to be "the first man who left Huntsville after the Federals came in."[31] After hiding in the nearby mountains, Clay eventually worked his way to Knoxville, Tennessee, where he resumed his pro-Confederate newspaper.[32] Concern over Union soldiers' interference with the master-slave relationship sent slave owners scurrying for safety. The Scott family started gathering valuables from their Madison County home the moment they learned the "Yankees [were] coming." By the time the Federal troops reached their land, the men had made a successful dash with their slaves to the nearby mountains. Mrs. Scott, however, "was too fleshy to run fast, and the Yankees overtook her."[33] In a few instances, slaves reportedly aided their masters' flight. Marshall C. Wilson was too young to enlist in the Confederate army, but he still vividly remembered the events that transpired when the Yankees closed in on his parents' Franklin County home. As Joanna, a household slave, watched Wilson's father run "across the backyard" to evade capture, she "cried gleefully: 'I tell you, old master made the dist fly.'" When Union soldiers began interrogating members of the family, Joanna was on the verge of telling them of her master's whereabouts when a slave named Harriet "knocked [Joanna] senseless to the floor." This allowed Wilson to complete his escape and likely saved Joanna from punishment.[34] As Union soldiers extended their grip over the Tennessee Valley, more civilians packed up and left. According to Catherine Fennell, "Scores of refugees from Madison County" were traveling past her parents' property on their way to the southern bank of the Tennessee River.[35] An unknown number of these refugees would eventually return home once the dust from the invasion settled. The initial decision by these Confederates to elude Union soldiers did not indicate a lack of commitment to Confederate independence. Rather, fleeing was a pragmatic response to the uncertainty over how they might be treated by Union soldiers.

Joshua Burns Moore sharply criticized affluent slaveholders for seeking refuge in the "hills and mountains" of North Alabama. This prosperous lawyer supported Confederate independence, though he was prone to disparage Confederate leaders and question their motives. As the Third Division advanced west from Huntsville, Moore wondered what had happened to all the "boasted chivalry" in the region. For well over a year, prominent slave owners had promised that "when the time came, each one of them would shoulder his *shot gun* and meet the invaders and fight until death for every inch of the soil of Alabama." But, with the arrival of Union soldiers, they instead "took to their heels" and "concealed themselves where ever their friends let them." As a slave owner himself, Moore assailed men who fled and left behind "defenseless families of females [without] protection" from male slaves. If there were no white men to ensure slave obedience, Moore worried, male slaves, "through idleness will become demoralized [and soon] commence the commission of crime of the deepest dye."[36] When the Union invasion turned into an occupation, Moore briefly contemplated joining his fellow slaveholders and becoming a refugee, but changed his mind when his wife refused to leave.[37]

Civilians who remained behind did their best to help the small number of

Confederate soldiers who were in the area escape. A young Thomas Washington Peebles of Limestone County had recently enlisted when the Third Division arrived in North Alabama. Rather than stay and confront the enemy, Peebles took the advice of his fellow Leighton residents and fled into the nearby woods. As Peebles made his way to safety, he grieved that his friends and neighbors would soon see "their glorious city . . . polluted by the disgraceful footsteps of Lincoln's Hordes."[38] Confederate women went to great lengths to protect their menfolk. During the first weeks of the invasion and subsequent occupation, nineteenth-century attitudes on gender and white femininity insulated Confederate women from being targeted or punished by Union soldiers. Confederate women—and men—used this to their advantage. Rowena Webster, who came to Huntsville after fleeing from Union soldiers in Tennessee, stated that "every woman" in Huntsville dressed soldiers and male civilians up in "female attire" to help them escape. While Webster does not state if this gender-altering ploy challenged established attitudes toward southern masculinity, she did note its success: "Soon they had all escaped."[39] Laura Wharton Plummer commented that the "wildest confusion" reigned when the Federals first entered Huntsville. Plummer, who was in her mid-twenties, observed Union "soldiers on horses and soldiers on foot were everywhere—galloping, shouting, halting, swearing, cursing and pounding on doors and rushing into the houses searching for Confederate soldiers who might have escaped." One Confederate soldier trying to evade capture knocked on Plummer's back door seeking a place to hide. Moments later, this man found himself in Plummer's wardrobe behind the hanging clothes. When Union soldiers came to the house demanding she turn over any Confederate soldier, she threw open her wardrobe, exclaiming, "Search the house, if you wish; you will see there is no soldier here." According to Plummer, "My promptness to open the door put them off their guard. They looked everywhere else and left." Shortly thereafter, the soldier made his escape.[40] There is little indication that these Confederate women resented shielding the very men who were supposed to be defending the region from invasion. They likely considered hiding soldiers from the enemy as part of their responsibility as good Confederate women. By helping these soldiers escape, civilians might have assumed that they would be rewarded with the return of a Confederate force strong enough to drive out the enemy.

With the Memphis and Charleston Railroad and key cities along the route firmly in Union hands, Mitchel wondered how long he would remain in the region. Even though the general had performed an important service that won the esteem of army personnel and the nation at large, he sought military glory on the field of battle. After a few weeks in North Alabama, Mitchel felt he had accomplished his objective and that it was now time for the Third Division to leave.[41] Given his location in North Alabama, two potential objectives beckoned the onetime astronomer and his men. To the west were Buell and Halleck, who were laying siege to Beauregard and thousands of Confederate soldiers at Corinth. According to one Cleveland, Ohio, newspaper, Mitchel was within "prompt striking distance" of the place.[42] While a successful assault on Corinth would bring additional accolades, it was not the task Mitchel coveted most; he preferred heading east to fight generals E. Kirby Smith and Braxton Bragg for Chattanooga and East Tennessee. The forward-thinking commander told his friend Salmon P. Chase that he had "spared the Tennessee bridges near Stevenson" when he first invaded North Alabama "in the hope I might be permitted to march on Chattanooga and Knoxville."[43] Mitchel waited for the go-ahead from Buell or Halleck, but as days turned to weeks without orders, Mitchel's frustration grew. At one point, he suggested to Secretary of War Edwin Stanton that he could offer "more effective service" in the Army of the Potomac.[44] Stanton replied, "We would be very glad to have you on the Potomac, but the President thinks that at the present juncture it would not be advisable to remove you from a command where you have rendered such distinguished service and where your abilities cannot be supplied."[45] Lincoln remained eager to liberate East Tennessee and would need a general with Mitchel's capabilities.

As Mitchel and his men transitioned from an invasion army to an occupation force, they were expected to adhere to the Union's prevailing policy of conciliation. This policy was based on the assumption that deep down, the majority of southerners were loyal to the Union but had been duped by aristocratic slaveholders into supporting secession and war. In numerous speeches, Lincoln had reminded secessionists of their enduring connection to the Union and reassured them that he would not interfere with slavery where it existed, but as of yet, his words had not taken hold. Lincoln and like-minded supporters of conciliation hoped to have better success using the Federal army to rekindle Confederate civilians' loyalty to the United States. As Union soldiers came into contact with secessionist civilians, they would conduct themselves in a manner that embodied the policy of conciliation: safeguarding the rights of noncombatant slave owners and treating Confederate civilians as if they were still citizens of the United States. By showing that the government had no intention to coerce or deny southerners their rights, Federal soldiers would show secessionists the error of their ways. By the time the Third Division arrived in North Alabama, this conservative civil-military approach had seen success in West Virginia and parts of Kentucky.[46] The successful implementation of conciliation in North Alabama could have important repercussions for the Union war effort. Pro-Union North Alabamians would begin the process of taking back control of their state, and conciliationists could use North Alabama to show other Deep South whites that they had nothing to fear by returning to the Union.

Buell was the chief advocate of conciliation in the western theater. Throughout his tenure as commander of the Army of the Ohio, this former slave owner sought to treat Confederates as if they were still protected under the U.S. Constitution and ordered his subordinates to do likewise.[47] The foundation for Buell's conciliatory civil-military policy came from General Orders 13a, which he issued soon after Nashville came under Federal control.[48] The former West Pointer started off by congratulating his men for restoring "the national banner to the Capital of Tennessee," noting that "thousands of hearts in every part of the State will swell with joy to see that honored flag reinstated in a position from which it was removed in the excitement and folly of an evil hour." To ensure that they maintain proper soldier conduct during the occupation of the city, Buell instructed his men to treat Confederate civilians in a cordial manner and reminded them that "We are in arms not for the purpose of invading the rights of our fellow countrymen." The commanding general then announced that, "Peaceable citizens are not to be molested in their persons or property." Soldiers were also forbidden from arresting or entering "the residences or grounds of citizens . . . without [proper] authority." If a civilian was suspected of committing an offense or impropriety against the Union, Buell stated he would handle the situation himself or have "authorized persons" do so. Union soldiers suspected of violating General Orders 13a would be dealt with in a way that would not "bring [further] shame on their comrades and the cause they are engaged in."[49] Adherence to a limited-war strategy and conciliation advanced Buell's desire for the Union to be victorious, but in a way that did not result in any far-reaching changes to the southern status quo.[50]

As a West Point graduate, Mitchel shared Buell's commitment to maintaining order and punishing soldiers who engaged in unbridled aggression against a nonviolent civilian population.[51] In the weeks leading up to the invasion of North Alabama, Mitchel issued a series of orders that shared strong similarities with General Orders 13a. While still in Nashville, Mitchel issued General Orders 81, which stated that "All plundering or pillaging or depredation upon property of any kind is strictly prohibited." To help insure that officers kept a close eye on those under their command, Mitchel stated that officers would be punished for the misbehavior of their men.[52] As the Third Division reached the outskirts of Murfreesboro on their march toward North Alabama, Mitchel issued General Orders 85. Under this directive, soldiers "engaged in any depredations, or in robbing of private property" would "be handed over to the civil authorities of the neighborhood in which the offense is perpetrated . . . and dealt with by them according to their laws."[53]

While there are striking similarities between Buell's and Mitchel's respective approaches to conducting an occupation, there were also fundamental differences. Mitchel was much more concerned with maintaining order among his men rather than protecting the civil liberties and property rights of Confederate civilians. By no means was this abolitionist-minded general a staunch conciliationist.[54] Conciliation for Mitchel was contingent upon civilians' willingness to be conciliated. If they rejected conciliation or acted in a manner Mitchel considered belligerent, he would adjust his policies accordingly. The general had articulated this philosophy at a Union meeting in New York City shortly after the firing on Fort Sumter: "When the rebels come to their senses we will receive them with open arms; but until that time, while they are trailing over our glorious banner in the dust [and] trample it under [their feet] I must smite, and in God's name I will smite."[55] While in North Alabama, Mitchel intended to maintain order within his ranks. He also planned to adhere to his superior's conservative civil-military policy, but only insofar as that did not hinder his military objectives and the Union war effort in general.

The angst that Confederate civilians surely felt when they realized that the enemy would be around for a while left them with a tough choice: accept conciliation or resist their occupier any way they could. As Union soldiers settled into the occupation, Confederate men and women collectively chose not to give up on independence or become a pacified population. In the struggle that lay ahead, they looked to Confederate soldiers, God, and themselves for protection and defense.

Civilians' faith in the Confederate military remained strong throughout the occupation; these Rebels were certain that a Confederate force would eventually arrive in the region and vanquish the enemy. Mary Chadick, whose husband W. D. Chadick was a preacher and a colonel in the Confederate army, remarked that the people of Huntsville "are in daily expectancy [that] Gen. Kirby Smith or Gen. Morgan is coming to our relief."[56] Little did she or others know that Smith considered a "movement on Mitchel at Huntsville impracticable, because bridges west of Bridgeport, on the Tennessee River, have been burned by the enemy." Smith considered the best way to drive Mitchel out of North Alabama was to make a move on Nashville, which would force his withdrawal.[57] Civilians' zealous faith in their army led some to take for fact rumors of an advancing Confederate army. Mary Fielding, a teenager who lived with her family near Athens, took to heart reports that "Gen. Smith is between Chattanooga and Stevenson on his way here."[58] In early May, Catherine Fennell heard that 26,000 Union soldiers had been wounded or killed during a battle at Corinth and that there was "fighting all along the railroad from Corinth to Bridgeport." She also learned that Mitchel was in a "deadly conflict" for control of Huntsville.[59] The often petulant Joshua Burns Moore also expected that a "large force" would soon arrive "to drive the Yankees out of the valley."[60] The knowledge that their male relatives and neighbors were stationed at Confederate camps in close proximity to occupied North Alabama reinforced civilians' expectation that help was on the way. While there were skirmishes between Union and Confederate forces, there was no large-scale plan by Confederate authorities to fight the Union army for control over North Alabama. Even so, Confederate civilians remained confident that at some point Confederate soldiers would come to their rescue.

As Confederate women awaited Confederate soldiers to rescue them, they looked to the Lord as well. The unshakable belief that God backed the Confederacy strengthened their trust in their military and gave them the motivation to endure what lay ahead. Since Catherine Fennell was convinced that "God is on the side of the Right," she had no reason to doubt that the Third Division would be driven from North Alabama or that the Confederacy would ultimately be victorious over a morally inferior enemy.[61] Sarah Rousseau Espy, a widowed mother of seven from rural Cherokee County, asked God to alleviate the suffering of North Alabama Confederates by sending Union soldiers "back to their own country."[62] Confederate women held to their religious convictions even when the situation in North Alabama, and for the Confederacy as a whole, appeared bleak. During a religious service in Athens, Rebecca Vasser and her fellow parishioners were "sadly demoralized" by rumors that McClellan had taken Richmond. "The presence of the enemy" in the church, according to Vasser, did "not add to the feeling of devotion." Yet she and many other Confederate women did not despair, though the same could not be said for the men. According to Vasser, "God alone can help us, but only the women seem to think so: but the prayers, and faith of women may do much even in such dire emergencies as this."[63] The faith these women had in God and the Confederacy likely grew stronger when they learned the capital had not fallen. Faith in the Almighty served as a crucial cornerstone in the development of secessionist women's Confederate nationalism and as a source of solace and strength as they continued to support their government while living under military rule.

As Confederate civilians waited for military and heavenly intervention, they were committed to doing their part to defend their hearth and homeland from their occupiers. After recovering from the initial shock of the invasion and occupation, civilians started engaging in acts of defiance toward the enemy. Confederates' methods of resistance, which ranged from verbal assaults to severing communication lines to killing enemy soldiers, sent an unequivocal message to Federals that they would not peacefully return to the Union. While assaults occurred across the occupation zone and in outlying areas, they were concentrated in the Tennessee Valley due to the Union's frequent use of the railroad and the decision by General Mitchel to make Huntsville his headquarters. These attacks created a volatile environment for occupation soldiers and indicated to Union military personnel and officials in Washington that convincing Confederate civilians to return to the Union was more difficult than previously assumed.

Interfering with enemy supply routes and communication lines were among the earliest and most conspicuous acts of defiance. Until Buell and the soldiers under his command arrived from Corinth at the end of June, Mitchel only had about 7,000 men to guard the Memphis and Charleston Railroad and other rail lines, all the while maintaining control of strategically important places. Confederates began targeting transportation routes as soon as the bluecoats entered North Alabama. A forward-thinking man by the name of Helm slowed Union soldiers' progress into northwest Alabama by damaging a bridge near Courtland (Lawrence County).[64] As the number of Confederate civilians engaging in irregular warfare increased, Mitchel found protecting his men and lines of communication quite difficult. After only a few weeks in North Alabama, Mitchel told Buell that "scarcely a day passes without some attack upon our bridge guards, our trains, or telegraph wires." He made a similar statement to the Secretary of War.[65] E. H. Tatem reported that "each day [the Rebels are] developing some new and bolder outrage. [Near the] Courtland station, [they] destroyed several culverts, burned a lot of cotton and cut the telegraph wires." Later that day, the same individuals were believed to have been the culprits behind the destroyed water stations near Decatur.[66] On occasion, civilians joined forces with roving guerrilla warriors and partisans. In early May, Mitchel sent word to Stanton that "straggling bands of mounted men [are wreaking havoc] along my entire line," completely destroying at least one bridge.[67] Efforts to combat these attacks were difficult since they were occurring "whenever there is the slightest chance of success."[68] James Monroe Mason was one of the many Confederate civilians who helped destroy railroad tracks. Since this future Methodist minister was too young to join the regular Confederate army, he left his Huntsville home and joined a group of armed men led by Frank Gurley. "Even when our numbers were small," Mason recalled, "we had several times interfered with [Union soldiers'] use of the [Memphis and Charleston Railroad], by removing rails at different points."[69] Although Confederate men did most of the damage to the railroad and telegraph lines in North Alabama, there were instances of Confederate women getting involved as well.[70] Confederate civilians' participation in these acts or knowledge that they had successfully occurred certainly buttressed their morale. Confederate efforts to damage railroads and telegraph lines could also prove devastating for Union forces in the western theater. An interruption in communication between Union personnel might lead to missed opportunities to defeat the enemy, while the disruption of supply lines might lead to soldiers being placed on reduced rations.

When the opportunity presented itself, Confederates fired into the rail cars transporting the enemy. This act of defiance served as a dangerous and potentially deadly reminder to Union soldiers that they were dealing with an implacable foe. Union efforts to counter these assaults or locate the Confederates responsible would not be easy as assailants could simply blend back into society after an attack had occurred. On more than one occasion, Mitchel reported that "Armed citizens" were firing into trains transporting his men, severing telegraph lines, and damaging bridges.[71] With so many Union soldiers being transported in to and out of Huntsville, attacks became common in Madison County. According to Corporal Caldwell, the county "is literally swarming with the enemy, fighting Guerilla fashion." As Union soldiers from the Third Ohio Volunteers passed the town of Paint Rock, which was several miles to the east of Huntsville, civilians fired into the train and wounded several soldiers."[72] In a separate incident, "a party of perhaps 20 bushwhackers" killed two soldiers and wounded another nine when they fired into a train.[73] Such attacks were frequent enough in Madison County that Lieutenant Robert S. Dilworth of the Twenty-First Ohio Volunteers developed "Considerable uneasiness" when a number of his comrades failed to arrive at the Huntsville depot on time.[74] This lieutenant had previously lost three men and had thirteen wounded during an attack near Athens in Limestone County.[75] One southern newspaper commented that the "Federals are greatly incensed by citizens of the country burning bridges, cutting telegraph wires, shooting scouts and pickets, and firing into Railroad trains."[76] When Union soldiers arrived in North Alabama, they quickly realized that federal officials had badly misjudged the strength of Confederate nationalism in the region. Even after Union soldiers adopted more punitive measures to put down the rebellion in North Alabama, they still had trouble stopping Confederates from firing into trains. In mid-August, Sergeant William M. Austin of the Twenty-Second Illinois Infantry noted that the "Secesh" near Bear Creek, Alabama, "are continually firing into and throwing off the cars."[77]

Federal soldiers out on patrol, standing guard, or in search of food encountered similar dangers. These attacks, like the ones on trains, started before Union soldiers were fully aware of the hatred Confederate civilians harbored toward them. In some cases, Confederates assaulted Union soldiers after appearing to offer hospitality. As a group of Union soldiers patrolled the countryside in rural northeast Alabama, one of the men became hungry and stopped to ask for food from a local resident. The homeowner enthusiastically responded that there were "some nice hams in his smokehouse" that he could have free of charge. The man's outward generosity was a ruse. Upon reaching the smokehouse, the owner pulled a knife on the unsuspecting soldier and stabbed him six times before the commotion alerted the others to what was happening. His comrades concluded that the attempt on the soldier's life was premeditated because they "found a hole dug in the smokehouse where [the man] intended to bury someone."[78] In Woodville, the promise of food from a Confederate nearly got one Union soldier killed. After the northerner followed the man into the house to retrieve the victuals, he was accosted and lost possession of his bayonet. The Confederate then pushed the soldier "against the wall of the room, presented the bayonet to his bosom and swore that if he moved or cried out he would kill him on the spot." The bluecoat yelled for help and was rescued. Union soldiers soon discovered that the man was a Confederate soldier wearing civilian clothes.[79] A less fortunate Federal in Jackson County was killed after a Confederate tricked him into laying down his gun while the two were in a smokehouse. This assailant was arrested, but he soon escaped.[80]

Because Union soldiers often were unfamiliar with the local terrain and did not know exactly where the enemy was, they were vulnerable to ambushes. Union soldiers patrolling the outskirts of Huntsville in mid-April came across a comrade who had been taken by surprise and hanged.[81] Several men from the Tenth Wisconsin were ambushed by residents of Woodville who fired upon them while hiding behind rocks and bushes. This incident left three Yankees gravely wounded.[82] Small groups of Union soldiers traveling long distances by horse or foot could readily be shot at or captured. A correspondent for the *Cincinnati Gazette* reported that four "post couriers" from the Fourth Ohio Volunteers had been killed by civilians along a nearly fifty mile route between Huntsville and Shelbyville, Tennessee. According to the correspondent, civilian attacks along this road were "becoming too frequent."[83] Such assaults played a crucial role in pushing soldiers away from conciliation. When soldiers from the Tenth Wisconsin learned that a "party of hidden enemies" had shot and killed Captain Moore near Larkinsville, they took a "solemn oath that they would never take another prisoner. They intended to kill."[84] With an insufficient Confederate force in North Alabama to drive out the enemy, Confederate civilians sought to engage the enemy on the best terms possible. This decision quickly proved how a conciliatory policy was, in soldier parlance, "all played out."

Under nineteenth-century gender conventions, women were considered passive individuals reliant on white male relatives for protection.[85] The absence of husbands, brothers, and sons and the inability of the Confederate army to protect the region challenged such beliefs. Instead of remaining docile in the presence of Union soldiers, Confederate women joined the resistance. Early efforts by these women to impede or frustrate their occupiers' military objectives were generally successful as Union soldiers were hesitant to punish white women. As these women took on both maternal and paternal characteristics to defend their communities and protect their families, they occasionally thought of themselves as soldiers. After Mary Fielding's first contact with the enemy, she commented that she had "seen the Elephant" at last.[86] Yet, even as women transcended prevailing attitudes on gender, there were limits to what they were willing to do, as there are only isolated reports of women engaging in violent acts toward their occupiers. Much more common were nonviolent methods of resistance to demonstrate the extent to which they supported the Confederacy.

Almost immediately after they reached North Alabama, Union soldiers became acutely aware of Confederate women's attitudes toward the war and reunification. One Union soldier remarked that the "ladies . . . are more vicious, fierce, and rampant than the men."[87] Since these "vicious" women were generally not the ones physically attacking Union soldiers or damaging Union supply lines, this soldier might have been referring to their vocal public support for the Confederacy. Colonel John Beatty considered the conduct of Confederate women in Huntsville more bothersome than their male counterparts. He remarked that "the men of Huntsville have settled down to a patient endurance of military rule. . . . The women, however, are outspoken in their hostility, and are marvelously bitter." If Confederate women in North Alabama and across the Confederacy were not so supportive of the war effort, Beatty insinuated, the conflict might already be over. According to the colonel, "The foolish, yet absolute, devotion of the women to the southern cause does much to keep it alive. It encourages, nay forces, the young to enter the army, and compels them to continue what the more sensible Southerners know to be a hopeless struggle."[88] As Corporal Henry Ackerman Smith of the Twenty-First Ohio stood guard over wounded Confederate soldiers, several Confederate women from Huntsville arrived with food for the prisoners. As these women tended to the soldiers, Smith was taken aback by how the women encouraged the prisoners "to be good rebels" and not to give up hope. Smith realized that even though these women shouldered no weapons, they remained dangerous. He commented that "if Jeff Davis, Beauregard, or half of organized rebeldom [*sic*] had been there, they could not have confirmed so much treason as these *incognito* traitors did."[89] From these initial interactions, Union soldiers came to understand that Confederate women in North Alabama were not innocent bystanders, but a crucial component to the Confederate war effort, and therefore, a threat to the Union.

Confederate women's contribution to civilian resistance efforts went well beyond encouraging Confederate men to stay true to the cause. Using silence as a political tool was one of the more common tactics women employed against their occupiers. By refusing to acknowledge the enemy, Confederate women sent an emphatic message to their occupiers that their ideological commitment to independence was resolute. After Mitchel had occupied North Alabama for only a few weeks, Mary Chadick commented that he had started complaining that "the ladies of Huntsville have given his officers the 'cold shoulder' by not having received them into their social circle!"[90] When in public, Confederate women went out of their way to ignore their occupiers. Rowena Webster stated "I shut my eyes after passing a bluecoat for the first time."[91] Robert S. Dilworth witnessed a similar situation. According to the lieutenant, as Union soldiers approached Confederate women on the street, the women "draw their veils . . . to hide their southern beauty from the vulgar gaze of the . . . Yankees."[92] In Florence, Confederate women rose from their lawn chairs and went inside as a Union soldier was about to pass by. As the last woman entered the house, she slammed "the door with a marked and unmistakable vehemence."[93] Some Union soldiers had difficulty handling rejection from the opposite sex. When Captain Moore of the Tenth Ohio saw two Confederate women stepping into a carriage in Huntsville, he gallantly stepped forward to close the door for them. Before he could do so, "one of the [ladies] put forth her hand and pushed the door most violently." For a brief moment, Moore "looked crestfallen," but regained his composure and exclaimed to the Rebels: "Excuse me, I thought you were ladies." The women ignored his comment and proceeded on their way.[94] Incidents of Confederate women shunning Union soldiers were more than innocuous or amusing forms of resistance; these acts of defiance informed Union soldiers that Confederate women did not publically fear them and that Union occupation had not squelched their loyalty to the Confederacy.

Even when they did speak with their foes, Confederate women remained unabashed about their Confederate sympathies. Some women tried to unhinge their occupiers by telling them that Confederate cavalry were nearby, poised to attack. The subterfuge worked. Rowena Webster claimed, "We often kept the Yankees in hot water, reporting that [Nathan Bedford] Forest [sic], [John Hunt] Morgan or some famous General was in the neighborhood, when we had no tiding from them." Webster admitted that it "was a mere ruse" but that it was necessary "to defend ourselves from insult."[95] This and similar acts of deception empowered Confederate women by momentarily giving them control over Union soldiers.[96] False alarms also disrupted soldiers' routines and occasionally deprived them of sleep. Henry Ackerman Smith noted that there "is something so particularly unpleasant in being called out at night from a warm bed into the chilly air and stand probably an hour to see whether there is any reality in the alarm or not."[97] Taunting soldiers proved equally popular. As Union cavalry passed by Tom Burton's home, his wife emerged and waved a Confederate flag while shouting "Hurra [sic] for Jeff Davis & the Southern Confederacy!"[98] Although her brother was inside the house recuperating from wounds suffered at Shiloh, Mrs. Burton appeared confident that the Union soldiers would not stop. When Confederate women verbally assaulted their occupiers, they assumed existing gender conventions would protect them. Ohio soldier James Thomson wrote of an incident in which a Confederate woman gave him "a good tongue lashing," but he did not retaliate. Even young girls made their Confederate loyalties well known to Union soldiers. Thomson stated that "In one house while I was sitting on the porch I looked around suddenly and saw a girl . . . holding a broom under her arm in the position of a gun and [pointed] at me."[99] Laura

Wharton Plummer's frustration with supposedly haughty soldiers boiled over into a direct attack on one soldier's masculinity. This Confederate poignantly asked him "Why do you bring this war on defenseless women and children?" Plummer then offered the Yankee some unsolicited advice: "Go to the field and meet our brave boys there and leave us alone—that would be manly."[100] During the initial phase of the occupation, recalcitrant women had the opportunity to interact with enemy soldiers in a way that was unavailable to their menfolk, and they were confident that their gender would insulate them from harm as they engaged in acts of trickery, verbally assailed soldiers, or openly questioned their occupiers' manhood.

While Confederate women's gender provided them with security as they harangued Union soldiers, this protection was not absolute. Repeated incidents of female defiance led Union soldiers to question the policy of conciliation and whether they needed to rein in "secesh females." When Corporal Caldwell learned that women had "spit upon our soldiers," the Ohioan decided this far exceeded acceptable feminine behavior. "It [is] quite a lucky thing for them that they have never used me in that manner," he tartly commented. "There is a point beyond which I cannot control my temper, and that would be quite a piece beyond that point."[101] In a few instances, women were taken into custody. Union soldiers arrested Sarah Patteson for "attempting to convey improper news" to her infirm husband, Brigadier General Benjamin Patteson, who was in hiding south of the Tennessee River.[102] The most infamous case involved Rowena Webster, Sallie Matthews, and Rosa Turner, who had refused to hand over a small Confederate flag to a Union officer. Webster sharply commented that he would take a "baby flag from a woman" because he lacked the "bravery to capture one on the battle field." The confrontation quickly escalated when the officer threatened to "put a case of smallpox" in the surrounding houses if they ignored his command. The women stood their ground. After being arrested, the three were taken to Mitchel's office.[103] The general realized that little could be done to these young women, so he released them with a tepid warning to behave themselves in the future.[104] Even though this arrest showed that there were limits to what headstrong Confederate women could get away with, their gender saved them from what could have been a much more harsh punishment.

From a military standpoint, the Third Division's invasion of North Alabama was a resounding success. Soldiers had taken control of strategically important locations and severed one of the main railroad routes linking the eastern and western theaters with minimal bloodshed to themselves. With an aggressive-minded Union general in North Alabama, Confederate officers and soldiers in Corinth and Chattanooga had to be prepared for a potential assault by the Third Division.

But the invasion and subsequent occupation of North Alabama also revealed a glaring miscalculation by Lincoln, Buell, and other supporters of conciliation. While there were a few isolated cases of Confederates in North Alabama returning to the Union, the majority remained committed to breaking away from the Union. These individuals' loyalty to the Confederacy was not transitory; it had been nurtured and maintained by their faith in the Confederate armies, God, and themselves. Confederates' defiant opposition to the Union presence in North Alabama placed Mitchel in the difficult position of deciding whether to stick to conciliation or reconfigure the Union's civil-military policies in the region. Mitchel and his men chose the latter.

3

"IN THE SERVICE OF

JEFF DAVIS"

The advocates of conciliation had not anticipated the type of response Union soldiers in North Alabama received from Confederate civilians. Proponents of conciliation had been so confident that their conservative civil-military strategy would work that a back-up plan had been deemed unnecessary. Without a well-defined contingency plan, Union soldiers in North Alabama were in a precarious situation. Mounting acts of defiance from Confederate civilians led an exasperated Mitchel to notify Buell "I have done my utmost to conciliate the people . . . but the genuine rebels will not listen to reason."[1] Even though Buell was aware of the threat Confederate civilians posed to Union soldiers' safety and military readiness in North Alabama, he still expected his men to adhere to the tenets laid out in General Orders 13a. Mitchel, on the other hand, had already seen enough unruly civilian behavior to know that continued attempts at conciliation would be futile. Therefore, Mitchel and his men replaced conciliation with punitive civil-military policies designed to overwhelm

Confederate civilians' commitment to independence. As Union officers and enlisted men adapted their civil-military policies to meet the gravity of the situation in North Alabama, the war in that region lost its conservative character. The decision by Mitchel to ignore key components of General Orders 13a drew Buell's ire, but he had the support of high-ranking officials in Washington. Union soldiers' use of hard war tactics in North Alabama placed them at the vanguard of a budding recognition among northerners that southern civilians who rejected conciliation had to be dealt with accordingly.

To Mitchel's way of thinking, conciliation was conditional upon Confederate civilians' acceptance of Union overtures. The decision of Confederate civilians in North Alabama to remain committed to independence and to defy their occupiers compelled the pragmatic general to adopt counterinsurgency measures. On the same day Mitchel emphasized to Buell that he had tried his "utmost to conciliate the people," he notified Confederate civilians of a change in Union policy. The division commander started off by stating that "Armed citizens have fired into my trains on the railway, have burned bridges, have attempted to throw my engines from the track, have attacked my guards, [and] have cut the Telegraph wires." In a clear break with the policy of conciliation, Mitchel warned that in the future, "All these acts will be punished by death, if the perpetrators can be found." Civilians who knowingly concealed Rebels suspected of committing a crime would incur the same punishment. Under General Orders 13a, Confederate civilians were to be treated as American citizens deserving of protection under the United States Constitution. By targeting Union soldiers, Mitchel believed that Confederate civilians had given up these privileges. According to the general, "Unorganized bodies of citizens have no right to make war. They are outlaws, robbers, plunderers, and murderers, and will be treated as such."[2] Even though the general's statement to North Alabama Confederates went against the Union's existing civil-military policy, the division commander deemed his change in strategy crucial to effectively combating civilian-led attacks on his lines of communication and assaults on his soldiers.

Union soldiers backed Mitchel's plan to hold defiant Confederates accountable for their anti-Union activities. Even before arriving in North Alabama, the typical Union volunteer soldier had not been enthusiastic about the policy of conciliation.[3] As these soldiers penetrated further into the South, they came into contact with outspoken Confederate civilians. Some had been targeted or at

General Ormsby M. Mitchel (Library of Congress)

least knew of a fellow soldier who had been on the receiving end of civilian resistance efforts. With acts of defiance by Confederate civilians becoming com-
monplace in North Alabama, support for conciliation largely vanished. Captain
E. H. Tatem agreed with Mitchel that civilians' recent conduct ended any reasonable expectation that civilians should be left alone. The captain called for the
"most stringent" Union policy to be inaugurated to restore order.[4] More than
one Union soldier in North Alabama wanted see their civilian attackers dead.
Liberty Warner, a son of an Ohio Methodist minister, stated that he and his fel-

low Buckeyes wanted to "kill the wreches [*sic*] that gorrillo [*sic*] through the country and make such enormous costs by keeping up this rebellion."[5] Civilians' rebellious spirit led another soldier to comment that "the hemp should take the place of the Bible" in North Alabama.[6] Union soldiers favored abandoning conciliation because they had seen firsthand what committed Confederate civilians were capable of achieving. If Confederate civilians wanted to target their occupiers, soldiers felt that retaliation was surely in order.

Union efforts to end Confederate civilian hostility brought Federal soldiers face-to-face with their most daunting civil-military challenge of the war. Confederate civilians participated in assaults toward their occupiers because they were defending their hearth and home from what they perceived to be a foreign invasion and because they were certain that their nation would ultimately prevail. For Union soldiers to stop these acts of violence, they had to do much more than execute suspected culprits: they had to stop civilians from wanting to inflict harm on them. By taking a punitive approach to combating Confederate's nationalistic spirit, Union soldiers sought to convince civilians that opposition to the occupation and reunion was futile. When James A. Garfield arrived in North Alabama after participating in the siege of Corinth, he quickly surmised that Union victory hinged on punishing the Confederate home front. The future president of the United States claimed that "Until the rebels are made to feel that rebellion is a crime which the Government will punish, there is no hope of destroying it."[7]

The punitive strategies used to restore federal authority in North Alabama varied greatly in severity. These approaches can be broken-down into two categories: "weak punitive policies" and "strong punitive policies." Strong punitive policies led to the confiscation of Confederate foodstuffs and the destruction of Confederate property, and placed the physical well-being of Rebels in jeopardy. Weak punitive policies included but were not limited to arrests, loyalty oaths, censorship, and the confiscation of cotton. While treated separately, "weak" and "strong" tactics were simultaneously implemented and were interlocking components designed to pacify North Alabama Confederates. Generally, enlisted soldiers engaged in punitive tactics based on the orders from their superiors. They also had sufficient autonomy to implement these approaches without prior authorization. This discretion was not the result of officers' inability to control their men. Rather, such instances resulted from the absence of a clearly defined national plan to counter defiant civilians and the need for Union soldiers to root out resistance in a timely fashion. Whether from official orders or ad hoc responses, Union officers and soldiers were determined to suppress all forms of anti-Union behavior and bring the rebellion to an end in North Alabama.

Arrests served as a key component of the Union's weak punitive measures during the 1862 occupation. Most of those arrested were men, but Confederate women were also taken into custody. Those most likely to be incarcerated were Confederates suspected of being involved in hostile acts against Union soldiers. In late April, Mary Chadick commented that Union soldiers arrested a Mr. Wilson and "kept [him] in confinement [for] several days" for not giving the enemy "information [they] desired."[8] After Confederates fired on trains transporting soldiers past Paint Rock, Alabama, several Confederate men were rounded up and taken to the Huntsville jail. Among those arrested was a Mr. Scott. Upon convincing the bluecoats that he was not involved in the ambush, he was released. Soon thereafter, Scott arrived at Catherine Fennell's parents' house where he recounted his harrowing experience. Scott told Fennell that "there is a complete reign of *terror* in and near Huntsville. Nearly every man there has been arrested on mere suspicion."[9] Former Alabama governor Clement Comer Clay was among those incarcerated. C. C. Clay, Jr., his son, considered the arrest an unjustified act by "tyrants," and he accused Union soldiers of punishing "the poor old man for the rebellious acts of his sons."[10] While the elder Clay's stature in the community and the ardent pro-Confederate feelings of his sons might have contributed to his arrest, they were not the main causes. The former governor had been taken into custody for his alleged involvement in orchestrating the attack at Paint Rock and several others. One Union correspondent remarked that there was sufficient evidence to "fix upon Clay a large share of the responsibility for all these nefarious transactions." This northerner was not surprised by Clay's potential involvement: "The entire Clay family, in Alabama, is apparently composed of traitors of the deepest dye."[11] Despite the supposed evidence connecting the former governor to violent anti-Union activities, he was eventually released. Because acts of violence against Union soldiers and their supply lines were often clandestine affairs, Union soldiers had trouble identifying the perpetrators. When they lacked sufficient proof to convict an incarcerated Confederate, as in the cases of Scott and Clay, Union soldiers generally let the suspect go.

Wealthy and prominent Confederates were among the most conspicuous individuals arrested. Union officers and enlisted men often blamed powerful or politically connected southerners for attempting to destroy the Union and for inciting civilian resistance. As strikes against the Union increased during the latter part of April and beginning of May, General Mitchel decided to hold well-known men accountable. On the same day he issued his stern warning to North Alabama Confederates, Mitchel ordered the arrest of twelve community leaders living in Huntsville. J. W. Clay sent word to his brother C. C. Clay, Jr. that "prominent citizens were held as hostages for the good behavior of the citizens in the country, who were worrying Mitchell's [sic] scouts."[12] Clay sent a similar letter to his other brother Huey that these men were "hostages for the good behavior of the country people, who were burning bridges & cutting telegraph wires."[13] Among the men incarcerated were noted quinine doctor and former Alabama legislator Thomas Fearn, Episcopal bishop Henry C. Lay, cotton merchant William McDowell, and planter Stephen W. Harris. George P. Beirne and Samuel Cruse, the director and treasurer of the Memphis and Charleston Railroad, respectively, were also arrested. Combined, the value of the twelve men's personal property was estimated at over one million dollars.[14] By tying the fate of these men to the activities of Confederate civilians, Mitchel clearly intended to demoralize these powerful men while enticing the Confederate citizenry to stop waging war on his men.

Before the outbreak of war, Henry C. Lay had moved from North Alabama to Arkansas where he served as a missionary bishop. When the Confederate clergyman feared Union soldiers were about to invade the state, he returned to North Alabama. During his incarceration in Huntsville, Lay meticulously recorded the events that transpired. According to Lay, "No information was given as to the grounds [for our] arrest."[15] The detained men remained unaware of the charges for two days before Mitchel finally told them that he had "arrested us [simply] to show that no one in the community was beyond arrest: the innocent must often suffer for the guilty."[16] The general then launched into a lengthy diatribe against the "unfriendly spirit manifested by private citizens, and complained of the acts of hostility committed against his force by persons unauthorized to wage war." Mitchel unequivocally demanded that these leading Confederate figures in Madison County condemn violence that left his soldiers wounded or dead and his lines of communication in ruin. He further told the men that they must do their part to convince Confederate civilians to peacefully accept the present situation in North Alabama. The arrested men were informed that they would remain behind bars until they pledged not to engage in or support civilian defiance. Having issued his ultimatum, Mitchel ordered that the men be returned to their cells.[17]

Soon, Union guards handed the twelve men a statement that they were required to sign. Lay transcribed the declaration into his diary:

> We the undersigned citizens of Northern Alabama hereby solemnly pledge ourselves, that so long as our state North of the Tennessee [River] is in possession of the armies of the United States we will not only abstain from any act of hostility, but will do our utmost to persuade others to do the same. We disapprove and abhor all unauthorized and illegal war: and we believe that citizens who fire upon Railway trains, attack the guards of bridges, destroy the telegraph lines and fire from concealment upon pickets deserve and would receive the punishment of death. We even disapprove all guerilla warfare as calculated to embitter feelings already too much excited.[18]

After consulting with each other, the prisoners unanimously refused to endorse the document because they had "never engaged in unauthorized or illegal warfare." Their refusal earned the respect and backing of the Rebel community. Mitchel, however, became incensed. When he informed Secretary of War Edwin Stanton that "I hold under arrest a few active rebels, who refuse to condemn their illegal warfare," Mitchel suggested that "some of them should be sent to a Northern prison."[19] Rather than follow through with this suggestion, he decided to place all but Dr. Fearn—who was released for medical reasons—in solitary confinement.[20] During the initial stages of their isolation, the deep-seated commitment these eleven men had to the Confederacy provided them with the necessary resolve to endure the silence. Mary Chadick privately encouraged them to stay strong and "be true to themselves—let the result be what it may."[21] After several days, solitary confinement began to take a toll on Lay and the others. When they were finally permitted to talk to each other, they agreed they could not remain indefinitely in isolation. They had to sign the statement and hope that the Confederate community would realize it had been done under duress.[22] In addition to Mitchel's initial demands, Lay and his cohorts further acknowledged that Confederate civilians "cannot engage in offensive hostilities without the express permission of their sovereign: and if they have not a regular commission as evidence of that consent, they run the hazard of being treated as lawless banditti not entitled to the protection of the rules of modern warfare."[23] Even though these well-known men had spent nearly two weeks in isolation and signed the document under protest, their capitulation disappointed the Confederate community. When Mary Chadick heard the news, she lamented: "Who would have believed it! Every one of those 12 men have signed the paper!! . . . We actually cried tears of shame and resentment when we heard it." Mitchel reportedly commented that he "knew they were a set of cowards."[24]

While Mitchel achieved his immediate objective of forcing several prominent Confederates to sign a statement condemning civilian attacks on Union soldiers, the long-term significance of this affair was negligible. The Confederate population—despite their momentary resentment toward the men—would have still considered the signatures a form of Yankee coercion and therefore not binding. When the general attempted to capitalize upon his victory by demanding all Huntsville Confederates sign a similar statement, he encountered stout opposition. According to J. W. Clay, residents were confident that the general would not arrest the entire city. After only a few civilians signed it, Mitchel relinquished his demand.[25] More importantly, the signatures made minimal advancements toward stopping violent civilian demonstrations against Union soldiers. Indeed, North Alabama remained an inhospitable region for the Federals.

Requiring Confederate civilians to take an oath of allegiance to the Union, which became a cornerstone of President Lincoln's Reconstruction strategy in 1863, was another weak punitive policy implemented during the 1862 occupation. While captured or wounded Confederate soldiers were among those who took the oath, most loyalty oaths were administered to Confederate civilians. Proponents of the plan anticipated that once civilians—and captured soldiers—swore allegiance to the United States, they would abide by their promise. In addition to professing their rediscovered loyalty to the Union, Confederates generally had to promise not to provide the "so-called Confederate Government, or its officers [with] any information pertaining [to] the movements of the U.S. troops."[26] Individuals suspected of or caught breaking their pledge faced arrest and even death if their betrayal to the federal government seemed particularly egregious. If enough oaths were gathered, advocates of this plan expected North Alabama to become much more hospitable, setting the stage for repatriating the region back into the Union.

Soldiers' ability to secure loyalty oaths from Confederates in North Alabama was largely based on whether or not civilians wanted to take the oath. Confederates who feared Mitchel would make good on his promise to punish civilians who were behind the attacks on his men and lines of communication sometimes took the oath to distance themselves from the more violent Confederates. A Savannah, Georgia, newspaper claimed that people in North Alabama "are in such moral dread of [Mitchel] executing his threat, that the strongest secessionists (hitherto) are now clamoring for submission . . . and many have already taken the oath."[27] More often, citizens were coerced into promising fidelity to the Union. In late June, a Union officer gave the "stockholders" of a recently opened hotel in Huntsville three days to take an oath of allegiance to the federal government. Failure to comply would result in the confiscation of the property. Dr. Thomas Fearn, who had been among the twelve well-known men arrested by General Mitchel, was among the shareholders.[28] At the same time this demand was made, residents of the city learned that "all provisions . . . are forbidden to be brought to town, or passes given" unless they took an oath.[29] Confederates seeking reimbursement for provisions confiscated by Union soldiers had to swear allegiance to the Union before they would be given a redeemable voucher.[30] Confederate women were also required to take the oath. When Catherine Fennell learned that Union soldiers "made several ladies take the Oath of Allegiance," she prayed that she would not suffer the same fate.[31] Detained civilians often had to take an oath before being released. This was the case for an acquaintance of William Cooper, who was arrested near Florence but "paroled after taking [the] oath."[32] Regardless of the method Union soldiers employed to get the oath, their objective remained consistent: weakening Confederate resistance and morale.

Although some civilians might have adhered to the oath, the shortcomings of this policy made it largely ineffective. With tens of thousands of Confederates living in North Alabama, Union soldiers could not realistically gather loyalty oaths from every one. Numerous Confederates who came into contact with the enemy evaded taking the oath or rejected Union efforts outright. When Lieutenant-Colonel Jason M. Neibling told a group of Athens residents that they would be required to take an oath before being allowed to leave town, they "refused to take the oath under any circumstances."[33] Joshua Burns Moore rebuffed a Union officer he called "Major Quackenbush" for attempting to force him to take an oath. Moore informed the major that since "the Southern Confederacy [was] a de facto government," they had no right to force him to take an oath of allegiance to another country. He then lectured Quackenbush, declaring that "war should not be levied against [civilians] but against the armies in the field."[34] Buell's conservative civil-military agenda further undermined the loyalty oath policy. The general believed that only certain Confederate civilians should be required to swear loyalty. Colonel James Fry, a member of Buell's staff, told General Robert L. McCook, a Union brigade commander stationed in North Alabama, that Buell "does not desire the oath of allegiance presented to all citizens." In the future, Fry told McCook, Buell "wishes you to exercise a wise discretion in . . . the restrictions you place upon [citizens]."[35] The problems associated with logistical issues of administering the oath, Buell's conciliatory strategy, and Confederate resolve made this punitive approach in North Alabama difficult to enforce and only minimally effective.

Arguably the greatest stumbling block was a simple one: taking the oath did not result in a newfound devotion to the Union. Civilians, even those who had participated in anti-Union activities, could take the oath and still remain ideologically committed to Confederate independence. Henry Ackerman Smith noted that Confederates were taking the oath of allegiance, but this did not mean these men and women no longer supported the Confederacy.[36] Since they considered the oath an act of coercion by a foreign force, Confederates felt that they were under no obligation to keep their promise. Captain Tatem spoke for numerous soldiers when he noted that the Rebels were routinely disregarding their promises. "The oath is taken to be broken, and instead of a binding obligation it is regarded as a farcical transaction by those who resort to it, as they would to any measure freeing them from military surveillance," Tatem wrote.[37] The Union's use of loyalty oaths was arguably the most ineffective method employed to subdue the Confederate population in North Alabama. Ultimately, loyalty oaths did little to unhinge Confederate civilians' commitment to independence.[38]

Union officers and enlisted men had better success at protecting themselves and sapping civilian spirits when they censored or suppressed outspoken Confederates. Preventing Rebel civilians from gathering in pubic, confiscating Confederate letters, and discontinuing mail deliveries all struck hard at civilians' morale. Since Mitchel was unsure who were the main instigators of anti-Union activity, he did his best to break up Confederates gathering in public. The *Daily Morning News* (Savannah) reported that when the division commander saw a group of "half a dozen or more citizens together," he would, "in the most haughty and imperious manner, cry out, 'Disperse, you d—d rebels!'"[39] Although Union soldiers did not stop every Confederate letter or note from reaching its destination, their ability to intercept mail delayed or thwarted some would-be attackers. Toward the end of the occupation, Union soldiers in Athens engaged in a concerted effort to control information in the town. According to

Mary Fielding, Union soldiers "have grown a great deal more particular & strict here in the last week or two; [they] search people as they come in & leave town & say they have captured a mail or two." Dr. Coleman was one of the Athenians arrested; he had written a letter calling for the creation of a company of Confederate soldiers.[40] Confederate women were also arrested for sending illicit information, indicating that some Union soldiers intended to hold women just as accountable as men.[41] The Union's ability to bring the delivery of Confederate mail to a complete stop around Florence appears to have demoralized a petulant Joshua Burns Moore. This northwest Alabama resident commented that "ever since the advent of the Federals, there has not been a mail arrival in the valley—consequently we cannot hear of anything of what is transpiring, except for rumors."[42] Disrupting Confederate civilians' access to pro-Confederate information was one of the Union's most well-thought-out plans to curtail Rebel defiance and the enemy's redoubtable commitment to independence.

The Union's censorship policies disrupted Confederate women's ability to maintain communication with loved ones in the army and those living outside the occupation zone. Some women went days, weeks, or much longer without hearing from their family and friends. The lack of information from their menfolk in the Confederate army tested women's continued support for war. The absence of news from relatives was particularly hard after rumors circulated that a major battle or military offensive had taken place. When Mary Chadick first learned of the Battle of Seven Pines (May 31–June 1), she became distraught: "O, when will this dreadful war be over! And how many weary days, weeks, and perhaps months will lapse before we can know who of our friends are among the slain!"[43] Mary Fielding shared Chadick's sentiments. "I do wish they would make haste & fight & have this thing decided," she wrote in her diary. Fielding longed to be reunited with her two brothers or at least learn that they were safe. Not hearing from them during the first month of the occupation was a heavy burden for her to carry: "I feel sometimes as if I could not stand this much longer, not hearing from Henry or Eppa, & I know they are anxious to hear from home."[44] Rebecca Vasser of Athens characterized the dearth of information from her relatives in the Confederate army as a "deathly calm [that] is most hard to bear."[45] Even though these women and numerous others continued to support the war effort, their inability to stay in contact with loved ones and neighbors was one of their most difficult challenges during the five-month occupation.

Confederate men outside the occupation zone who had strong ties to the area expressed feelings of powerlessness over intermittent communication with loved ones and not being able to do more. Southern men would have considered defending their families from harm as one of their most important roles. The idea of protecting one's family from northern abuses had even been used as a central justification for disunion. Anxiety over the safety of their relatives and the indefinite length of the occupation sent some Confederate men to the precipice of despair. While in exile in Knoxville, J. W. Clay remarked that unless "Beauregard shall soon whip Halleck at Corinth," he saw "no immediate prospect" of his family being rescued.[46] In the coming days, Clay became increasingly anxious over feelings that he "ought to be doing, or trying to do something to wrest my home from Vandals & to rescue my relatives and friends from their oppression & persecution."[47] Edward D. Tracy adopted an even more urgent tone. Three weeks after the invasion of North Alabama, the Confederate officer nervously wrote that his "house is in the possession of the enemy & I am [in] suspense as to the fate of my wife & little ones, as I can hear not a word from them. God help us!"[48] The lack of information from family members was a distraction for Confederate soldiers and could hurt their performance on the field of battle. Robert Bliss, a native of Florence who enlisted in the Confederate army, was one of many Confederate soldiers who hoped "that soon North Alabama may be cleared of the scoundrels."[49] Bliss did not receive a single letter from his family during the entire occupation. While he still sent letters home, he could never be sure whether they reached his loved ones. In one of them, he told his mother that "I have thought a great deal about you all lately and what would I not give to hear directly from home."[50] The scant information some Confederate men received created moments of intense nervousness and apprehension. During these emotionally draining times, more than a few Confederate men might have wondered how far they were willing to go to support the Confederate war effort.

Union forces in North Alabama could not always keep civilians in the dark about Confederate military victories or Union setbacks. Confederate forces' successful defense of Richmond during General George B. McClellan's Peninsular Campaign ranked as the most significant military event in the eastern theater during the 1862 occupation. News of a Confederate victory would likely strengthen civilians' resolve to resist their occupiers. Confederates in North Alabama were aware that an important battle had taken place in Virginia, but they were unclear as to the outcome. During a church service in early June, Rebecca Vasser commented that she and her fellow parishioners were momentarily more worried over the fate of Richmond than their salvation. According to Vasser, "Mr. M. gave us a solemn sermon on the Judgment this morning," but "more minds in the assembly were . . . praying [to] God to protect our capital than listening to the learned arguments used to prove the judgment." Later that day, rumors began spreading in Athens that Union forces had prevailed, though Vasser's unwavering faith in God and the Confederate army helped her to not give up "hope till it is further confirmed."[51] The lack of verifiable information concerning the campaign frustrated Mary Chadick. At one point, she heard people claiming that the Confederates had prevailed and McClellan had been killed, though she considered the information unreliable rumor. This wife of a preacher longed for "our great suspense to be relieved and the truth be known! What would we not give this moment to set eyes on a Rebel newspaper!"[52] Over the ensuing weeks, she continued to receive questionable information. Fanny Mayhew told Chadick that she learned from a Union soldier that the Yankees had won a great victory.[53] It is unknown if this soldier had attempted to deceive Mayhew or if he himself had relied on unconfirmed reports. By early July, an exasperated Chadick commented that "It is really tantalizing the state of suspense we have to remain in before we can get the truth."[54] Over in Lauderdale County, Joshua Burns Moore noted that "we are totally cut off from all sources of information" about the campaign, but thought something was amiss. When he learned that there were no Union newspapers circulating among the occupiers, the observant slave owner decided that "the Yankees have had a reverse."[55] Union officers and soldiers could not indefinitely suppress or hide the news of their crushing defeat; civilians would eventually learn that their army had saved Richmond and driven McClellan off the peninsula. According to Rebecca Vasser, "We can bear all things here if our capital can be saved."[56]

Union soldiers did their best to censor pro-Confederate religious expression. The belief among Rebels that God was on the side of the Confederacy was a central component to their nationalistic spirit and fostered determination to resist their occupiers' punitive policies. Obviously, the Yankees could not prevent Confederate civilians from privately praying to God for solace and deliverance. While some civilians might have wondered why God had brought the enemy to their doorsteps, they were nonetheless confident that He would protect "us from our enemies."[57] During civilians' darkest moments, they found strength in the belief that the Almighty was on their side. Shortly after Catherine Fennell wrote that "all is lost and that it is useless to try any longer," her confidence rebounded. A reenergized Fennell concluded that "He will take care of us for I believe we are right."[58] For those living outside the occupation zone, faith soothed concerns over their loved one's well-being. J. W. Clay remarked that he had "an abiding trust in the goodness & mercy of God through Christ, & in His promises not to forsake those who put their trust in Him, but to hear & answer the prayers of those who ask."[59] Confederate civilians' deeply rooted conviction that God was on their side offered them a powerful tool to combat Union soldiers' punitive measures.[60] At least in the private sphere, Union soldiers could not stop Confederates from looking to providence for comfort and guidance to sustain them during the occupation.

Cracking down on public pro-Confederate religious demonstrations was a different matter. In a few instances, Union troops were able to silence the moral leaders of the community. Virginia Clay, wife of C. C. Clay, Jr., recalled that Union officers in Huntsville instructed Reverend Bannister about the "limited petitions with which he might address his God on behalf of his people."[61] When Union soldiers attended Confederate churches, their presence annoyed parishioners and forced some preachers to tone down their anti-Union sermons. Mary Fielding arrived at one springtime service expecting the preacher "would pray for the success of our cause & for the confusion and defeat of our enemies." This young Confederate was shocked when several bluecoats walked through the doors of the chapel for Sunday school; they then stayed for the service. Even worse, according to an irate Fielding, they had "the impudence to join in the singing with us." On this occasion, the clergyman toned down his pro-Confederate sermon, much to the chagrin of Fielding and other Confederates in attendance. He did, however, ask "the Lord [to] bring this unholy war to a close."[62] For good measure, a Union chaplain sat alongside the cleric during the service and gave the closing prayer.[63] On this particular Sunday, the Union preacher and the soldiers in attendance were able to largely prevent the Confederate parson from overtly preaching about God's support for the Confederacy and were able to frustrate Confederate civilians in the process. Their presence, however, hardly diminished Confederates' faith that God would see them through the occupation and lead them to victory.

The attendance of Union soldiers in Confederate churches did not persuade every Confederate clergyman to temper his sermon. Some preachers held such a fervent conviction that giving pro-Confederate sermons was God's will that they were prepared to incur earthly punishment. Reverend Frederick A. Ross, a Presbyterian minister from Huntsville, and Reverend William Henry Mitchell, a Presbyterian minister from Florence, aroused the ire of Union officers and enlisted men for their fiery anti-Union sermons.[64] After Lieutenant Robert S. Dilworth attended one of Ross's services, he wrote that the preacher did not hold anything back: "He throws all at us. Oh. What a church."[65] Both Ross and Mitchell were known for encouraging civilians to defy their occupiers, even if it meant resorting to violence. During one sermon, Ross assured his flock that if anyone died while "in the service of Jeff Davis" they would be rewarded by the Almighty in Heaven and would be remembered across the Confederacy as a hero.[66] Ross's steadfast defiance led to his arrest on more than one occasion.[67] The *Louisville Daily Journal* reported that Reverend Mitchell openly prayed for the "President, Cabinet, [and] General[s] . . . of the A.C.S." during a service in early July.[68] Within a month, his actions became more unabashed. With Union soldiers in attendance, Mitchell urged his congregation to pray for "Jeff Davis, for the success of the Confederate armies, and for the attainment of the independence of the Confederate people." Soldiers surprisingly allowed Mitchell to finish the sermon before taking him into custody.[69] When Confederate preachers were willing to suffer the consequences, Federals had few options besides making an arrest. They could send the preacher to a northern prison or shut down the church, but even these measures were problematic. Deporting a man of the cloth to a prison in the North would almost surely make him a martyr. Shutting down a place of worship would prove to Confederates that northerners were in fact ungodly people; closing a church might only intensify local opposition. Successful censorship of Confederate preachers such as Ross and Mitchell epitomized the challenges facing Union soldiers in occupied North Alabama: enacting measures that would end civilian defiance and overwhelm Confederate civilians' commitment to disunion.

Mitchel's decision to involve the federal government in selling cotton to northern merchants ranks among his most successful—and controversial—weak punitive policies. Seizing cotton from Confederate civilians and selling it to northern merchants was a pecuniary strategy that defrayed the costs of conducting an occupation. In addition to weakening Confederate civilians' ability to make a living, the strategy had the ancillary benefit of straining the relationship between Confederate civilians and nearby Confederate soldiers. Surprisingly, historians have generally ignored the important implications of a policy that simultaneously added cash to Union coffers while punishing those in rebellion.[70]

Less than a month into the occupation, Mitchel sent word to Stanton that his quartermaster was running low on money to operate the railroad and to pay "good Union men [who are] very poor and very needy." As the general waited for

Stevenson, Alabama (*Harper's Weekly Magazine,* August 30, 1862)

additional funds to arrive, he told the secretary of war that he intended to sell to northern merchants cotton that had been bought or confiscated from Confederates. The general made clear to Stanton that this cotton trade would not interfere with the transportation of soldiers or supplies and the program would "meet the approbation of the Government." Although there is no record of Stanton's reply, Mitchel's statement that he would charge "for the Government the usual prices" suggests that the secretary of war was aware of the policy and perhaps had approved it elsewhere.[71] Mitchel also informed Buell that cotton "buyers are in the market, and I have agreed to transport their cotton by rail and wagon, charging for the government the usual prices, using the empty supply train on its return."[72] By the beginning of July, the *New York Evening Post* reported that the sale of cotton to northern merchants had offset the costs associated with running an occupation and once again proved Mitchel's resourcefulness: "General Mitchel not only seized the railroads, but he has worked them, and he has made enough out of them to pay a considerable part of the expense of his troops."[73]

This policy was an economic blow to Confederate cotton growers in North Alabama and deprived the Confederacy of material necessary for uniforms, tents, socks, and other supplies. Confederate civilians had few options when approached by Union personnel in search of cotton. According to Mary Fielding, "Commanding officers at some places are forcing the people to sell their cotton; they say they will take it & pay nothing if they do not."[74] The *Cincinnati Gazette* reported that Union soldiers' threats to simply seize the cotton "compelled [Confederates] to submit, or else suffer for a want of the necessities of life." Few, if any, Rebels came out on top when the two sides negotiated the terms of the sale. With Union soldiers and northern cotton brokers determining the price, Confederates who sold their cotton often did so "at prices that . . .

scarcely cover[ed] the cost of cultivation."[75] The amount of cotton taken from Confederates and transported north was substantial. A few days after Mitchel's initial telegram to Stanton, he notified the secretary that "270 bales of captured cotton" were on their way to northern markets.[76] Toward the end of May, Union soldiers near Decatur took possession of 500 bales of cotton. This acquisition brought the total amount to "nearly if not over 6,000 bales" of cotton waiting to be sent to Cincinnati.[77] Some of this cotton might have been sent north on a convoy of wagons reported on by the *Southern Confederacy* (Atlanta). A correspondent for this newspaper stated that Union soldiers sent "400 wagons, loaded with cotton from Huntsville to Shelbyville," Tennessee, in early June. From Shelbyville, the cotton was taken to Nashville.[78] Even though not all Confederates were affected by this program, it had the potential to weaken the resistance movement in North Alabama. In all likelihood, the civilians who owned this cash crop were at least moderately wealthy and were thus the same type of people whom Union soldiers blamed for causing the war and encouraging civilian defiance. If enough of these wealthier Confederates became disheartened to the point that they were no longer willing to participate in or support attacks on Union soldiers, North Alabama might become safer for the Federals. Mitchel's cotton program was not only an insightful strategy to make money, but it also had the potential to make some Confederates suddenly more loyal to the Union.

Confederate military personnel could not simply stand back and allow Mitchel and the Union to commandeer such a valuable commodity. On several occasions they destroyed the cotton before it could be shipped north. Generally, Confederate civilians or cavalrymen made fleeting raids on Union-controlled warehouses and stores to incinerate the cash crop. In early June, Catherine Fennell remarked that 160 bales of cotton were destroyed by Confederates before the commodity could be transported from the southern to the northern bank of the Tennessee River.[79] In northwest Alabama, a small contingent of Confederate cavalry made a raid on Florence, where they "burned all the warehouses used for commissary and quartermaster's stores and all the cotton in the vicinity."[80] These might have been the same cavalrymen that Mary Fielding stated "burned a great deal of cotton that had been bought & deposited on the road between Pulaski & Nashville for shipment."[81] Because cotton is so combustible, it only took a brief moment for Confederates to set it on fire, frustrating Union forces and northern merchants alike.

Confederate military leaders sometimes ordered cotton fields to be burned before the bluecoats could seize the crop. According to a correspondent from the *Cincinnati Gazette*, General P. G. T. Beauregard issued a "ukase," or edict, for his men to burn cotton in northern Alabama and northeastern Mississippi.[82] Cotton fields not firmly within the Union's occupation zone were most likely to be targeted. On one day in late June, Catherine Fennell remarked that "our cavalry are burning all the cotton south of the Tennessee River" because "the Federals are taking all that they can find."[83] Fennell's sixty-year-old aunt Charity Lee was among those who had their fields set ablaze by Confederate soldiers.[84] Some Confederate civilians were dismayed that both armies were targeting civilian property. Joshua Burns Moore feared that North Alabama cotton growers faced certain disaster from both Union and Confederate forces. "If [civilians] sell their cotton [to the Union], the Confederates will raid on and destroy [the cotton]" Moore wrote. "If they refuse to sell it, the Federal soldiers deems [*sic*] their action suspicious and will raid on them. What in the name of common sense are they to do[?] . . . I can see ruin nothing but ruin, total ruin."[85] While some civilians might have considered the loss of their cotton a sacrifice for the cause, this Confederate strategy created internal turmoil for the segment of the population that questioned the military's decision to destroy private property under the guise of military necessity.

Despite the success of the cotton program, a disgruntled Union officer's claim that Mitchel and his family stood to profit from the venture has tarnished the legacy of the general and this punitive policy. In early June, Colonel Jesse Norton, an officer from the Twenty-First Ohio, left his post and traveled to Washington intent on testifying before the Joint Committee on the Conduct of the War about Mitchel's illicit involvement in the cotton trade. Once he was granted an audience with the committee members, Norton blasted Mitchel's leadership abilities and told them that the general made three cents for every pound of cotton sold to northern merchants.[86] Mitchel vehemently denied the allegation, noting that there had been no objection to this policy when it was first broached to the War Department.[87] With no proof linking Mitchel to any kickbacks, Norton's case fell apart. However, one arrest was made: Union military officials took Colonel Norton into custody for leaving his post in North Alabama without authorization.[88] By the time this occurred, the Union's confiscation of Confederate cotton had largely come to an end. After Buell moved his headquarters from Corinth to Huntsville in late June, he issued a directive heavily restricting northern merchants' ability to buy and transport the cash crop.[89]

—⇒•⇐—

Soon after Union soldiers arrived in North Alabama, General Mitchel and his Third Division realized that a conciliatory strategy was grossly inadequate for the situation they confronted. When Confederate civilians eschewed conciliation and turned to violent and nonviolent forms of resistance, the general abandoned the conservative policy. To counter this unexpected and potentially deadly welcome to North Alabama, Mitchel and his men devised a series of punitive measures designed to overpower Confederates' commitment to independence.

The success of the Union's "weak punitive policies" varied. Attempting to coerce Confederates into taking loyalty oaths barely lessened civilian defiance. Arresting Confederate civilians for illicit activities could potentially diminish violence, but only if the actual perpetrators were held indefinitely. Certain types of censorship and the confiscation of cotton rank as two of the most effective weak punitive approaches. While restricting the flow of information led to moments of hopelessness for Confederate men and women, the Union's seizure of cotton had the potential to demoralize an influential segment of Confederate society. Yet none of these approaches, either by themselves or collectively, substantially subdued Confederates' nationalistic spirit. Faith in divine providence and in their Confederate armies gave Confederates in occupied North Alabama the courage to withstand soldiers' hard war tactics while continuing to challenge Union soldiers for control of the region. Mary Fielding brazenly told one Federal that Confederate women in North Alabama would remain defiant until there were no more Confederate men left to defend them: "Maybe when all the men are killed you'll have the glory of conquering the women and children, but we won't give up before."[90] A few weeks later, Fielding wrote at length of how her occupiers' policies had done little to endear the Union to the region's Confederate population. Fielding remarked that "Never can I like anybody as well after they have mistreated me. . . . And I know the acts perpetrated under the folds of the 'stars and stripes' here are not calculated to make anyone love them." When a Union captain reassured the young woman that northerners and southerners would soon be reunited and at peace with each other, Fielding scoffed at such a thought: it would "be after this generation had passed away, then I think several more will have to pass away" before reconciliation would begin. "I think the theory of storms clearing the atmosphere of social & political life & the sunshine being brighter [is] humbug," Fielding told the officer.[91] Fielding's words were not idle rhetoric intended to fluster the captain. Rather, they were a firm statement from a Confederate woman who had no intention of abandoning the Confederacy. If Union soldiers were to have any success at subduing the Mary Fieldings of the area, they would have to implement punitive tactics that were much more harsh and destructive.

"'TWILL BE DONE AGAIN ALL

OVER THE SOUTH"

At the same time Union soldiers relied on weak punitive policies to overwhelm civilians' ideological commitment to the Confederacy, they also adopted much more severe measures. When necessary or militarily expedient, General Mitchel authorized his men to use "strong punitive policies" that threatened Confederates' personal safety and ability to provide for themselves. This approach to combating Confederate nationalism in North Alabama made Mitchel and Union soldiers among the earliest practitioners of destructive civil-military warfare. Even though these policies were an extreme departure from General Buell's conservative agenda and existing national legislation, Mitchel received the backing of the War Department and the president. The general's ability to carry out this brand of warfare ended when Buell arrived in Huntsville to assume command of the occupation, though Buell's efforts to resuscitate a more conciliatory strategy were mixed. The former slave owner was able to get rid of Mitchel, but he could not reverse Union soldiers' punitive mentality that linked the punishment of Confederate civilians to national victory.

Confederates in North Alabama hardly understood how their own actions had contributed to the Union's move to hard war measures against them. At the same time civilians participated in acts of defiance, they condemned their occupiers for engaging in what Rowena Webster labeled "daily depredations" or "arbitrary" acts against a civilian population.[1] Confederates naïvely assumed that they could retaliate against their occupiers with impunity. One border state correspondent remarked that "the rebels among us are clamoring for the guarantees of the Union and Constitution. That is all very well, but don't they tell us in every other breath that there is no Union and no Constitution?"[2] Since Confederate civilians had chosen to make war on Union soldiers, Colonel John Beatty of the Third Ohio argued that his government had the responsibility to "lay its . . . hand upon treasonable communities" until they came to their senses.[3] Union soldiers' harsh and unsympathetic treatment of Confederates hardly signified wanton depravity, though isolated incidents of egregious treatment did occur. The use of strong punitive policies was a calculated response to the threat dangerous Confederates posed to Union soldiers and the restoration of the federal government in Alabama.

The confiscation of foodstuffs was among the Union's most pervasive hard war policies.[4] Whenever Rebel soldiers or civilians disrupted the flow of rations into North Alabama, Union soldiers looked to civilians to furnish the difference. In mid-May, Colonel Beatty commented that recent attacks by Confederate General John Hunt Morgan on Union supply lines in southern Tennessee would not make the Third Division go hungry or drive them from the region. According to this officer, the "bread and meat we fail to get from the loyal States are made good to us from the smokehouses and granaries of the disloyal." Besides, "Our boys find Alabama hams better than Uncle Sam's sidemeat, and fresh bread better than hard crackers," Beatty wrote.[5] A few weeks later when Confederates prevented Union supplies from reaching the Huntsville depot, a Confederate correspondent reported that Yankee soldiers "robbed" from residents all the "bacon, beeves, poultry, corn, fodder, flour, groceries, horses, mules—in short everything that will replenish the exhausted quartermaster and commissary stores."[6] Because Federal troops could not realistically protect the entire supply lines between central Tennessee and North Alabama, Mitchel hoped to cow

Confederates into turning against those perpetrating the attacks. One southerner claimed that Mitchel was "oppressing the people and swears that he intends to starve them into submission. With his supply lines cut, he has resorted to stealing provisions from the people, taking everything he can find. What the people here are to do I cannot imagine."[7] Confederates could condemn the policy all they wanted, but it would not stop until supply lines ran uninterrupted and civilians accepted federal authority in North Alabama. Mary Fielding perceptively concluded that Mitchel was "trying to reach our loyalty through our stomachs."[8]

Although there were a few occasions when Union soldiers paid for their food, soldiers often embraced Mitchel's hard war mentality of relying on Confederate provisions when their own ran low.[9] On occasion, the seizure of foodstuffs was remarkably thorough. When Union soldiers entered Woodville and Larkinsville, they took "all the bacon, corn and killed all the [hogs], cattle, chickens, geese, and turkeys."[10] After Buell arrived in North Alabama, Federal soldiers accustomed to punishing Confederates did their best to continue with their ways. Mary Fielding's frequent verbal barbs against her avowed enemy might have played a role in Union soldiers arriving at her house one day in mid-July to confiscate all of "ma's milk . . . buckets & all."[11] Martin Moor, a Hoosier volunteer, commented that he and his comrades felt no guilt in taking the "potatoes, peaches, meal, [and] bacon" from secessionists near Stevenson.[12] Union soldiers hardened by Confederate civilians' unruly behavior and clandestine attacks were determined to make the Rebel population pay the price of disloyalty, even to the point of civilians wondering where their next meal would come from.

Soldiers in the Twenty-First Ohio Volunteers reveled in recalling such exploits. According to Private Liberty Warner, Confederate grocers were prime targets. While in Huntsville, he claimed that it "is extremely dangerous for a 21ster to go into a grocery, the stuff laying around naturally sticks to their fingers and the grocer wakes up to find things stept [sic] out, no one knows where."[13] As these men grew accustomed to taking what they wanted, their tactics became more brazen. While stationed in Athens, the men would go to a rich slave owning grocer "and present our case." These grocers, Warner wrote, "sometimes object, but the sight of our shineing [sic] bayonets argue the case. In fact, a bold face and a revolver at the side always win the grub."[14] Some soldiers, like Lieutenant Robert S. Dilworth, referred to livestock as defiant Confederates. On one July day, "Not less than 4 fine hogs took the oath of allegiance this morning." When the loyalty oath proved ineffective in stopping these hogs' unruly behavior, they were slaughtered and eaten. If they "cannot support the constitution, they will support the soldiers," Dilworth wryly commented.[15] Robert Caldwell considered consuming the enemy's victuals an act of patriotism. Upon eating a "good dinner" comprised in part of fresh mutton, he was pleased the meal "did not cost Uncle Sam nor ourselves anything." The Ohioan had no regrets about taking what he wanted from Confederate civilians: "This is a Secesh country and some [provisions] are now and then declared Contraband."[16] Caldwell's zeal for bringing the war to the Confederate home front apparently caught the eye of his superiors, and he was soon promoted to sergeant. From all appearances, the men of the Twenty-First Ohio fervently supported a punishing civil-military agenda designed to suppress rebellious activities and crush civilians' support for independence.

Confederates residing in the countryside likely incurred the greatest hardship from the Union's confiscation policy. Farms generally had larger quantities of food on hand, and Union soldiers wanted revenge against those who were behind the attacks on Federal troops, railroads, and telegraph lines. This was particularly the case for Confederates living in rural Madison County, which had been rife with anti-Union violence. Planters were prime targets. In late May, the *Charleston Mercury* alleged that Union foragers took "all the provisions from the plantations" in the county in an effort "to starve the people into submission."[17] Catherine Fennell claimed that the enemy ruined two of her cousins who lived in the county. After taking all the meat and corn, they decided to tear "up their beds, [break] their furniture and [steal] their money" for good measure.[18] When Union soldiers approached Confederate farms in search of food, outnumbered civilians had few options but to submit to their occupiers. Confederate soldier Nimrod Ezekiel Long, who returned to the area after the occupation ended, learned from a Confederate woman that enemy foragers took what "they wanted and paid for it or not as they pleased."[19] In some instances, Confederates on the lam inadvertently endangered their compatriots. After a few "Secesh" eluded capture in southern Madison County, George M. Kirkpatrick of the Forty-Second Indiana and his fellow soldiers refused to return to camp empty handed. To assuage their frustration, they rounded up "some hams and shoulders of meat and chickens" to take with them on their journey home.[20] With Huntsville serving as the headquarters for Union forces, the outlying region became one of the most contested areas in occupied North Alabama. Depriving Confederates of their sustenance was one of the many approaches Union soldiers took to subduing their enemies.

Of course, Confederates living elsewhere suffered too. Illinois soldier William M. Austin sarcastically wrote that he killed several chickens out of "self defense" while encamped outside Athens.[21] The extensive amount of grain taken from Limestone County alone led Henry Ackerman Smith to predict that soon "*corn* will be *king* instead of *cotton*."[22] When soldiers first arrived in northwest Alabama, they relied on civilian foodstuffs until supply routes were secured. Josephine Thompson Bryan recalled that during the first weeks of the occupation, the Yankees "passed our plantation near Florence and took by force all of our wagons and mules." Soldiers then "loaded the wagons with hams and cured bacon and corn."[23] When Union provisions ran low near Florence, foragers were sent several miles into a hostile interior to gather food. They returned safely with wagons full of supplies, including "four loads of corn [from] Dr. McConnel's plantation."[24] Bluecoats' proclivity for commandeering foodstuffs in northwest Alabama left an indelible mark on Marshall C. Wilson. Decades after the war he remembered that "Gen. Mitchell's [*sic*] troops swept the valley clean," leaving only a "little food" to see his family through the near future.[25] Whether they lived in towns or in the countryside, many Confederates experienced this harsh Union strategy firsthand.

Despite the severity of this policy, there is no evidence indicating that large numbers of North Alabama Rebels succumbed to the enemy. Yes, the loss of food and potential income caused many to suffer, but they bore this setback and remained committed to resisting their occupiers until help arrived from Confederate soldiers or the Almighty. There is little evidence of civilians blaming each other for what had occurred, and there certainly were no large-scale calls for the resistance to end.[26] Instead, Confederate nationalists placed the blame on vindictive northerners who did not know how to properly treat noncombatants. Some Confederates might have become even more committed to disunion as a result of the policy because they feared a worse fate if they surrendered. Instead of giving in to their occupiers' demands, they made do with what remained or sought help from their Rebel neighbors.[27]

Just as Confederates confronted the prospect of having their food supplies decimated, they also faced the possibility of having their property damaged or destroyed. The 1862 occupation of North Alabama marked a new stage in the war: Federals specifically targeted civilian property. Generally, instances where Union soldiers unleashed their destructive capabilities resulted from acts of civilian defiance that threatened soldiers' well-being and military preparedness. Naturally, Confederate civilians considered themselves victims of a barbaric northern military policy that needlessly punished civilian men, women, and children. Only in a few occasions did Confederates acknowledge that their defiance had contributed to the creation of one of the Union's most devastating hard war policies. The implementation of this strategy made Union soldiers in North Alabama the predecessors of a civil-military strategy made famous by General William Tecumseh Sherman.

One of the greatest challenges confronting Union officers and enlisted men in North Alabama was knowing whom to blame for violent anti-Union activity. Whenever possible, the Federals sought out their assailants and punished them accordingly. In situations where the attackers could not be found, the troops often held responsible all Confederates in the region where the attack occurred. The people in Paint Rock experienced the destructive power of the Union forces firsthand after local Confederates severed telegraph wires and fired into a train that wounded at least six Federals. A furious Colonel John Beatty ordered the train stopped and marched his men back to Paint Rock. Upon rounding up the townspeople, Beatty told them that "this bushwhacking [must] cease." The Ohioan warned them that from here on out, "every time the telegraph wire was cut we would burn a house; every time a train was fired upon we would hang a man; and we would continue to do this until every house was burned and every man hanged between Decatur and Bridgeport." To prove his point, he "set fire to the town [and] took three citizens" before proceeding on to Huntsville.[28] Beatty considered his response to the Paint Rock affair necessary to "preserve us from constant annoyance." The colonel later wrote that Mitchel was "well pleased with my action in the Paint Rock matter," and that his vigorous response to the attack was "spoken of approvingly by [fellow] officers and enthusiastically by the men."[29] By holding the townspeople of Paint Rock responsible for the violent deeds of a few Confederates, Colonel Beatty and his men sent to Rebels throughout the occupied region a clear message: attacks on Union soldiers would have dire consequences.

Officers and enlisted men echoed Beatty's call for swift retaliation. When soldiers were unable to catch the perpetrators behind several deadly attacks near Woodville, Mitchel issued a sweeping edict that if the townspeople "did not cease shooting his men, he would hang every private citizen he caught doing it and wd. burn every barn within ten miles."[30] Apparently, these civilians did not heed Mitchel's warning; several days after his announcement, Catherine Fennell reported that the general sent soldiers to burn Woodville, along with the towns of Larkinsville and Bellefonte.[31] When Union soldiers were unsure if the assailants were civilians or regular Confederate soldiers, there was a good possibility that civilians would still suffer. Mary Chadick stated that this was the fate for numerous Confederates between Huntsville and Stevenson who had their property "plundered and destroyed" after an ambush by Confederate soldiers or citizens resulted in thirteen Union casualties.[32] Madison County guerrilla fighter Frank Gurley provides one of the rare documented cases of a Confederate acknowledging that their violent actions contributed to Union reprisals. Gurley commented that after he and his gang killed eighteen soldiers and wounded another six aboard a train, "the Yank[s] paid me back [by] burning [Confederate] houses" in the vicinity of the attack.[33] Whether an attack on Federal soldiers came from private citizens, Confederate soldiers, or bands of guerrilla fighters, the slightest bit of perceived civilian involvement could lead to the destruction of Rebel property.

During the initial days of the occupation, Confederate women made their Confederate sympathies well-known to their occupiers because they assumed that prevailing gender conventions would shield them from harm. Female defiance and persistent incidents of anti-Union activities gradually wore down the Federals' patience. When soldiers participated in retaliatory attacks, whatever special protection Rebel women had been given quickly evaporated. In some situations, women were targeted for the deeds of their sons or husbands. In Jackson County, a Mrs. Dillard was unable to stop revenge-minded Union soldiers from torching her home as punishment for her son having killed one of their comrades.[34] There were also claims that Union soldiers roughed up Confederate women while destroying property. The homes of several Confederate women living near New Market were set ablaze by Union soldiers. At one point, they reportedly "kicked Mrs. Word" through the doorway and "slapped Miss Anna's jaws."[35] At least one Confederate woman paid the ultimate sacrifice for her government. The shelling of Guntersville by Union forces resulted in the destruction of more than a dozen homes and the death of "Mrs. Sarah Bayburn, [who] was greatly beloved by all her acquaintances."[36] Confederates were aghast at Union soldiers "making war on women and children."[37] After Mary Chadick heard soldiers had burned the town of Whitesburg, she blasted them for leaving the women and children of the town "houseless and homeless."[38] Rowena Webster singled out Mitchel: "A greater tyrant never lived in revolutionary times."[39] When Mitchel and his men moved toward destructive measures to subdue defiant civilians, Confederate women quickly learned that their gender no longer afforded much protection. As Confederates, they faced a very real possibility of incurring the wrath of punitive-minded soldiers just as their menfolk did.

When Frank Gurley and his men killed General Robert L. McCook in northeastern Madison County, Union soldiers accused civilians of leading Gurley to McCook, who was suffering from dysentery and being transported in an ambulance. Retaliation swiftly followed. General George H. Thomas sent word to Buell that McCook's men were so "enraged" that "before they could be stopped [they] burned and destroyed some four or five farm-houses."[40] Confederate sources suggested greater mayhem. The *Charleston Mercury* claimed that the "death of [General] McCook was fearfully avenged. His regiment, hearing of his death, seized their muskets, and, breaking through all discipline, dashed forth with feelings amounting to frenzy." After Union soldiers accused their scout of nefarious involvement, they "hung" him "up between two saplings and riddled [him] with bullets." When this failed to quench their thirst for revenge, the soldiers set their sights on "the adjoining town and plantation" where they killed every male Rebel they could find.[41] Mary Fielding made a similar charge. McCook's "enraged soldiers hung seventeen citizens & destroyed all the plantations in the neighborhood." She learned from Miss Sue Sneed that Union soldiers "burned all the houses within five miles" of where the general died.[42] Decades after McCook's death, Reverend James Monroe Mason, a member of Gurley's gang, stated that Union soldiers enacted "their vengeance upon the defenseless inhabitants of the country." According to the preacher, "These citizens were wholey [*sic*] innocent of complicity with us."[43] In the days following McCook's death, Buell offered no official condemnation of the attack, though he was also silent on the actions of his men.[44] A correspondent for the *Cincinnati Gazette* was much more vocal on the killing of McCook and insisted that "the blood of this murdered officer cries out from the ground for a [national] war policy that shall exterminate the whole guerrilla system."[45] Although the actions of these soldiers straddled the line between a justifiable retaliation and egregious vengeance, the general's death and reports of civilian involvement ultimately encouraged the use of harsh methods to subdue hostile Rebels.

Confederate newspapers echoed the accusations made by Rebel civilians. By bringing to light the plight of Confederates in North Alabama, editors reminded their constituents of northerners' efforts to terrorize civilians. A Savannah, Georgia, newspaper issued a scathing report on Mitchel's "cowardly disposition" for "oppressing the people" of North Alabama.[46] The *Charleston Mercury* condemned Federals for their attack on civilians after McCook's death, stating

Searching for Rebels in North Alabama (*Harper's Weekly Magazine,* August 16, 1862)

that the general was a "bloody and unscrupulous tool of the tyrant Mitchell [*sic*]."[47] Phrases and words such as "reign of terror," "atrocities," "outrage," and "cowardly" were commonly used to depict the enemy as the aggressors and Confederate civilians as the victims. The *Fayetteville Observer* (N.C.) argued that "Yankee outrages have produced such a reign of terror . . . that no citizen dare raise so much as a little finger by way of protesting against the barbarism of the invading force."[48] The editor of the *Charleston Courier, Tri-Weekly* claimed that "the Yankees have violated all the decencies and proprieties of life" in North Alabama and deserved "the heartfelt execration of the people of the South, and contempt of the world." They "have made the name of Yankee a synonym for all that is base, cowardly, and cruel."[49] These reports served an important ideological purpose by stirring Confederate civilians outside of North Alabama to continue sacrificing for their government—otherwise, they might share a similar fate.

The most severe incident of Union soldiers targeting Confederate civilians and their property occurred in Athens. On May 1, Confederate Colonel J. S. Scott and his cavalry made a clandestine raid into Athens, forcing surprised officers and enlisted men from the Eighth Brigade to make a hasty retreat.[50] When the Athenian men saw their Confederate liberators give chase to the enemy,

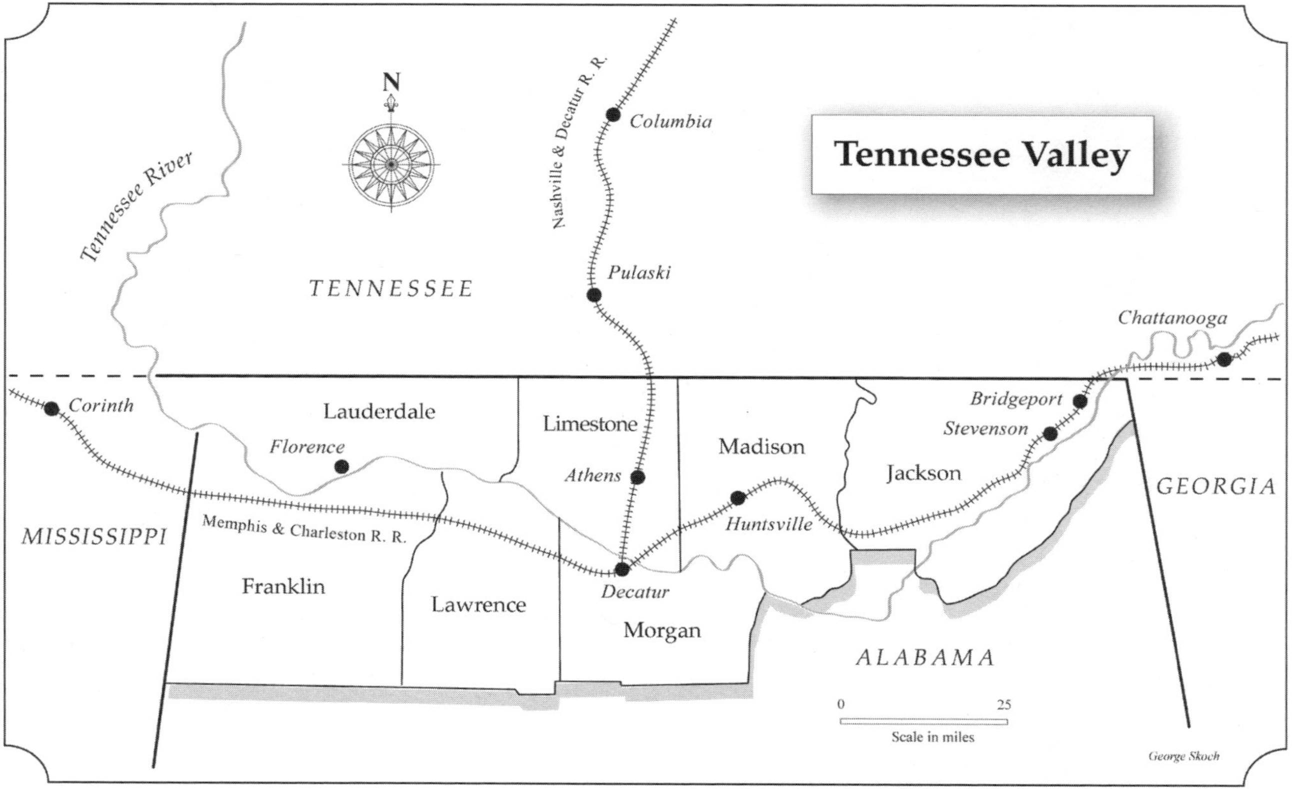

Map 3. Tennessee Valley

they experienced an upwelling of patriotism and reportedly "seized their guns, mounted their horses and joined the rebel gang and pursued" the fleeing enemy.[51] Confederates also fired on the Yankees from the windows of houses, though it is unclear if the shooters were men or women.[52] Those who did not arm themselves showed their disdain for the enemy in other ways. As Union soldiers fled, elated civilians "laughed, snired [sic], hurrahed, threw up their hats, [and] cursed the Yankees."[53] The boldness of Confederate women stood out to Reverend T. M. Eddy of Illinois. He noticed how the women "jeered at [Union soldiers] with the vilest epithets, spat upon them, and the rabble followed them, throwing filth and garbage."[54] Once the last bluecoat had been driven from the town, Confederates rejoiced. Colonel Scott and his men "were greeted with cheers & a waving of hats & handkerchiefs by the citizens on the square," wrote Mary Fielding. Soon thereafter, the "ladies at the tavern brought to light a Confederate flag that hasn't seen the light in some time."[55] Confederate civilians' wait for the return of their fighting men had ended. Some likely felt that it was the first step in reclaiming all of North Alabama from their hated foes. Their celebration, however, was short-lived.

Colonel John Basil Turchin, who commanded the Eighth Brigade and had previously spent time as an officer in the Russian Imperial Army, was adamant about retaking the town and punishing those who joined or stood by and cheered Scott's cavalry unit. On May 2, Turchin drove the enemy from Athens. Then, he ordered his men to sack the town. Lieutenant Robert S. Dilworth, who did not participate in the "Sack of Athens," claimed that "General Turchan [sic] ordered his men to do their own will for 3 hours."[56] Captain Spillard F. Horrall of the Forty-Second Indiana Volunteers heard that Turchin was so mad about the conduct of Confederate civilians that he told his men, 'I shust [sic] mine eyes for two hours.'"[57] Some Confederates mistakenly assumed Mitchel ordered Turchin to lay waste to Athens. "No worse order was ever given in the days of the French Revolution than that he issued to old Gen'l Turchin . . . to give the soldiers the liberty of the town for two hours," wrote Rowena Webster.[58] Even though Confederates were already well aware of the Union's harsh tactics, they were still aghast at the Russian's order. Mary Fielding remarked that she had "perfect contempt [for] a man that will give permission to his soldiers to sack a town & lock himself up to keep from being appealed to."[59] For soldiers under Turchin's command, the order gave them the opportunity to avenge the preceding day's humiliation as well as previous acts that left their comrades wounded or dead. Once Turchin recused himself, his men "let . . . loose upon the town and citizens of Athens."[60]

When Mary Fielding first tried to describe what happened, she did not know "where to begin or what to say, so many things are jumbled together in my brain 'tis like a tangled skein not to be easily unraveled." As she worked through the raw emotions, she depicted Union soldiers as callous men with an inner "will" to destroy property and terrorize Confederates. Fielding reported that soldiers broke into several Confederate stores and either "destroyed" what was inside or gave it to blacks. At the same time soldiers looted businesses, others searched Confederate homes for weapons.[61] During these searches, they often ransacked the place. At Catherine Fennel's uncle's house, bluecoats "did all the mischief they could; breaking up the furniture, boxes, trunks, [and] tearing up clothes."[62] Some of the aggressors reveled in their authority to punish the enemy with apparent impunity. Rowena Webster claimed that a "chief delight" for soldiers "was to strew molasses and lard all over the carpets, break up furniture and smash the mirrors, and to leave nothing that they could possibly destroy."[63] When the opportunity presented itself, Union soldiers humiliated Confederate women. The *Newark Advocate* (Ohio) reported that Confederate "ladies were robbed of all their wearing apparel, except what they had on."[64] A friend of Mary Fielding was among those who had their clothing ruined or confiscated. According to Fielding, this woman became "madder and madder every time she [thought] about it. They took her finest silk dress & worst of all, nearly everyone of [her] underclothes."[65] At other times "wives and mothers [were] insulted." If a husband or father "dared to murmur" in protest, he was arrested.[66] Soldiers' conduct was more than one woman could bear. When soldiers turned Mrs. Hollingsworth's home upside down, the "alarm and excitement" resulted in a miscarriage and her subsequent death.[67] Mr. Hollingsworth was unable to comfort his wife in her final moments or take care of his children because he had fled to escape punishment for joining Colonel Scott's cavalry.[68] Over the course of a few hours in early May, Union soldiers unleashed their most destructive attack on a Confederate town during the 1862 occupation. In addition to striking back at civilians' recent acts of resistance, some soldiers likely assumed that their assault on Athens would completely demoralize Confederate morale and civilians' ideological commitment to independence.

While Athenians were certainly frightened by the events of May 2, they were not ready to abandon resistance. Over the ensuing weeks, Confederate nationalists inundated Mitchel with demands to launch an investigation. In a few instances, the general made a feeble attempt to recover missing items.[69] He balked, however, when Confederate civilians presented him with a petition seeking criminal charges against Turchin and his men and nearly $55,000 to cover their losses. Mitchel told them he could not "arraign before a court, civil or military, [an entire] brigade."[70] When Secretary of War Edwin Stanton learned of the Sack of Athens, Mitchel acknowledged that "terrible excesses" had occurred, but he insisted Confederates had instigated the affair by supporting the Confederate cavalry and by cursing at and spitting upon his men as they fled the town.[71] Mitchel's report to Stanton was apparently enough to satisfy the secretary of war. For the time being, no charges would be leveled at Turchin or any of his men. Inaction by Washington officials meant tacit support for harsh punitive policies against southerners who had spurned conciliation.

Mitchel and his men did not face their first significant internal objection to their punitive ways until Buell arrived in Huntsville in late June, following a painstakingly slow march from Corinth.[72] Buell's efforts to rein in the Third Division's punitive measures and reinstate conciliation as the guiding civil-military policy in the region were fraught with difficulty. As commander of the Army of the Ohio, he had the authority to order the Third Division to follow General Orders 13a, but he was unsuccessful at convincing them to accept a return to more limited warfare. Nor could the general stop soldiers who came with him to North Alabama from promoting a punitive response to unruly civilians. As the nation became increasingly aware of Confederate civilians' defiance, the general faced an additional hurdle from officials in Washington who began pushing for policies similar to those implemented by Mitchel. Throughout his time in North Alabama, Buell's conservative agenda encountered resistance from Union soldiers and the nation at large. To ever-growing numbers of Federals, punishing Confederate civilians now seemed a military necessity.

Despite soldiers' opposition to conciliation, they had few options when Buell intervened. Incidents where the general sided with defiant civilians fueled speculation by Federal troops that their commander cared more about the welfare of Confederates than his own men. John Otto of the Eleventh Indiana Battery recalled how Buell released a Rebel named Farrier even though the man was suspected of firing into a train carrying Union soldiers near Stevenson. Otto mordantly remarked that "I suppose he proved himself innocent as usual. These Southern conspirators [are] always innocent [to Buell]."[73] A Wisconsin officer fumed after Buell released a member of a guerrilla gang that killed two of his comrades. Adding to the officer's frustration was Buell's *"order . . . for [the*

General Don Carlos Buell (Library of Congress)

man's] horse to be returned." This Midwesterner remarked that Buell's "conduct makes my blood boil."[74] Union soldiers feared that their commander's regular intercession on behalf of Confederates threatened their safety and the
restoration of federal authority in North Alabama. Sergeant Robert H. Caldwell
claimed that Buell was ignoring his military responsibilities by coddling "the
sensitive feelings of the high bred sons of the chivalric South."[75] Colonel Geza
Mihalotzy of the Twenty-Fourth Illinois questioned how Buell could expect his
soldiers to follow General Orders 13a when a "strict . . . construction" of the pol-

icy posed a dangerous risk to the "gallant soldiers under his command."[76] Buell's continued insistence on conciliation did not endear him to his men, nor did it make the region more hospitable for the Federals.

Hardened soldiers ridiculed their commander for promoting an archaic strategy that empowered Confederates and shielded them from harm. Charles W. Willis, an Illinois soldier, claimed that Buell's conservatism bolstered Confederate civilians' nationalistic spirit. "These people, safe in the knowledge of our conciliatory principles, talk of seceshism [sic] as boldly as they do in Richmond," Willis wrote.[77] In areas of North Alabama where a conciliatory approach was restored, albeit temporarily, Rebels had less reason to fear that their food would be confiscated. Captain Spillard F. Horrall of the Forty-Second Indiana Volunteers commented that Buell's "very strict rules forbidding foraging," even after supplies to the region had been interrupted, left some bluecoats with "very meager allowances" of food.[78] The commanding general's theories on proper civil-military warfare certainly perplexed the region's unionist population. James A. Garfield had seen enough of Buell's conciliatory ways to know that it was "better in this country . . . for a citizen to be a rebel than to be a Union man."[79] Sergeant Caldwell spoke for countless Union soldiers when he expressed frustration that Buell was "endeavoring to win back the traitors, by acts of kindness" despite the "most vindictive, and uncalled for cruelty committed on the part of the rebels."[80] After turning to punitive tactics to put an end to civilian resistance, few Union soldiers wanted to return again to more conciliatory measures. Buell, however, remained oblivious to the potential peril his policy might have on his soldiers, their morale, and Union victory.

Given the differences between Mitchel's and Buell's views on conducting the occupation, the two were bound to clash. Within days of Buell's arrival in Huntsville, they argued over a potential attack on Chattanooga.[81] The aggressive-minded Mitchel came away from the heated discussion convinced that his talents could be put to better use elsewhere and asked Stanton to remove him from North Alabama. This was not the first time Mitchel had approached the secretary of war for a transfer. In late May, he had requested reassignment to the Army of the Potomac "simply and solely because I am confident I can do there more effective service than here in Alabama," but Stanton and Lincoln both felt he would be needed for the assault on East Tennessee.[82] With Buell en route to Huntsville, Mitchel received a similar response after he again appealed to Stanton for a transfer to the eastern theater. The secretary of war stated that "it would also gratify me very much to have your eminent military genius employed actively in the East, but the President regards the advance on East Tennessee as only second in importance to Richmond."[83] This time, when Mitchel threatened to resign his commission, Stanton relented and recalled him to Washington.[84]

For nearly three months, recalcitrant civilians endured an array of punitive policies devised or supported by Mitchel. While some of these hard war tactics would continue after Mitchel's departure, proponents of punitive civil-military policies in North Alabama had lost their unquestioned leader. With their arch-nemesis gone and Buell in command, Confederates had reason to expect the vestiges of Mitchel's policies would be overturned. Soon after Buell arrived in Huntsville, Mary Chadick stated that he "did not approve of the course [Mitchel] had pursued toward the citizens here" and she assumed that Mitchel's policies would be done away with.[85] Mary Fielding claimed that Buell was "mortified at the course pursued by Gens. Mitchel & Turchin" in North Alabama.[86] Both of these women suggested that the departed general would receive a stiff rebuke, if not a court-martial, for his conduct in North Alabama.[87] With Mitchel out of the way, Confederates looked to Buell to restore their civil liberties. Governor John Gill Shorter learned from one North Alabamian that once Mitchel left the region "Gen'l Buel [sic] revoked many of his offensive orders against our citizens."[88] Even though North Alabama Confederates were still living under an occupation, they were hopeful that Buell would bring an end to Mitchel's punitive policies and treat them in a manner befitting their self-proclaimed noncombatant status. Confederate civilians did not, however, indicate that their defiance would cease.

Mitchel's willingness to punish recalcitrant Confederates had created a faithful following among Union soldiers and correspondents. Both groups championed his use of punitive policies in North Alabama. Lieutenant Robert S. Dilworth longed for Mitchel's aggressive style of warfare when it became apparent to him that Buell had no intention of launching an offensive against Chattanooga anytime soon. "Oh! if we had Gen. O. M. Mitchell [sic] with us. . . . We would be in our glory. Hurrah! for the brave old gen. I love the name of Mitchell [sic]."[89] According to this officer, if "there were a few more Mitchells [sic] in the field, seceshia [sic] would be obliterated in a twinkling."[90] A correspondent for the *Cincinnati Gazette* asserted that the general's efforts to combat a hostile population in North Alabama would be duly recorded in the annals of American history. He wrote that "instead [of] the future historian . . . complaining that [Mitchel] did not do enough, [he] will point with enthusiasm to what he did perform, as a striking illustration of the power of genius and energy to [achieve] wonderful results, even with comparatively insignificant means."[91] The *New York Times* praised the onetime astronomer for a style of warfare that treated "rebels as if they *were* rebels."[92] The editor of the *Daily Cleveland Herald* made a similar statement, applauding the "fiery mars of the west" for "prosecuting the war with vigor."[93] For the past few months, Mitchel had relied on unbending tactics to protect his men from attacks and to crush Confederate civilians' nationalistic fervor. In doing so, he earned the enduring admiration and respect of like-minded compatriots and left a legacy of becoming one of the first and foremost practitioners of bringing the war to the Confederate home front.

Upon Mitchel's arrival in the nation's capital, members of Lincoln's inner circle met with him and praised the general for his recent services to his country. One morning in late July, John Hay, Lincoln's private secretary, had breakfast with Mitchel and three other generals at Willard's boardinghouse. Later, Hay remarked that "history . . . will regard [Mitchel] as a giant." The enemy, according to the secretary, "has had little time for slumber when opposed by the earnest vigilance of this unwinking star-gazer."[94] As Mitchel awaited orders, cabinet members urged that he be given an assignment of the utmost importance. Mitchel's knack for living off the land and for aggressive tactical movements made him a candidate for leading the campaign to take Vicksburg and secure Union dominance on the Mississippi River. When Salmon P. Chase arrived at the War Department on July 21, he joined Stanton and Lincoln in a conversation about upcoming military operations. "We talked about the necessity of clearing the Mississippi and Stanton again urged sending Mitchell [*sic*]," Chase wrote. Intrigued by the possibility of naming Mitchel to the post, Lincoln requested an audience with the general. After Mitchel met with the president, Chase told the general that "now was the time to do great things."[95] While Mitchel had many influential supporters, he did not have the backing of General Henry W. Halleck, the general in chief of the army. According to Mitchel's son Frederick, Halleck refused to sign off on the appointment, perhaps out of jealousy for the recent accolades Mitchel had received.[96] The task of taking Vicksburg eventually fell to General Ulysses S. Grant. There were also rumors that Mitchel might be made commander of the Army of the Potomac or given a division in General John Pope's Army of Virginia, but nothing happened.[97] Instead, he was sent to the Midwest to recruit volunteers—where he likely stressed the importance of punishing the Confederate home front—until September, when he was appointed commander of the Department of the South with his headquarters in Hilton Head, South Carolina.

Mitchel's tenure in South Carolina was brief; in the latter part of October, he contracted yellow fever and soon died. Over the following weeks, northerners mourned the loss of a man who influenced the Union's acceptance of punitive policies against Confederates. The Cincinnati Astronomical Society, where Mitchel formerly served as director of the observatory, issued a statement that his death was "an occasion of mourning, not only to us as a Society founded and made efficient by him . . . but it is also a source of lamentation to our country—to the lovers of science and mankind."[98] The *New York Times* compared Mitchel's passing to the "loss of a great battle."[99] A writer for the *Daily Cleveland Herald* asserted that Mitchel left an indelible mark on the Union Army and the northern war effort. Of "all the Generals in the war, no one more emphatically stamped heartiness upon all his blows aimed at the accursed rebellion [than Mitchel]," the man wrote.[100] Confederates were equally strong in excoriating their dead foe. A contributor to the *Weekly Mississippian* (Jackson) claimed that Mitchel's "tyranny will not soon be forgotten by the people of North Alabama," adding that the general's conduct in the region was comparable to "Beast Butler in spirit and temper."[101] One North Alabama Confederate declared that "No man ever had more winning ways to excite people's hatred than [Mitchel]. We have no space to do justice to his vices." This man was certain that Satan himself would reward Mitchel for his malicious treatment of Confederate civilians by making him the "president" of the "new hell . . . established for the Yankees."[102] General Mitchel's military legacy and death elicited strong responses on both sides of the Mason-Dixon Line. While northerners grieved the loss of an aggressive-minded officer who made punishing dangerous civilians a top priority, Confederates condemned Mitchel for his harsh treatment of those who claimed to be noncombatants.

General W. S. Smith was initially tapped to take over for Mitchel as commanding officer of the Third Division, but he was soon replaced by General Lovell H. Rousseau, a career politician who had served in the Mexican War.[103] The appointment of Rousseau might have been at least partially driven by Buell's expectation that this Kentuckian would work with him to end the destructive methods of the Third Division. While Rousseau was more conservative than Mitchel, his civil-military philosophies did not coincide with Buell's conciliatory beliefs. Shortly after assuming command of the Third Division, he remarked that "Southern man as I am . . . I am for the Government of the United States against all its enemies."[104] Hard war advocates considered the general a capable successor to Mitchel. The *Cincinnati Gazette* claimed that Rousseau "will never make those soldiers cease to regret the loss of Gen. Mitchell [sic], but he may, in time, make himself equally loved."[105] Rousseau supported his soldiers' efforts to hold dangerous Confederates and their accomplices accountable for their actions. Colonel John Beatty was delighted that Rousseau "damns the rebel sympathizers [and] discards the rose-water policy of General Buell under his nose."[106] In one of Rousseau's most notable responses to unruly civilian behavior, the general ordered "a conspicuous secessionist, a preacher, or a member of one of the churches at Huntsville," to be placed on trains that had been previously fired on by Confederates; if the assailants were still determined to attack their occupiers, they would now risk wounding or killing one of their community leaders. Much like Mitchel, Rousseau was committed to making the Confederate population "feel heavily the consequences of forfeiting the protection of the Government."[107] Rousseau's aggressiveness did not sit well with his cousin Sarah Rousseau Espy. She wrote that Rousseau was "very zealously . . . engaged in fighting his Southern brethren," but held out hope that "he [may] see his fault and amend it."[108]

Perhaps Rousseau was able to continue Mitchel's brand of warfare because Buell had immersed himself in bringing to justice those soldiers who had violated General Orders 13a but had thus far escaped punishment. Colonel John Basil Turchin, who had ordered his men to sack Athens, was at the top of the list. On July 2, Buell relieved Turchin as commander of the Eighth Brigade.[109] Three days later, he charged the Russian with several counts of conduct unbecoming an officer, disobedience of orders, and disregarding a military directive prohibiting the wives of officers from establishing residences within camp. No other single event during the 1862 occupation more encapsulated the conflict between the proponents of punitive civil-military warfare and conciliation than Turchin's court-martial.[110]

On July 7, the trial convened in Athens with a jury of six colonels and one general.[111] Soon thereafter, the court proceedings were relocated to Huntsville.[112] The prosecution's case centered almost entirely on Turchin's refusal to stop his men from laying waste to Confederate businesses and homes. With such a large amount of the testimony focusing on the suffering of Confederate women, Captain P. T. Swaine, the judge advocate, likely hoped to persuade the jury that Turchin had given his men carte blanche to do their worst against docile women. One witness testified that when the bluecoats entered the home of Ms. M. E. Malone and Ms. S. B. Malone, they "ransacked it throughout, carrying off the money which they found, and also the jewelry, plates, and female ornaments of value and interest to the owners."[113] At Milly Ann Clayton's house, soldiers "opened . . . destroyed . . . or carried away . . . all the trunks, drawers, and boxes of every description."[114] The prosecution claimed that Turchin's men caused Mrs. Hollingsworth's miscarriage and death by firing into her house and threatening to set it on fire.[115] By bringing forth instance after instance of unrestrained fury against Confederate women and their property, Captain Swaine laid a solid foundation for arguing that Turchin bore the ultimate responsibility for telling his men that he would not intervene.

The prosecution presented additional evidence that soldiers made sexual comments toward Confederate women and sexual advancements toward female slaves. If the accusations were true, Union soldiers likely engaged in them to make clear to Confederates—female and male—that they held absolute power over them and their property. At John F. Malone's house, Union soldiers "used coarse, vulgar, and profane language to the females of the family."[116] Soldiers engaged in similar conduct toward the Rebel women in Thomas S. Malone's house.[117] Although there are no reports of soldiers raping white women, sexual assaults on female slaves reportedly occurred. After Federals trashed the contents of Milly Ann Clayton's house and "threatened to shoot her," they entered "the kitchen [where they] attempted an indecent outrage on the person of her servant girl."[118] The statements of some witnesses suggest greater indignation when such assaults or sexually-based comments toward slaves occurred in the presence of Confederate women, which would have been viewed as an affront to a white woman's respectability. After soldiers entered Mr. Irwin's residence and ordered Mrs. Irwin and her slave to fix them a home-cooked meal, they "made the most indecent and beastly propositions to [the slave] in the presence of the whole family." When the frightened slave left the kitchen, soldiers "followed her in the same manner, notwithstanding her efforts to avoid them."[119] At the same time Colonel Jesse Norton testified before the Joint Committee on the Conduct of the War that Mitchel had illegally profited from the sale of cotton, he also stated that soldiers from the Eighth Brigade raped female slaves "in the presence of their mistresses," though it is not known if the prosecutor in Turchin's trial was aware of this accusation.[120] When soldiers used sexually charged language or assaults to terrorize households, neither black nor white women were immune, though race did factor into who was more likely to be physically attacked. In either instance, the Confederate men of Athens were powerless to protect their women and slaves.

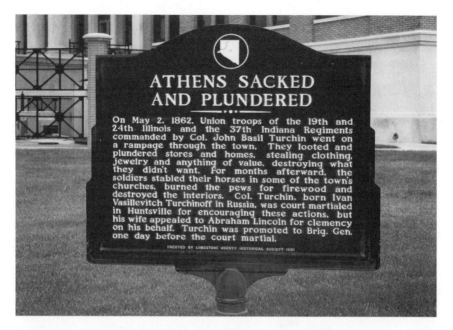

ATHENS SACKED
AND PLUNDERED

On May 2, 1862, Union troops of the 19th and
24th Illinois and the 37th Indiana Regiments
commanded by Col. John Basil Turchin went on
a rampage through the town. They looted and
plundered stores and homes, stealing clothing,
jewelry and anything of value, destroying what
they didn't want. For months afterward, the
soldiers stabled their horses in some of the town's
churches, burned the pews for firewood and
destroyed the interiors. Col. Turchin, born Ivan
Vasillevitch Turchinoff in Russia, was court martialed
in Huntsville for encouraging these actions, but
his wife appealed to Abraham Lincoln for clemency
on his behalf. Turchin was promoted to Brig. Gen.
one day before the court martial.

ERECTED BY LIMESTONE COUNTY HISTORICAL SOCIETY 1991

Historical Marker Commemorating the Sack of Athens (Library of Congress)

Turchin and his supporters denounced the prosecution's decision to have
Confederate civilians take the stand and testify against him. Some blamed
Buell. According to Lieutenant Dilworth, Buell "does not treat [Turchin] justly
[by allowing] the citizens to bear testimony against him."[121] When given an opportunity to defend himself, the Russian told the court that a dangerous prece-
dent was being established by permitting "the enemies of the Government [to]
be the judges as to how much harm shall be inflicted upon them by Government officers!" He claimed that if the Union allowed Confederate civilians to dic-
tate the severity of the Union's civil-military policies toward them, Union soldiers would be held "liable to arraignment before a Court-martial . . . anytime . . .
they exceed the bounds set for them by their rebel masters."[122] The colonel
urged the court to ignore the statements of Confederates and sustain his European style of warfare where "military necessity" dictated soldiers' relationship
with enemy civilians and their property.[123] James Fenton of the Nineteenth Illinois Infantry, which was part of the Eighth Brigade, commented that his former
brigade commander told the court that "you will never put down this rebellion
until you make war as war is made in Europe. Live off the country and destroy

the enemy's resources."[124] Anything less than hard war against Confederate civilians, Turchin argued, would prolong the war, or worse, end in the Union's defeat.

The private statements from two members of the jury suggested that some Union soldiers, even those who supported aggressively combating civilian led resistance, had a difficult time reconciling the actions of Turchin's men with the need to punish those who supported disunion. With the development of the Union's hard war mentality still in its infancy, these soldiers understandably struggled with the use of punitive civil-military policies and the damage it brought. After a few days of testimony by Confederates, an appalled General James A. Garfield could not "sufficiently give utterance to my horror of the ravages and outrages which have been committed by General Mitchel's army. There has not been found in American history so black a page as that which will bar the record of General Mitchel's campaign in North Alabama."[125] Yet, the future president of the United States also sympathized with and supported Turchin's defense arguments. According to this jury member, Turchin "has borne himself so much like a noble-souled man that he has quite won my heart." Even as the trial was proceeding, the two officers developed a budding friendship and held private discussions on the merits of retaliating against unwavering Confederate civilians.[126] Colonel John Beatty, who had set fire to the town of Paint Rock the same day the Eighth Brigade sacked Athens, shared Garfield's horror at the events in Athens. Beatty remarked that "Turchin has gone to one extreme, for war can not justify the gutting of private houses and the robbery of peaceable citizens."[127] The colonel stated that the Russian's order to sack the town was "the policy of the devil." Yet Beatty also asserted that "Buell's [conciliation] policy is that of the amiable idiot."[128] After reflecting on the state of affairs in North Alabama, Beatty denounced the assault on Athens, while supporting the theory behind it. "The policy we need is one that will march boldly, defiantly, through the rebel States . . . crushing those who have aided and abetted treason, whether in the army or out," Beatty wrote.[129] These officers' views were likely held by a number of Union soldiers who were still somewhat uncomfortable about making war on civilians while simultaneously acknowledging that something had to be done to put down Confederate civilians' resistance efforts.

The jury decided Turchin's fate after carefully weighing the evidence, as well as taking into consideration their disillusionment with Buell's conservative agenda and news that General George B. McClellan's Peninsular Campaign had failed.[130] McClellan's retreat was a devastating blow that emboldened Confederates. While these officers did not condone the specific actions of the Eighth Brigade, they felt that Turchin's argument of military necessity had some merit. In late July, the jury found Turchin guilty of conduct unbecoming an officer and violating General Orders 13a, but asked Buell to grant Turchin clemency on grounds that "the offense was committed under exciting circumstances."[131]

When Buell learned of the jury's plea, he scoffed at the notion of leniency for an officer who had blatantly violated his orders not to harm Confederate civilians. Turchin's conduct with the people of Athens, Buell remarked, "does not mean vigorous warfare; it means disgrace and disaster, and is punished with the greatest severity in all armies."[132] Buell intended to dismiss the Russian from the army, but he hardly controlled the colonel's fate. During the trial, Turchin's wife, Nadine, and prominent politicians from Turchin's adopted state of Illinois had traveled to Washington to defend the beleaguered general. Their defense of Turchin was well received by military and civilian leaders who were disgruntled with conciliation and gave additional weight to the recent actions taken by the secretary of war. Prior to their arrival, Stanton had submitted Turchin's name to Congress for promotion to brigadier general. When Buell learned of the idea, he protested to Stanton that Turchin "is entirely unfit for it. I placed him in command of a brigade, and I now find it necessary to relieve him from it in consequence of his utter failure to enforce discipline and render it efficient."[133] This biting critique from the commander of the Army of the Ohio failed to derail the promotion. When Congress concurred with Stanton's recommendation and Lincoln signed off on the promotion, Turchin became a general. His promotion invalidated the court-martial, for officers must be tried by their peers or superiors and Turchin now outranked six of the jurors.[134] Another trial was never convened. After his promotion, he returned to Chicago before returning to the field in September. According to historian Mark Grimsley, "Short of actually removing Buell [from command], it is hard to imagine what more devastating insult the administration could have offered him" than Turchin's promotion.[135]

The federal government's implicit endorsement of Turchin's "European" style of warfare occurred at the height of northerners' realization that conciliation had failed. Union soldiers and northerners alike now called for greater reliance on punitive measures to overwhelm Confederate civilians' support for disunion. General Buell's unwillingness to move away from his limited-war approach led to his vilification in the Union press. One correspondent suggested that Buell's strict adherence to conciliation did more to promote the Confederate, rather than Union, war effort. The general's policy to "protect the homes of rebels [has] emboldened" civilian resistance, while leaving "the Union men . . . to take care of themselves as best they could against unscrupulous guerrillas."[136] The *Ripon Weekly Times* (Ripon, Wisc.) published an article ridiculing Buell for releasing a son of a Confederate general even though the man had been suspected of committing "treasonable acts." Once freed, this man reportedly raised a Confederate company.[137] The *Cincinnati Gazette* was one of the most vocal anti-Buell newspapers in the Union. The paper regularly condemned the general for not punishing dangerous North Alabamians. One such instance occurred in Larkinsville when Buell let a suspected "bushwhacker" go without first conducting a thorough investigation.[138] The correspondent was convinced that if the general "continues . . . to follow his . . . miserable policy of 'conciliation,' the nation, with unparalleled unanimity, will pronounce him wanting in intelligence to comprehend the nature of the rebellion and destitute of the ability to command an army in the field." Buell's leniency toward Rebel civilians, his southern birth, and his status as a former slaveholder led a *Gazette* contributor to question the general's loyalty. "Everywhere [Buell] is regarded with suspicion and distrust [and] everyone [has] his own tale to tell of the working of that system which considers it the first duty of a loyal soldier to protect the property of traitors," the person wrote.[139] General Don Carlos Buell was, of course, no traitor. From the beginning of the war to the summer of 1862, his goal had remained the same: achieving Union victory without bringing social, political, and racial chaos to the defeated South.[140] The hard war policies advocated by Mitchel, Turchin, Stanton, and the northern public threatened this objective.

By the summer of 1862, the federal government's official support for conciliation was evaporating, and nothing short of the Confederacy's formal surrender or the pacification of Rebel civilians could stop it from ending. The use of destructive measures against defiant civilians in North Alabama played an important role in this process, but so too did the creation of punitive civil-military policies in other occupied areas. In eastern Florida, General Horatio G. Wright's efforts to stop ambushes against his men were comparable to Mitchel's May 2 proclamation. Assistant Secretary of War P. H. Watson told Mitchel that Wright "stopped the assassination of his sentinels by issuing orders to them to shoot . . . everything they saw approaching them at night." Watson informed Mitchel that "summary dealing with guerrillas [is] indispensable" to maintaining an occupation in hostile regions of the Confederacy.[141] Support in Washington for the hard war policies of General John Pope, commander of the Army of Virginia, further discredited conciliation. At the same time Turchin was on trial for the Sack of Athens, Pope issued General Orders 7 after his men incurred repeated attacks from Confederate civilians. Pope warned the Rebels that "If a soldier or legitimate follower of the [Union] army be fired upon from any house the house shall be razed to the ground. . . . Any persons detected in such outrages, either during the act or at any time afterward, shall be shot, without awaiting civil process." Pope promised "heavy afflictions to the population" if their violent ways did not cease.[142] Lieutenant Dilworth supported Pope's response. "I like Pope's order," the officer succinctly wrote.[143] When Mary Fielding learned that Lincoln had no intention of revoking Pope's order, she keenly understood that the use of punitive tactics to punish Confederate civilians was "to be the policy in the future." According to Fielding, "Turchin was only a little ahead of the times."[144] As the summer of 1862 wore on, Union personnel in occupied territories and leaders in Washington had come to the stark realization that violent civilian behavior against Union soldiers was not restricted to small pockets of the Confederacy but was occurring in many areas where Federal troops were stationed. Failure to combat these outbursts of Confederate nationalism threatened soldiers' lives and the restoration of the federal government in the seceded states.

Congressional representatives who supported taking the war to the Confederate home front did more than back the promotion of hard war officers; they also revised existing civil-military legislation that had become obsolete. During the summer of 1862, the passage of the Second Confiscation Act was the most significant contribution Congress made to furthering a punitive-based mentality toward Confederate civilians. Members of Congress had become convinced that the First Confiscation Act of August 6, 1861, failed to go far enough in punishing Confederate civilians. Several of the new provisions, such as soldiers' authority to confiscate property, foodstuffs, and slaves from Confederates, shared striking similarities with the policies enacted or supported by Mitchel.[145] From July 18 onward, Union officers and enlisted men in North Alabama could continue with their punitive and, when necessary, destructive ways, confident that Buell's conciliatory policies no longer applied. According to Colonel Beatty, the act "will have good effect. It will . . . enable us to weaken the enemy . . . and strengthen ourselves."[146] Northern proponents of harsh measures against Confederate civilians championed the change in official policy. One contributor to the *Cincinnati Gazette* argued that since the Union was carrying on a "just war" they had the "right" to make "the enemy's country contribute to the support of the army." In what was most likely an attack on Buell, the writer added that "the safety of the army is the paramount question, and a commander who permits his soldiers to suffer from hunger, or to fall into disease for want of vegetable food while there is food in the country, has not found out what the war is about, nor which side he is for."[147] Confederates in North Alabama were well aware of the implications of the act. Joshua Burns Moore commented that it would allow "generals to forage upon the districts of the Southern states occupied by [Lincoln's] armies [and] to seize upon all and any thing [*sic*] his armies may need."[148] Mary Fielding perceptively noted that since the northern Congress had sanctioned the same uncivilized policies used under Mitchel, proceeding with the Turchin trial was unnecessary. "I don't see any use in trying [Turchin or his men] for what they did here; 'twill be done again all over the South wherever they have the power," the Confederate woman predicted.[149]

As soon as Union soldiers arrived in North Alabama, Confederate civilians had chosen to resist their occupiers. Their defiance ranged from innocuous disruptive behavior to attacks that left Union soldiers maimed or dead. Civilians resorted to such conduct because the faith they had in God, their government, and men in the Confederate armies precluded any passive acceptance of occupation. Their decision to resist their occupiers, however, had local and national consequences. Initially, Union soldiers were not prepared to handle a belligerent civilian population; before arriving in North Alabama, most of these soldiers likely assumed that the war would be decided on the field of battle. As they became more accustomed to retaliating against cantankerous civilians, Union soldiers began to develop a mentality that helped lay the foundation for a national program of hard war measures against Confederate civilians. Born from necessity, Union soldiers' "strong punitive policies" were intended to inflict severe physical and emotional damage to Confederate civilians' resistance efforts and their ideological commitment to independence. When a Confederate—civilian or soldier—disrupted Union soldiers' food supply, bluecoats responded in kind. When the deeds of civilians were particularly egregious, such as killing a soldier, retaliation could be swift and relentless. Even though Buell rid himself of Mitchel, the hard war attitude the division commander instilled in his men remained long after his return to Washington and subsequent death.

While the retaliatory actions of Union soldiers likely caused some civilians to think twice about assaulting their occupiers, there was no discernable decrease in civilian morale and no calls for attacks on Union soldiers to cease. In some respects, Federal soldiers' harsh tactics appear to have reinforced Confederates' commitment to disunion and resistance. According to the *Charleston Mercury*, the Union's "bitterest foes" were now in Athens.[150] At the same time civilians redoubled their devotion to the Confederacy, a similar process occurred among supporters of the Union. Proponents of hard war measures recognized that to put down the rebellion and reunite the fractured nation, they had to achieve victory on the battlefield and on the Confederate home front. After being part of the 1862 occupation, Union soldiers were committed to bringing their hard war mentality to the doorsteps of Confederates throughout the South. For Private Andrew W. Johnson of the Twenty-Seventh Illinois Volunteers, this could not happen soon enough. Toward the end of the occupation, Johnson longed for an order from "Abe Lincoln [for] our Army [to] go through and swepe [*sic*] the country and save nothing but take everything . . . and kill every man that is in arms aganst [*sic*] our onest [*sic*] happy country." If necessary, Johnson was willing to "spiell [*sic*] my last drop of blood" for victory.[151] With both sides still determined to achieve their goals, Illinois soldier Charles W. Willis worried about the state of America once the war ended: "I hate them now, as they hate us, and I have no idea that we'll ever be one nation, even if we conquer their armies."[152]

"WE ALL READY TO FALL INTO

ABRAHAM'S BOSOM"

On August 15, 1862, Mary Chadick wrote that her slave, Corinna, "got into one of [her] rages this morning." Chadick, unaccustomed to dealing with insubordinate slaves, looked to an available male figure, a Mr. Franks, to punish the woman.[1] Before Franks arrived, Corinna "suddenly disappeared," presumably to a Union camp. Chadick, who owned four other slaves, blamed Union soldiers for Corinna's unmanageable behavior. They are "playing mischief with the Negroes, and the poor ignorant creatures don't now [sic] which way to turn, or who are their real friends," an irritated Chadick wrote.[2] A few days later, Corinna returned to her mistress, claiming she had not been with the Yankees but had been staying with "an old woman at the depot."[3] In the coming weeks, Chadick's control over Corinna and her other slaves continued to deteriorate. When another female slave, Vienna, escaped to the Union camp and Corinna professed to be sick, Chadick and her two daughters had to finish the housework themselves.[4] As "the only well person on the place who knows how to make a biscuit," Chadick had "to cook for the entire family." While she prepared the meal, her daughters Sue and Jennie cleaned the house and ironed. The increased domestic responsibilities for these three Confederate women led Chadick to predict that her family's toils were a "foretaste of what we will have to go through . . . when the rebellion is quashed, and the wonderful 'Yankee nation' gets possession of 'Niggerdom.'"[5]

By the time Chadick wrote of Corinna's defiance and Vienna's departure, the social and racial landscape had drastically altered for slaves and slaveholders in North Alabama. The occupation provided slaves with an unprecedented opportunity to resist their masters' authority and engage in bold actions that once would have been considered suicidal. The absence of white men, the hesitancy of white women to punish defiant slaves, and the Union's punitive policies toward Confederates gave new meaning and purpose to slaves' actions. Slaves in this Deep South region believed the arrival of Federals offered them their best opportunity to break the master-slave bond. For slaves, the occupation meant freedom.

As of the 1860 census, 63,000 of Alabama's 435,000 slaves resided in North Alabama.[6] The majority of these slaves lived in the counties heavily populated or traveled by Union soldiers during the 1862 occupation. Madison County, which served as the hub for Union operations in the region, had the largest number of slaves (about 14,600) of all the North Alabama counties. A few of these counties had more slaves than whites. Slaves in Madison County accounted for about 55.5 percent of the population, while 53 percent of the 15,300 residents in Limestone County were in bondage. Aside from Jackson County, whose slave population accounted for only 18 percent of the county's total population, the remaining Tennessee Valley counties had significant concentrations of slaves. In Lawrence County, slaves made up nearly 49 percent of the entire population, followed by Franklin County (45.6 percent), and Lauderdale (39 percent). One in three people in Morgan County in 1860 was a slave. Collectively, slaves represented roughly 42.6 percent of the total population in the Tennessee Valley in 1860. The area was also home to about 4,000 of the 6,000 slave owners in North Alabama. Not surprisingly, Madison County had the largest number of masters, approximately 1,100. Planters—those who owned twenty or more slaves—comprised at least twenty percent of the slaveholding population in Madison, Franklin, and Lawrence counties. Although these census figures would have fluctuated between 1860 and the start of the occupation in April

1862, a sizable slave population and slaveholding class would have still existed. Given the number of slaves and masters in the Tennessee Valley, Union soldiers likely came into contact with each group on a regular, if not daily, occasion.[7]

Initially, soldiers did not intend to come between a master and his slave; they were in North Alabama to guard the railroad line and engage the enemy, not to liberate slaves. Few soldiers felt the need to aid a race they considered inferior in all respects. Corporal Robert H. Caldwell's statement, "I am actually tired of seeing their black countenances" after only three days in the region expressed a typical sentiment among the bluecoats.[8] Obstructing a master's authority seemed unnecessary since soldiers were unaware of how long they would remain in the region. When a male slave near Tuscumbia promised a Union colonel that he and his fellow blacks would "do anything" if allowed to follow their perceived liberators, the officer warned him: "Go back to your plough you black villain or I will put a bullet through you."[9] As Alfred Lacey Hough marched through the countryside of northwest Alabama, he "could easily see that [the slaves] thought [of] us [as] their friends," but he and his comrades refused to commiserate with them.[10] A correspondent for the *Cincinnati Gazette* who had travelled between Decatur and Huntsville on a train reported that the "negroes were gathered in masses" along the route. "As the cars passed they bowed, they scraped, they grinned, they pulled off their hats, and in every way tried to secure a recognition from those whom they considered their friends."[11] Even if a soldier or correspondent empathized with a slave, existing federal policy gave them minimal authority to intervene on behalf of the slave. Shortly after arriving in North Alabama, a Union correspondent detailed a desperate attempt by a group of slaves to climb on board a stopped train. When a soldier ordered one slave to get down, the black man begged, "O for de good God's sake, let me go wid you." The correspondent noticed "a perceptible tremor" coming from the soldier when he once again told the slave to disembark. Later, this same correspondent had a heartfelt conversation with a man who expected soldiers to deliver him from bondage. The correspondent urged the slave not to flee to Union lines because he would "probably be turned out [at] the first place we encamp." Even if he was allowed to remain in the camp, the correspondent forewarned, "somebody . . . will come and take you back; and then, besides being severely punished for running away, you will in every respect be worse off than before."[12] While racism led some soldiers to ignore the pleas of slaves, the hands of more sympathetic soldiers were tied by the Union's conciliatory policy. As of the late spring and early summer, Union soldiers still were fighting to restore the Union; they had not yet linked defeating the Confederacy to the destruction of slavery.

Confederate masters were unaware that Union soldiers did not intend to come between them and their slaves; they were certain that their occupiers were about to do irreparable damage to the institution of slavery. Rowena Webster fully expected Union soldiers to steal what she considers Confederates' rightful property: "If you were about to be robbed of all your possessions and accumulation of wealth which was honestly gotten by your parents and your rightful inheritance, would you not [feel] the same way?"[13] To prevent Federals from confiscating their property, some masters fled with their slaves to the mountains south of the Tennessee River after learning that the enemy was in the region.[14] Those who remained instructed their slaves to assure the enemy that they were content and well treated. Mingo White, a former slave from Franklin County, recalled after the war that "Dey tol' us to tell [the Union soldiers] how good [our masters] been to us an' dat we [liked] to live wid 'em."[15] After years of anti-abolitionist and anti-Republican propaganda, Confederates were convinced that the arrival of Union soldiers in North Alabama meant nothing less than the loss of their property and a vital component of their white identity.

Numerous Confederates relied on violence or the threat of violence to control their slaves during the occupation. The threat of physical punishment sought to ensure proper conduct in the presence of Union soldiers and to dissuade blacks from running off to Union camps. In certain instances, masters were successful in stopping blatant pro-Union acts. As Ohio soldier James Wilson Davidson and his fellow soldiers marched outside of Florence, slaves "began to come around as thick as flea[s] [and] commenced dancing and singing plantation songs." One slave revealed to Davidson that they wanted to serenade him with Union songs, but they were afraid their master would "flog them like the debbil" if they gave any indication they supported the Union cause.[16] James A. Garfield feared for the safety of a group of slaves who, after expressing their discontent to soldiers, were not afforded sanctuary. This was not the first time the future president of the United States worried about the fate of slaves who had sought the aid of Union soldiers. He assured his wife, "I could chill your blood with the recital of horrors that have resulted to slaves from their expectation of deliverance. . . . But I have not time nor heart to write these things."[17] By threatening to inflict harsh punishment on those who communicated with Union soldiers, Confederate North Alabamians hoped to maintain black docility

General James A. Garfield (Library of Congress)

during the occupation. If a slave was caught disregarding this warning, they almost certainly faced some form of punishment from their master or overseer.

While Confederates relied on brutal force to maintain slave compliance, they accused their occupiers of mistreating blacks. Pointing out Union soldiers' rough treatment toward slaves helped reinforce southerners' belief that only they knew how to properly manage blacks. In mid-April, Catherine Fennell insisted that soldiers in Huntsville were treating "the negroes very badly." They had even "passed a law to shoot all [slaves] who come to them."[18] According to Fennell, soldiers had killed several slaves, leaving African Americans in "Madison and Limestone Counties . . . badly frightened."[19] Confederates also accused their occupiers of separating black families by taking male slaves against their will. One Sunday, Union soldiers surrounded a church conducting a biracial service. Hugh Lawson Clay remarked that Union soldiers proceeded to kidnap "fifteen to fifty" male slaves before leaving for Tullahoma, Tennessee.[20] Soldiers' statements to civilians that slaves had better lives than poor whites buttressed Confederates' claims that they had slaves' best interests at heart. Mary Chadick proudly recorded a conversation in which a Union soldier stated that "the Negro women live like ladies, compared to the poor women of the North [and that] the Negro men dress better than the poor men of the South."[21] Military occupation certainly generated concern among Confederates over how the arrival of Union soldiers would affect their slaves and the institution as a whole. Highlighting northerners' brutality toward blacks and statements by soldiers championing the peculiar institution were cathartic tactics Confederates used to lessen this anxiety and strengthen their argument that they were benevolent masters.

Confederates' unease over their ability to maintain firm control over blacks while enduring an indefinite occupation was well-founded. Union soldiers might not have intended to involve themselves in the master-slave relationship, but blacks took the occupation as an opportunity to rebel against their owners. By late April, Joshua Burns Moore reported that slaves had become "completely demoralized" after the arrival of Union soldiers.[22] This was particularly the case for slaves near Union camps. Moore defined demoralization as an increase in blacks' self-esteem and their demands for basic property rights.[23] Virginia Clay, wife of C. C. Clay, Jr., noticed a marked change in the behavior of slaves when Huntsville became an occupied city. The occupation and the hesitancy of Confederate women to discipline slaves led her "father's Negroes, and most of our own, [to conduct] themselves in an insolent manner." When there was work to be done, she stated slaves would take "to the mountains" but would eventually return "to feed upon [our] rapidly diminishing stores." The slaves of absentee owners were even more unmanageable, according to Clay. With their owners having fled from the Union advance into North Alabama, these slaves were reveling in the "opportunity to sleep in [their master's] bed or eat from the family silver and china."[24] Joshua Burns Moore predicted that slaves would continue to conduct themselves in disobedient ways as long as the Yankees were in the area. Their recent rebelliousness proved to Moore that "the Federal army, the negroes and white Southern people cannot inhabit the same country."[25]

The efforts by slaves to use the occupation to show their discontent clashed with prevailing Union policy. Whereas Union soldiers had no intention of inter-fering with the master-slave bond and Buell sought a continuation of the racial status quo, these African Americans were determined to use the arrival of sol-diers to challenge their masters for ownership of their own bodies. It did not take long for soldiers to support this objective. Civilian-orchestrated attacks on Federals and the willingness of slaves to aid the Union cause convinced soldiers to support measures that chipped away at the foundations of slavery in North Alabama. By early May, more and more soldiers supported punitive policies that eroded Confederates' absolute power over their slaves. While these sol-diers quite often retained their racist perception of blacks, they simultaneously viewed breaking the master-slave bond as a military necessity to help pacify the rebellious Confederate population and hasten an end to the conflict.[26] The inter-connectedness of civilian hostility, the Union's reliance on punitive policies, and blacks' self-determination led to a regional breakdown in the peculiar institution and contributed to the development of federal policies that, in time, would ex-tend rudimentary rights to slaves.

The ability of slaves to break away from their owners and potentially achieve freedom in Union camps depended on their individual circumstances. Slaves re-siding within occupied towns or within a short distance of a Union camp were the most likely to flee. When Joshua Burns Moore learned that several of Mr. Nathan's slaves were missing, he surmised they had fled to a nearby Federal camp.[27] By the end of May, several female domestic slaves from Mary Field-ing's neighborhood had found a new home with the Yankees in Athens.[28] When Union soldiers arrived in more remote areas of North Alabama with the intent to punish the Confederate population, slaves took the opportunity to flee. Catherine Fennell noticed a sizable number of slaves "running to the Yankees, expecting to be free" after soldiers laid waste to Confederate farms in northeast Madison County and northwest Jackson County.[29] Gender and age were often important factors in blacks' ability to run from their masters. As the distance from Union lines increased, pregnant women or those caring for young chil-dren were less likely to attempt an escape. This could have been why the wife of John Cockburn remained behind with their children while he ran for a Union camp in northwest Alabama. Joshua Burns Moore, who owned the female slave but not Cockburn, considered him a scoundrel for leaving "his wife and 6 chil-dren for us to feed."[30] The elderly and infirm would have had difficulties compa-rable to those of Cockburn's wife. Even young or relatively healthy black males attempting to reach Union lines miles from their owners' residence had to navigate around Confederate civilians and slave patrols. This did not stop John, a nineteen-year-old slave from Oxford, Alabama, from making a run for a Union outpost that was located several miles from his masters' home.[31] In some instances, the master's horses and mules were used to overcome the long distances or obstacles. Marshall C. Wilson awoke one morning "to find that about 25 of our negroes, mostly men and well-grown boys had slipped away in the night, taking with them every horse and mule in the stables."[32] For slaves who were able to elude their masters and potential slave patrols, they arrived at occupied towns and camps hoping they had taken an important step toward lasting freedom.

The freedom that awaited blacks in occupied towns and Union camps was often partial at best. While black women performed domestic duties for Union soldiers, black men typically engaged in manual labor. When Union soldiers feared a Confederate attack, they often relied on male slaves to erect defenses. A southern correspondent reported over "500 negroes [were] employed in digging entrenchments and building fortifications" to secure Huntsville. A similar scene played out near Stevenson.[33] Black men were also used to repair severed communication lines. After Confederates burned a bridge near Decatur, Guy Morgan put "about 15 or twenty negroes" to work repairing the span.[34] Still, slaves were reportedly enthusiastic about contributing to the Union war effort. Colonel John Beatty stated blacks "are delighted when we give them an opportunity to serve us."[35] The *Cincinnati Gazette* reported that slaves eagerly responded to Colonel Turchin's request for manual laborers. Soon, "one hundred and fifty pairs of stout, honest, dusky hands were working away at the bridge" near Florence.[36] William M. Austin noted that slaves in Huntsville were "anxious to get in the service of Uncle Sam" and were being used to "drive teams, [while] others cook, and build fortifications."[37] While these statements undoubtedly reflected blacks' commitment to Union objectives, they also reflect northerners' assumption that blacks enjoyed or were well-suited for toiling with their hands. But the use of slave labor was not without risk. When Union soldiers and blacks were miles from the nearest outpost, they could be assaulted by the Confederate population. This fear led Captain James Thomson, who was in sole command of slaves repairing a railroad line between Athens and Decatur, to make sure he returned to camp before dusk. As the "only soldier in the crowd," Thomson expected he would be assaulted if captured.[38] The types of labor blacks performed for the Union did mirror the menial labor they carried out under the threat of their masters' lash. Yet their decision to work for the

Union freed up a greater number of soldiers to seek out unruly Confederates, and it demonstrated their value to the Union war effort. African Americans anticipated that their commitment would be duly rewarded by their assumed liberators.

Slaves did much more than perform tedious labor. Providing sensitive information about their masters and other Confederates to Union soldiers was arguably one of their most important contributions to the 1862 occupation. Their knowledge of the whereabouts of wanted civilians, hidden supplies, the location of small bands of Confederate cavalry, and other useful information proved to be an invaluable asset to Union soldiers. With information supplied by a Limestone County slave, Captain Thomson and his men entered the home of a Southern sympathizer, where they found "six guns, double barreled shotguns, rifles, [and] $4000 in coin and paper . . . collected for the use of the C.S.A."[39] Slaves acting as spies helped Union forces disrupt Rebel communications. According to Captain E. H. Tatum, "the statement of negroes, that their masters leave home at night and return in the day time, is a strong confirmation of who the guilty parties are."[40] Some blacks went to great lengths to seek out additional knowledge for Union soldiers. When Colonel John Beatty told a field slave he needed more information before acting on his tip that Confederate soldiers were at his master's house five miles away, the man began his long journey home with the promise to return. Later, Beatty reflected on this particular slave's thoughts "about the war, and its probable effects on his own fortunes." The colonel rhetorically asked himself: "Is it the desire for freedom, or the dislike for his overseer, that prompts him to run five miles on a Sunday to give this information?" He concluded it was "Probably both."[41] Throughout the occupation, slaves worked tirelessly to strike a blow against the Confederacy and their masters. This information vastly improved Union soldiers' ability to protect themselves, and when possible, enact counterinsurgency measures against the enemy.

Slaves who were caught or suspected of furnishing information to Union soldiers in North Alabama were dealt with accordingly by Confederates. Generally, Confederate women abstained from punishing accused spies, preferring instead to have their menfolk do it. Mary Chadick saw slaves "giving information of the arms and [Confederate] soldiers who have been concealed" to Union soldiers soon after the soldiers' arrival, but the diarist did not record any occasion where she confronted an African American spy.[42] A few months later she witnessed a slave by the name of Granville engaging in "very intimate [conversations] with the Yankees" and reported the incident to Granville's master.[43] What exactly transpired between the two men is unknown, but it was enough for Granville, and Chadick's slave Vienna, to runaway soon thereafter.[44] Confederate men were more likely to use corporal punishment on slaves suspected of spying. A Union correspondent described a particularly unnerving incident of a slave being whipped for disclosing the location of hidden pistols. To teach the male slave a lesson, he "was stripped of his clothing and tied securely to a post." After, "the whips were brought" out, a Mr. Townsend and his "accomplished overseer . . . acted as executioners." The correspondent relayed to his northern audience that, with "zeal," Townsend and his overseer "plied their chivalrous task, until the wretch before them, lacerated from head to heel . . . fainted from exhaustion and loss of blood."[45] Confederate men were also known to execute black spies. While in Huntsville, Colonel Beatty learned from a slave "that a colored man was whipped to death by a planter . . . for giving information to our men."[46] The risk involved for blacks who passed along information to the Union was immense. When a Confederate male got hold of a slave turned informant, the suspected African American would most always be assaulted and possibly killed for their crime against their master and the Confederacy.

The willingness of slaves to gamble their physical safety and lives to supply soldiers with intelligence presented a dilemma for the Union. As a result of slaves' courageous actions, soldiers had become substantially more knowledgeable about the region, Rebel activities, and the location of Confederate supplies. If Union personnel did not extend an incentive to blacks or offer some form of protection, informants might become hesitant to aid the Federals, which would make pacifying the rebellious population more difficult. As it stood, existing national policy offered Union soldiers minimal authority to target Confederate masters' ownership of slaves. The First Confiscation Act, passed in August 1861, applied only to slaveholders who were using their slaves to supply Confederate forces with food and provisions. In March 1862, the War Department issued General Orders 27, which prohibited Union "officers or persons in the military or naval service [from] returning fugitive slaves" to their Confederate masters. Soldiers found guilty of engaging in such actions would be "dismissed from the service."[47] General Orders 27 was an earnest attempt to punish Confederates and protect runaway blacks, but its flaws were readily apparent. The directive did not prohibit masters from entering Union camps to collect their property, leaving open the possibility of a slave informant being returned to his owner. The lack of a federal policy protecting these spies irritated Union soldiers. Colonel

Beatty remarked, "We worm out of these poor creatures a knowledge of the places where stores are secreted, or compel them to serve as guides, and then turn them out to be scourged or murdered." The colonel believed prevailing policy had to "change . . . before we shall be worthy of success."[48]

In the absence of a viable national policy, General Mitchel took it upon himself to protect the Union's black allies. On May 4, he sent word to Stanton attesting that slaves are "our only friends" in North Alabama and that in two instances he owed his "safety to their faithfulness." The abolitionist general informed the secretary that he had worked out an agreement with slaves and that very soon there would be "watchful guards among the slaves on the plantations bordering the river from Bridgeport to Florence." In return, Mitchel informed Stanton, he "promised [these slaves] the protection of my Government." Without this agreement, Mitchel stated it would be "impossible for me to hold my position."[49] He reiterated his policy to the secretary of war in another telegram: "I have promised protection to the slaves who have given me valuable assistance and information. My river front is 120 miles long, and if the Government disapproves what I have done, I must receive heavy re-enforcements or abandon my position." Mitchel concluded that with "the aid of the negroes in watching the river I feel myself sufficiently strong to defy the enemy."[50] Grounded in military necessity, these two telegrams superseded existing federal policies, and, if endorsed by Stanton, would irrevocably change the legal relationship between certain Confederates and their slaves.

Stanton surely took time to consider the implications of Mitchel's policy before replying. Offering protection to spies would sever the master-slave bond and validate Confederate claims that the abolitionist North was indeed fighting to free blacks. In the end, Stanton sustained Mitchel's strategy because the "assistance of slaves is an element of military strength which, under proper regulations, you are fully justified in employing for your security and the success of your operations." Stanton's statement suggests a willingness in the War Department to use all available resources in a particular region to defeat the Confederacy. The secretary of war considered protecting informants a "high duty" and that anything short of that "would be a failure to employ means to suppress the rebellion and restore the authority of the Government."[51] Support from the War Department's highest ranking official gave Mitchel and his men the authority to proceed beyond existing congressional legislation, previous civil-military directives, and Buell's conservative agenda. The protection of slave spies was now a federal policy.

Edwin Stanton (Library of Congress)

With that matter settled, Mitchel asked Stanton if he could use "the testi-mony of the blacks" to convict Confederate civilians of crimes against the Union. This advocate of hard war told Stanton that he currently held "prisoners (citizens) against whom the negroes will prove charges of unauthorized war."[52] If this too were to become policy, the Union would have another punitive tactic to add to their arsenal, while extending basic citizenship rights to North Ala-bama blacks. During the antebellum era it was highly unusual for a slave to pro-vide evidence against a white person. To do so would place blacks in a position of authority over a white.[53] Military necessity pushed Stanton to enthusiastically support Mitchel's spy policy, but the secretary was unwilling to make an un-equivocal statement regarding the use of black testimony to convict whites. Instead, he offered Mitchel a statement that supported but did not explicitly permit slave testimony: "You are allowed to inflict the extreme penalty of military law upon persons guilty of crimes specified in your telegram and upon those guilty of irregular or guerrilla warfare."[54] Stanton's guarded response on the subject might indicate his unease over the request, his perceived lack of authority to make such an important decision, or his preference to leave such a sensitive issue for Lincoln or Congress to decide. Although Mitchel could have pressed the issue further or gone ahead and used slave testimony without Stanton's overt support, there is no evidence suggesting he did so.

In working with Stanton to extend federal protection to black spies, Mitchel achieved greater success than more high-profile attempts by Union officers to weaken the master-slave bond. The previous fall, John C. Fremont, a military commander in Missouri, issued a sweeping proclamation freeing the slaves of Confederates "who . . . take up arms against the United States" or aid Confederate soldiers.[55] While Fremont considered it a military necessity to deprive Confederates of the use of slave labor, Lincoln admonished the general for exceeding his authority. At this stage in the war, Lincoln still needed to placate border state citizens and what he believed was a sizable southern unionist population.[56] The president also overruled General David Hunter's attempt to free blacks only a few days after Mitchel received authorization to extend federal protection to slave informers. On May 9, 1862, Hunter, who commanded the Department of the South, declared slaves in "Georgia, Florida, and South Carolina . . . forever free."[57] General Orders 11 received broad support among northern leaders. Carl Schurz—a native of Prussia who became a brigadier general during the war—told Lincoln a decree such as Hunter's was inescapable under current circumstances. The Prussian advised the president, "If you should feel obliged to modify Hunter's proclamation, I would entreat you to consider this: As our armies proceed farther South the force of circumstances will drive us into measures which were not in the original program, but which necessity will oblige you to adopt."[58] Mitchel's friend and the current Secretary of the Treasury, Salmon P. Chase, told Hunter the "proclamation merely recognized an inevitable necessity."[59] Despite Republican support, the president refused to endorse a far-reaching proclamation by a field general that would fundamentally alter slavery and the nature of the war.[60] Whereas Lincoln overturned Fremont's and Hunter's respective orders, he remained silent on Mitchel's policy. Given Mitchel's regular communication with Stanton and Lincoln's May 28 statement—sent through Stanton—praising the general's tactics in North Alabama, the president likely knew of Mitchel's policy but chose not to act.[61] Lincoln might not have countermanded the policy since it was narrow in scope. It is possible Mitchel astutely pressed to have only a few slaves freed because he realized Lincoln would not allow a broad proclamation. Sam Gardiner was one of the slaves rewarded through Mitchel's policy. When told by the general that he would be free in return for spying, Gardiner's face "gleamed."[62] As of mid-1862, few generals rivaled Mitchel's ingenuity in permanently breaking the bond between some masters and slaves.

The Union's ability to make good on their promise came into question when Mitchel returned to Washington in early July. As the general awaited reassignment, he received word that Buell had returned some escaped slaves to their owners. Mitchel asked Stanton for the War Department's "interference on behalf of these slaves . . . for I fear if they fall in to the hands of their masters their lives will not be safe."[63] An investigation immediately commenced. Assistant-Adjutant General E. D. Townsend demanded Buell respond to Mitchel's claims and reminded the former slave owner that "whenever the protection of the Government has been duly promised to any person, whatever his color or condition, the promise must be kept inviolate." In what surely irritated Buell, Townsend told him that in the future he was to extend federal protection to all slaves who have "rendered valuable services or given important information," even if no explicit promise had been made.[64] Buell responded by stating he had no knowledge of the policy. According to Buell, "General Mitchel did not, to my recollection, speak to me of protection promised to any slaves; certainly he gave me no statement in regard to those who merited protection for their services." The conservative general further stated that even though he knew nothing of the policy, no protected slave had been handed over to their master.[65] Mitchel's replacements were also ordered to respond. General W. S. Smith knew of no instances where a Confederate retook ownership over a protected black.[66] General Lovell H. Rousseau offered the same response as Smith, but he did mention an incident between Captain Cyrus O. Loomis, a protected slave, and himself. When Loomis attempted to put the slave on a northbound train, Rousseau intervened. Loomis protested, stating "Mitchel had set the negro free and . . . that he should serve no man again." Rousseau replied that Mitchel "had no power to free slaves" and ordered Loomis to take the black man back to camp.[67] Technically, this black had been freed from his owner, but his status remained unclear. The War Department's investigation reveals the potential limitations of Mitchel's policy. The investigation soon ended with no evidence to support Mitchel's accusation against his former superior.

Punitive war advocates still had reason to be wary of Buell's views toward slavery and the limits to which his men should interfere with the rights of Confederate slave owners. Back when the Third Division helped oversee the occupation of Nashville, Buell instructed Mitchel to "permit no fugitive slave to enter or remain within your lines."[68] As the general worked his way from Corinth to Huntsville in late June, he issued similar orders. Before General Robert L. Mc-Cook and his Second Division crossed the Tennessee River, he was told to expel "all unauthorized persons [including] fugitive slaves" from his ranks.[69] As a former slave owner, Buell was committed to largely leaving slavery alone. A senior member of Buell's staff instructed Rousseau to tell soldiers near Indian Creek who were relying on slave labor to "send the negroes out of camp [and] do the work themselves." The newly minted commander of the Third Division was told that Buell would be the one to decide if and when the use of slave labor was necessary.[70] By restricting the interactions between Union soldiers and North Alabama slaves, Buell sought to keep any interruption in a master's absolute control over his property at a minimum.

With Union soldiers and correspondents beginning to accept the military need to target Confederates' ownership of blacks, Buell's policy proved unpopular. According to the *Cincinnati Gazette*, Buell is "so conservative that he orders commanders of regiments to let citizens search the camps for fugitives, and to deliver [them] up when claimed."[71] When Confederate women informed Buell that the loss of runaway slaves had left them in a state of despair, he was apt to remedy the problem in their favor. In one instance, he told Colonel C. O. Harker, who was stationed near Stevenson, to return two slaves, Zack and John, to a Mrs. Cole. His justification: they were needed to "take care of the place, there being no hands left for that purpose."[72] If officials from the War Department had been more thorough in their investigation into Buell's return of protected slaves, they would have learned that the commanding general allegedly returned protected blacks to their masters. A soldier in the Fourth Ohio Cavalry asserted that since "the arrival of Gen. Buell our services seem to be turned in a new channel, that of catching negroes and returning them to their masters—even those Gen. Mitchell [*sic*] offered liberty to for valuable information given, and for which death is their [fate] if returned to their masters."[73] Colonel Turchin attested during his court-martial that Buell knowingly reversed Mitchel's "eminently proper" protection policy. This proved deadly for several slaves near Tuscumbia who were hung "because they had given us some valuable information."[74] Buell's inability to adapt his civil-military policies to meet in-the-field realities hindered the Union war effort in North Alabama and placed slaves in mortal danger. If Turchin and the Ohio cavalryman's respective accusations were indeed correct, the commanding general of the Army of the Ohio knowingly deceived War Department officials.

Union soldiers did their best to undermine Buell's archaic and dangerous military policies. The *Cincinnati Gazette* reported that several of Buell's "best officers" were willing to "stand court-martial or [tender their] resignation before they will become slave catchers for rebels."[75] General Garfield told Buell neither he nor his men would follow an order to help slave owners locate their runaway slaves. Buell's blatant attempt to disregard General Orders 27 brought a swift reply from the future president: "I sent back word that if the general wished to disobey an express law of Congress, which is also an order from the War Department, they must do it themselves for no soldier or officer under my command should take part in such disobedience."[76] Union soldiers considered interfering with Confederates' ownership of slaves and assisting slaves' efforts to undermine their masters an indispensable component of the war. The more Union soldiers interacted with defiant Confederates and fugitive slaves, the less willing they were to tolerate Buell's conservative strategy. According to one northern correspondent, "The number of those in the army who will not voluntarily bow . . . to slave-hunting traitors is rapidly increasing."[77]

During the second half of the summer, congressional legislation began to reflect the changing nature of the conflict between the Union and Confederacy. A determined Confederate home front and McClellan's disastrous defeat in Virginia led to the passage of a harsher confiscation act. Republican Senator John Sherman asserted that the indefinite length of the conflict had prepared the "North for a warfare that will not scruple to avail itself of every means" to defeat the enemy.[78] The Second Confiscation Act, passed in mid-July, established the criteria under which Confederates would permanently lose their slaves. If a Union court found a citizen guilty of treasonous activity or giving "aid and comfort" to Confederate forces, their slaves would be freed. The act further liberated fugitive slaves, confiscated slaves, and slaves left by fleeing Confederates. Congress also empowered Lincoln to enlist or draft "persons of African descent" for military service.[79] The president signed the bill into law, but not before voicing his concerns about certain aspects of the act. He especially challenged the idea that the power to arm blacks rested with Congress. Lincoln un-equivocally stated that even "without this law I have no hesitation to go as far in the direction indicated, as I may at any time deem expedient."[80] After learning of its passage, Colonel Beatty felt the act "will have good effect" on Union sol-diers. He predicted that if "we can tear down [slavery], the rebels will lose all in-terest in the Confederacy."[81] A correspondent stationed in North Alabama told readers the act reflected soldiers' desire to "cripple the rebellion and [bring] terror to disloyal hearts."[82] Confederates felt the act would prove disastrous for the Union cause. A South Carolina correspondent asserted that the Yankee army near Bridgeport appeared "much demoralized" by the act. This south-erner assured his readers that the enemy "will not fight in conjunction with the negroes."[83] In Huntsville, Mary Chadick considered the act evidence of the Union's despair: "So they are arming blacks. Truly their course must have be-come desperate."[84] These two Confederates could hardly understand how or why the Union's objectives had evolved from their conservative origins. North-erners, they seemed to think, were willing to make immeasurable changes to American society to attain victory.

As Union soldiers went about dismantling the institution of slavery, their in-teractions with blacks often created paradoxical reactions.[85] For many Union soldiers, the occupation was their first in-depth experience living in a society that was heavily populated by slaves. Southerners' brutal attacks on African Americans produced an empathetic reaction from Union personnel. When Cap-tain Thomson and his fellow soldiers were between Decatur and Athens, they came across a slave who had been shot by his overseer. Thomson, who was al-ready taking one slave back to camp, offered protection to the injured slave. Had the overseer not lived so far away, Thomson stated, he and his men "might have paid him a visit and combed his hair the wrong way."[86] After three months in North Alabama, Liberty Warner better appreciated the routine of slaves who worked in the field. "In this country," Warner remarked, "big black stinking Sambo grows in all his glory. It is here this beloved, industrious, trodden down [individual] toils all day long . . . and gets nothing but pork bread and whatever he raises in his little garden and hen coup."[87] Charles Willis, a Union soldier from Illinois, noted a particularly gruesome moment when he encountered a male and female slave with "marks of severe punishment" that left the man "a cripple for life from blows by a club on his ankles and knees" and "the woman . . . badly cut [from] a horsewhip."[88] Violent assaults on blacks reaffirmed soldiers' desire to punish the enemy and support the eradication of slavery. After Thomson wrote of the slave being shot by his overseer, this Union officer added, "I used to be called an abolitionist and since in 'Dixie' I am not getting any better."[89]

Soldiers also had compassion for newly married blacks. Under slavery, the bonds of matrimony were tenuous at best, and even a marriage recognized by a master could be easily broken through sale or sexual exploitation. While stationed in Athens, Lieutenant Robert S. Dilworth attended the wedding of "a colored man and girl." Although the ceremony was a day for celebration, Dilworth somberly reflected that as long as the institution of slavery remained, the "vows of these poor colored people" could be "disregarded . . . by a tyrant master."[90] A *New York Times* correspondent shared Dilworth's sentiment on the fragile nature of slave marriages, commenting that "a system that denies marriage, shuts out knowledge, chattelizes [*sic*] humanity should be sanctioned by none."[91] Some slaves went ahead with their marriages in the expectation they would soon be free. Colonel Beatty marveled at the determination of two newly married slave couples who traveled from Jackson County to Huntsville "confident that the rainbow and bag of gold were in the camp of the Federal Army."[92] Slave marriages during the occupation served as a moment when black couples took greater control over their lives and looked to the future with an anticipation that their days in bondage were nearly over.

But, while soldiers sympathized for those in bondage, this compassion did not greatly alter their racial attitudes toward those of African descent.[93] Soldiers' racism remained firm even as their actions helped dismantle slavery in North Alabama and contributed to national policies that would eventually bring slavery to an end. Charles Willis and his comrades often focused on the actions of slaves that supported their stereotypical perception of blacks. Willis stated that his "pet negro got so lazy and worthless" he was "compelled" to get rid of him.[94] Liberty Warner considered periodic breaks taken by African Americans as a sure sign of laziness. When Warner used slaves to construct a tunnel near Athens, he observed, "You have to keep on the lookout as they will mosey off into [somewhere] shady and lay down." After all, Warner informed his friends, "Nigger heaven is a place where they can dance and lay in the shade all day."[95]

Orchestrating deceitful tricks was another manifestation of northerners' racism. As the Fourth of July approached, soldiers from Colonel Beatty's Third Ohio Infantry played a hoax on a "good-natured Ethiopian, named Caesar." These Buckeyes convinced Caesar that he would be the main course when they celebrated the nation's birthday. Soldiers used the absence of a sizable black population in the North as proof to Caesar that "Yankees always dine on roast[ed] nigger" on Independence Day. Caesar subsequently disappeared on the Fourth of July.[96] In another instance of deception, soldiers from the Forty-Second Indiana created a bogus fifty-dollar bill to scam a "darkey" out of a "whole wagon load of melons and potatoes."[97] The ability of soldiers to separate their entrenched racism from military necessity allowed them to degrade blacks while undermining slavery.[98] In spite of soldiers' awareness of the inhumanity of slavery and of the valuable services blacks were performing for the Union war effort, they often could not transcend their own prejudices.

On occasion, soldiers severely abused blacks. While the exact catalyst behind acts of violence varied, hardened northern racism, slaves' vulnerability, and soldiers' pent-up anxiety over being stationed in a hostile environment contributed to these vicious attacks. After residing in a slave region for an extended length, some Union soldiers started to act like slave owners. Lieutenant William Nazareth Mitchell, an Illinois soldier and a father of fifteen, wrote about a soldier named Fogarty who decided to go "into the negro business [and purchase] six negroes" while they were stationed in Tuscumbia.[99] If a black man did not work hard enough, he might be whipped by a Federal. General Thomas J. Wood's merciless treatment of a black man near Jackson's Ferry, Alabama, earned him the nickname "Nigger Whipper." According to a northern correspondent, Wood became irate when a slave "didn't move as lively as he (Gen. W.) thought he should." The general subsequently "directed another contraband to tie the hands of the offending darkey." Once the slave's shirt had been removed, Wood brought out the lash. The slave "begged piteously" after each blow, but Wood refused to stop. When the bleeding slave managed to release one of his hands, the enraged general turned to the slave who had tied him to the post and warned "that if he didn't tie him up more securely, he'd whip him as well."[100]

Black women faced the ever-present possibility of being sexually assaulted by their supposed liberators. Accusations arose after the Sack of Athens that soldiers raped or made sexual advances toward female house servants, but none were ever charged with a crime.[101] However, if a black male was accused of sexually assaulting a white woman, he faced certain retribution. Union soldiers would not tolerate black-on-white rape against any woman. After two slaves named Wilson and Henry were found guilty by a military court of raping Mrs. Ann Blair, they were sentenced to be hung in Athens.[102] Union soldiers were very much a product of a society that often tolerated the humiliation, abuse, and killing of blacks by whites. Even though soldiers favored measures that would lead to the demise of slavery, blacks were still not treated as equals.

By the end of the 1862 occupation, Union soldiers, Confederate civilians, blacks, and officials in the War Department had irrevocably weakened slavery in North Alabama. Confederate civilians' dogged resistance led to punitive policies targeting their personal well-being, homes, crops, and ownership of blacks. Had these Confederates endured the occupation peacefully, there is a strong possibility that soldiers would have felt less of a need to liberate slaves. Without question, the actions and sacrifices of African Americans prodded Union personnel to devise tactics stripping Confederates of full authority over blacks. Slaves' collective efforts to aid the Union demonstrated that they were a crucial asset to the North and deserved to be rewarded. Although soldiers retained their racially prejudiced views of blacks, they generally supported slaves' acts of defiance against Confederates. A statement made by Joshua Burns Moore shortly after the occupation began predicted the effect a prolonged occupation and war would have on the peculiar institution. Moore wrote prophetically: "The object of the war says Mr. Lincoln is the restoration of the Union as it was. He may think so and doubtless does—But from the very nature of the contest, so sure as the war continues it is the death blow to negro slavery."[103] The 1862 occupation of North Alabama ultimately played an integral role in leading the Union toward emancipation.

The occupation of North Alabama came to a close in early September after Buell ordered his men to halt Bragg's invasion into Kentucky. The two armies fought at Perryville on October 8, 1862, with the Union achieving a strategic victory. When the occupation finally ended, civilians rejoiced. Sarah Lowe offered her "inexpressible . . . thanks to the Ruling Power that their stay, though a long disagreeable one, was not permanent." According to this resilient Confederate, there was now an "air of freedom on the wind."[104] With no bluecoats in sight, Rebecca Vasser was once again able to "enjoy the calm night air, and the sweet moonlight that falls around me and is reflected in brighter gleams from my ring."[105] Huntsville residents gave partisan fighter Frank Gurley and his men a hero's welcome when they entered the town following the Federal's departure. The accused killer of General Robert L. McCook stated that the "streets [were] crowded with ladies [who] paved the streets with roses and clothed the soldiers with flags and bocuets [sic]."[106] After five months, Confederate civilians had regained their independence, though immeasurable damage had been done to their communities, countryside, and the institution of slavery.

When the Union soldiers left North Alabama, so too did thousands of African Americans. Even though their future remained uncertain, they preferred the unknown to staying. In northwestern Alabama, Joshua Burns Moore estimated that "10,000 negro men and women and children" left with Union soldiers.[107] The *Charleston Mercury* reported about "1500 negroes" from Madison County followed Union soldiers out of the region.[108] Confederates claimed to be better off without their slaves. Catherine Fennell asserted that citizens from Huntsville were "glad to get rid of them."[109] Others damned soldiers for pilfering their workforce and investment. An irate Guntersville woman told Confederate soldier Nimrod William Ezekiel Long that the "Yankees stole a great many negroes."[110] As Sergeant William M. Austin readied himself to leave North Alabama, two "very bitter" Confederate men remarked that the "North ought to be ashamed for taking their negroes." Without a black workforce to harvest their crops, these men predicted their families would surely starve.[111] The Union's punitive policies and blacks' self-determination had created an opportunity for thousands of blacks to renounce their status as slaves. Confederates were incapable of stopping this mass exodus.

The sizable black population attached to the Army of the Ohio generated concern among Union soldiers. Military necessity drove soldiers to shatter the bonds between masters and slaves, but few wanted their camps or northern states inundated with blacks. When more than one-hundred field slaves arrived at a Union outpost in northwest Alabama with the intent of following soldiers out of the state, Charles Willis suggested only half be allowed to leave with them. Willis' desire to limit the number of blacks following the army stemmed from his dread that a mobile black population might relocate to the North. Willis hoped they would remain in the South so "our Northern states [are not] degraded by them."[112] As Lieutenant William Nazareth Mitchell and his comrades billeted out of North Alabama, he noticed the army was "getting full of negroes of all sorts and sizes," including "stark naked" children. Mitchell saw little reason for them to remain in North Alabama. According to Mitchell, "Slavery as an institution here seems doomed for they are all running off and their masters are in no scituation [sic] to recover them, or take care of them." With long marches and autumn on the horizon, Mitchell doubted women and children could keep up or provide for themselves. He suggested that even if the women were able to keep pace, they might become victims of sexual assault.[113] The success Union soldiers had in disrupting the institution of slavery in North Alabama had unanticipated consequences. As officers and enlisted men left the region with a large black population in tow, they now had to address a host of logistical, gender, and racial issues unleashed by the occupation and their punitive tactics.

In the coming weeks, northerners' unease over the racial implications of their actions continued to take a back seat to military necessity. By the summer of 1862, President Lincoln began to make private statements indicating a desire to free slaves from their Confederate masters. At a meeting in mid-July, he told Secretary of State William Seward and Secretary of the Navy Gideon Welles that "we must free the slaves or be ourselves subdued."[114] North Alabama slaves had longed for such a decision by Lincoln. As soldiers from the Forty-Second Indiana Volunteers traveled through the countryside of North Alabama, they were approached by a group of slaves. The slaves' de facto leader proclaimed: "Bress Mars Abraham foh, long time sah, we all ready to fall into Abraham's bosom."[115] Soon after McClellan's Army of the Potomac defeated General Robert E. Lee's forces at Antietam, the president issued his preliminary Emancipation Proclamation. On January 1, 1863, "all persons held as slaves within any state, or designated part of a state, the people whereof shall then be in rebellion against the United States shall be then, thenceforward, and forever free." The proclamation prohibited military personnel from returning slaves to their Confederate owners and ordered the enlistment of African American men "into the armed service of the United States."[116] Prominent Union officers who had served in North Alabama supported Lincoln's strategy. General Garfield claimed that the "President's proclamation gives great satisfaction among all strong vigorous men." Given the significance of the proclamation, Garfield prayed for the president to "have the strength to stand up to his convictions."[117] General Mitchel remarked to his friend Salmon P. Chase that "a large majority of the People of the North are now desirous of . . . destroying the institution of Slavery as a War Measure." Had Lincoln arrived at this conclusion while Mitchel had commanded the Third Division in North Alabama, the general was confident the "entire region, would have remained without cultivation, no crops would have been planted or harvested, and in this the most terrible blow would have been struck."[118] As a whole, Union soldiers backed Lincoln's decision to make the eradication of slavery in Confederate-controlled states a military objective.[119]

Coinciding with the preliminary Emancipation Proclamation was the removal of Union generals whose conservatism was no longer in line with official policy. In early November, General Ambrose Burnside replaced McClellan as commander of the Army of the Potomac. That same month, Buell defended himself in front of a Court of Inquiry investigating his conduct as commander of the Army of the Ohio. The commission chided Buell for his reluctance to liberate East Tennessee and for not living off the Confederate countryside. Although the court concluded that Buell's conciliatory policies were "at that time understood to be the policy of the Government," he, like McClellan, was never appointed to another command.[120]

With no end to the conflict in sight, the Union needed military leaders and soldiers who were capable of defeating Confederates on the field of battle and who were willing to use unbending force to demoralize a defiant Confederate home front. North Alabama Confederates hoped they had seen the last of their bitter foe, but after a winter reprieve, their commitment to Confederate independence would again be tested.

6

"A CONTINUAL DROPPING OF WATER

WILL WEAR AWAY A ROCK"

During the spring and summer of 1862, North Alabama Confederates weathered a Union storm that had devastated their region and loosened the shackles of slavery. Although civilians continued to feel the effects of the occupation and war, their Confederate nationalism sustained them during the winter.[1] Southerners, and at least one international observer, were particularly stirred by the determination of the region's female population not to succumb to the burdens of war. A contributor to the *Daily Southern Crisis* (Jackson, Miss) noted how North Alabama women were doing their part in the perilous conflict by forgoing "the lightly-worn pleasures and luxuries of peace." They "have betaken themselves to the reality of war, and without a murmur cheerfully assumed its duties of self-denial and self-sacrifice."[2] D. P. Lewis, a Moulton, Alabama resident, reported that women were "plowing, grubbing, rolling logs, [and] milling" while their men folk fought in the Confederate army. Such work had even been embraced "by some women who [before the war and occupation] were in circumstances of ease, affluence, and refinements."[3] When Sir Arthur Fremantle, a British chronicler of the war, traveled through Huntsville, he recorded women's hatred for the Union and their determination to resist Yankee domination. Fremantle remarked that these "Southern women" were still "furious . . . by the proceedings of Butler, Milroy, [and] Turchin, [and] prepared to undergo any hardships and misfortunes rather than submit to the rule of such people."[4] The ruin Union soldiers brought to North Alabamians in 1862 and the inconclusiveness of war had failed to quell these civilians' drive for independence. At the dawning of a new year, secessionists' ideological devotion to the Confederacy remained as vibrant as ever.

Southern nationalists' ability to remain committed to their cause and overcome adversity was not inexhaustible. When Union soldiers started raiding the region in April 1863 and settled down into another occupation in the fall, Confederate civilians' collective morale began to deteriorate. The hardship civilians experienced from the Union's unrelentingly punitive policies and Confederate military setbacks created cracks in the foundation of their Confederate nationalism. As civilians became demoralized, African Americans and the region's small unionist population grew more defiant. The inability of the Confederate military and state government to protect North Alabama Confederates or alleviate their suffering further weakened their morale. Even though civilians' ideological commitment to independence had not yet collapsed, it had reached its lowest level since the beginning of the war.

The Union's ability to undermine Confederate morale in North Alabama stemmed from the abandonment of conciliation during the winter of 1862–1863. Northern citizens and soldiers had come to demand a destructive brand of warfare to bring the Confederate home front to its knees.[5] For President Lincoln, that meant following through with his preliminary Emancipation Proclamation. His objective was not to incite a slave rebellion or race war, but rather to embolden slaves to defy their Confederate masters in ways that would contribute to the collapse of the Confederate home front.[6] The decree, which went into effect on January 1, 1863, signaled the death knell of the Union's limited warfare strategy and demonstrated Lincoln's willingness to fundamentally reshape the contours of American society to attain victory.[7] The debate over the president's motives mattered little to Bill Towns, a one-time slave from Tuscumbia. Towns remarked that "Some say dat Abe wan't intrusted so much in freein' de slaves as he was in savin' de union. Don' make no diff ence iffen he wan't intrusted in de black folks, he sho' done a bug thing by tryin' to save de Union."[8] When the proclamation went into effect, the closest Union encampments to North Alabama slaves were in northeast Mississippi and southern Tennessee. Although the proclamation and proximity of Union soldiers influenced some North Alabama slaves, and even those farther south, to make a run for these camps, most African Americans remained with their masters during the months between the proclamation and the reappearance of Union soldiers in the state.[9] When Federal soldiers began conducting raids in North Alabama during the spring and settled into an occupation later in the year, Confederate civilians experienced firsthand the power of the Emancipation Proclamation to lift the morale of blacks while causing their own to plummet.

Just as soldiers began raiding North Alabama for provisions and livestock in late April 1863, the War Department issued General Orders No. 100, "Instructions for the Government of Armies of the United States in the Field." The document contained a series of civil-military guidelines to better address the realities of the conflict and promote the use of hard war tactics against Confederate civilians. Orders 100 shares undeniable similarities to the punitive policies used by General Mitchel the previous year. Francis Lieber, a prominent antebellum intellectual who had written an essay on partisan and guerrilla warfare, is regarded as the main architect of Orders 100.[10] Lieber's Code, as Orders 100 is commonly referred to, did not sanction "the infliction of suffering for the sake of suffering or for revenge. . . . nor of the wanton destruction of a district."[11] Rather, Lieber and his co-authors detailed the various circumstances in which military necessity justified the punishment of the civilian population. One code stated that "Military necessity consists [of] measures which are indispensable for securing the ends of the war."[12] A central tenet of Orders 100 was to make the Confederate home front suffer the "hardships of the war."[13] When necessary, soldiers were authorized to punish Confederate women and had the right to take civilians' foodstuffs even if it meant that "the hostile belligerent [would] starve."[14] Lieber and his cohorts were confident that by incorporating the punishment of Confederate civilians into the Union's overall strategy, the war would end more quickly than if the Union relied solely on battlefield victories: "The more vigorous wars are pursued, the better it is for humanity."[15] Issuance of the code reflected the government's determination in the spring of 1863 to wage an aggressive war against all who were ideologically opposed to the Union.[16] With Union soldiers resuming their raids in North Alabama, they had at their disposal a national policy that encouraged the relentless use of hard war tactics against a rebellious population in an effort to bring a swifter end to the conflict.

Union forays into North Alabama were generally launched from encampments in or near Nashville and Murfreesboro, Tennessee, or Corinth, Mississippi. The first significant raid into the region occurred in April 1863. In addition to gathering needed provisions and supplies from towns and farms in northwest Alabama, Union soldiers stationed near Corinth were hoping to create a diversion while Colonel Abel D. Streight and 1,700 soldiers from the Army of the Cumberland traveled across North Alabama in an attempt to cut Confederate supply lines and destroy military equipment in Rome, Georgia.[17] According to Joshua Burns Moore, the Union soldiers marching into northwest Alabama were "so superior in numbers" to Confederate cavalry in the region that Yankee advances "could not [be] resist[ed]."[18] Soldiers' subsequent actions toward the civilian population embodied the civil-military philosophies of Mitchel and the tenets embedded within Lieber's Code. Union soldier Thomas Hoffman stated that as they neared Tuscumbia, soldiers "burn[ed] everything within five miles of the road on either side." According to this Iowan, "smoke [was soon] seen in all directions curling up from cribs, out houses, and fine mansions."[19] Tuscumbia was mostly vacant by the time soldiers entered the town. This did not surprise Hoffman. "Like most of the towns that have fell into our possession [a] great [number of Confederates] have fled on our approach," Hoffman wrote.[20] Given the flight of Confederate civilians from advancing Federals, some soldiers must have been surprised when they reached Florence and realized that a number of townspeople had chosen to stay. Even though these Confederates were in a "state of alarm" over the reappearance of the enemy, rumors of Union soldiers "burning dwellings & destroying as they go" likely compelled residents to stay put and try to protect their property.[21] When the citizens refused to surrender Florence, Union soldiers responded by shelling the town. Olivia Moore O'Neal considered the Union's actions a shameful display of northern aggression that could have maimed or killed "innocent women & children."[22] Two days after the attack, the citizens of Florence admitted defeat and turned the town over to the Union.[23] Union soldiers did not stay long. After replenishing their supplies, drawing attention away from Colonel Streight, and targeting those who remained committed to disunion, the Federals returned to Corinth.

Streight's mission did not go as planned. Diseased horses and mules, poor communication, inclement weather, exhausted soldiers, and civilians alerting Confederate cavalry to the Union's whereabouts doomed the expedition. After skirmishes with General Nathan Bedford Forrest's cavalry, the two opposing forces fought a minor engagement near Gaylesville (Cherokee County), Alabama. According to Streight, his men were in no shape to repulse the enemy: "Our ammunition was worthless, our horses and mules in a desperate condition, the men were overcome with fatigue and loss of sleep, and we were confronted by fully three times our number, in the heart of the enemy's country." On May 3, the Union force, which actually outnumbered Forrest's cavalry, conceded defeat.[24] When Captain D. Coleman, a Confederate soldier in the Army of Tennessee and Athens native, learned of Streight's surrender, he gave thanks to "the Giver of all victories."[25] Zillah Haynie Brandon, who lived near Gaylesville, interpreted Forrest's triumph as "a blessing from almighty God."[26] Captured Union enlisted men were eventually exchanged for their Confederate counterparts, while Union officers were sent to Libby Prison in Richmond.[27]

While no other military action similar to "Streight's Raid" took place in 1863, foraging occurred regularly. Florence native Joshua Burns Moore, who often wrote of the Union's hard war tactics during the 1862 occupation, considered the Union's "visit to the valley" in early 1863 even worse. According to Moore, soldiers "robed [sic] the people . . . of every horse, mule . . . wagon . . . corn and meat."[28] The confiscation of foodstuffs in 1863 served the same function as it had in 1862: adding to Union supplies while seeking to demoralize the enemy. When General David S. Stanley learned of a large quantity of foodstuffs in and around Huntsville, he urged General William Rosecrans, commander of the Army of the Cumberland, to seize the goods.[29] The subsequent confiscation of provisions in the area included "all [the] meats, stock and, so forth" from the home of Susanna Clay, the wife of a former Alabama governor and mother to prominent Confederate statesmen.[30] When additional raids on Huntsville left civilians without wheat and flour, Clay predicted her fellow Confederates "will be hard pressed for bread" in the coming months.[31] Union soldiers occasionally took what could be considered luxury items from Huntsville homes. At Ms. Fearn's house, one Union officer took her cache of wine in addition to more essential goods.[32] In areas hit hard by raiding parties, Confederates' ability to procure provisions became exceedingly difficult. After Union soldiers thoroughly confiscated supplies from the small towns and countryside east of Huntsville, Catherine Fennell commented that she "never dreamed anything could be so scarce."[33] Even though the family of Confederate soldier Kinnion S. Lee lived in southern Alabama, he feared Union foraging expeditions in northern Alabama and Georgia would likely lead to a scarcity of food for his wife and children.

While stationed in Chattanooga, he instructed his wife to stockpile corn and wheat to see the family through the next several months.[34] North Alabamians who were constantly subjected to Union foraging did not always have that option. By summer's end, Susanna Clay asserted that there was enough food for her family "to last, with care a month perhaps."[35]

As Union soldiers raided North Alabama for supplies, they were unequivocal about their hatred for Confederates.[36] Whether they were motivated by military necessity, the indefiniteness of war, or a loathing for the enemy, Union soldiers left a path of destruction in their wake and generated feelings of dread and shock among Confederates. Confederates living along the path taken by D. Leib Ambrose in late April received no reprieve from this Seventh Illinois Infantry soldier and his comrades: "To-day we witness war's desolating scourge. . . . The devouring elements of fire are doing their work." Marching with Ambrose were cavalrymen from an Alabama unionist regiment and "Kansas Jayhawkers," whom Ambrose characterized as hardened punitive-war advocates. According to Ambrose, these two groups "are on the war-path: their day has come—their day of retribution."[37] As Union soldiers neared Huntsville, Mary Chadick wrote that "Everybody is hiding their silver and valuables, and dreading we know not what. Anxiety and dread is upon every countenance."[38] The cumulative effect of soldiers' unrelenting punishment convinced a Mrs. Cunningham of Franklin County that the Union intended to "subjugate the South by burning and destroying everything in sight."[39] With the absence of large numbers of Confederate men, women were left to bear the brunt of the Union's harsh policies. Some were subjected to unwanted advances and intrusive searches. Ellen Virginia Saunders, a teenager from Courtland, wrote of Union soldiers looking for hidden contraband by "running their hands into [the] pockets" of women.[40] Others lost substantial portions of their crops. Mrs. Pearsall of Lawrence County had nearly eight hundred bushels of corn and a gin house containing roughly one hundred bushels of peas set ablaze by Union soldiers.[41] When Union forces returned to the outskirts of Florence and again shelled the town, Olivia Moore O'Neal hid her family in a neighbor's cellar.[42] She and her loved ones survived, but she informed her husband that "I never was as badly frightened as I was when the drunken Yankee came in and threatened to *burn my house*."[43] The Union's use of hard war tactics against Confederate civilians during their raids led one northern correspondent to comment that General Turchin's aggressive approach in 1862 had been fully vindicated. The correspondent reminded his readers that "little more than a year ago this brave, chivalrous, earnest and patriotic leader was persecuted by Gen. Buell and dismissed [from] the service . . . for no other offense than simply preferring the rights and interests of Union soldiers to those of the miserable traitors whom they came to subdue!"[44] North Alabama Confederates had reason to fear the enemy's return: a punitive and retaliatory mentality had taken hold among Union soldiers, and they intended to unleash it on those who stood in their way.

The Union raids of 1863 contributed to a visible decline in Confederates' morale. The loss of provisions, property, and the general uncertainty surrounding the return of an unrelenting foe weakened Confederates' faith in their cause. Confederate women internalized these raids as a sign they had lost divine favor. After suffering through several Union raids, Susanna Clay prayed she would be able to "bear all His discipline patiently!" A repentant Clay wrote that the absence of God's protection forced her to remember "what a 'bitter and evil thing sin is.'"[45] Frequent Union incursions into northeast Alabama convinced Sarah Rousseau Espy that God "has given us over into the hand of our cruel foe."[46] Diminished morale and the apparent futility of harvesting crops only to have them taken by the enemy led some Confederates to abandon their fields. A northern correspondent reported that "scarcely one [plantation] in a hundred [is] being cultivated. . . . [T]he plows were standing as if deserted in mortal fear of the coming Yankees."[47] Susanna Clay unknowingly concurred with this depiction: "Our people appear paralyzed" by the prospect of raiding Union soldiers.[48] Rather than live in fear, some Confederates became refugees. This was particularly the case in Madison County, which Union soldiers raided often. By mid-July, Catherine Fennell noted a sizable number had left the region.[49] That same month, Mary Chadick remarked that the "country on the other side of the [Tennessee] River is filled with refugees."[50] When Confederate Lieutenant Robert Anderson McClellan learned his family had chosen to flee their Limestone County homes, he could barely contain "a rising tear" knowing they had been "driven from their homes, by the . . . minions of the ungodly North."[51] The Union's incursions of 1863 had a noticeable effect on Confederates who experienced these raids or feared they soon would. With Union soldiers showing minimal remorse about or inclination to change their ways, North Alabama Confederates' resolve began to waver.

These raids also produced the first conspicuous occasion in which Confederate women questioned the ability of their menfolk to protect them. Female discontent resulted from a breakdown in reciprocity. In return for sacrificing for the Confederacy, women expected to be protected from their northern foe. The inability of their government to stop the Union's raids created a backlash among the female population. Olivia Moore O'Neal bluntly wrote "If we don't have a different commander" to protect the region, "we will [see] the Yankees frequently."[52] The apparent ease with which Union soldiers traversed the region led a frustrated O'Neal to accuse Confederate soldiers of failing in "*their duty*" to protect the civilian population.[53] General Braxton Bragg's decision to retreat to Chattanooga in July instead of engaging the enemy in southern Tennessee or northern Alabama led Mary Chadick to question a military strategy where "we are again exposed to the incursions of a ruthless foe."[54] Sarah Rousseau Espy felt abandoned by Confederate soldiers who were "leaving the country to its fate instead of protecting it."[55] Confederate women's attitudes toward the army were increasingly affected by the inability of their menfolk at home to offer protection. Espy remarked that "the few men who are left here must conceal themselves" whenever Yankee soldiers are nearby.[56] Some even suggested to their menfolk in the Confederate army that it was time to return home and protect their family. Olivia Moore O'Neal wrote to her husband Edward Asbury O'Neal that "I would vote my husband to *come home*. If any man has ever done his duty . . . you have."[57] Union incursions into North Alabama tested the limits of Confederate women's willingness to sacrifice for a nation whose army or available men were unable to shield them from harm. These Confederate women had not yet admitted defeat, but without some protection from their men, they could not indefinitely continue to place the demands of the Confederate government above their own or their families' needs.

Confederate civilian morale was further shaken as thousands of Confederate soldiers came to North Alabama, not as liberators but as deserters, wounded soldiers, or parolees. Confederate soldiers who no longer believed in the viability of an independent South sometimes moved civilians to think likewise. By the summer of 1863, upwards of 10,000 Confederate men were hiding out in the mountains of northern Alabama.[58] The motivation to desert varied. A Pennsylvania soldier stated some of the deserters had returned "to protect their families from our reported depredation."[59] Others gave up hope and deserted after the Confederacy's defeat at Gettysburg and loss of Vicksburg in early July. Governor John Gill Shorter ordered available Confederate forces to hunt down the deserters, but Union soldiers stood in their way.[60] The appearance of paroled or wounded soldiers provided Confederate civilians with irrefutable evidence that the war was not going well. Sarah Rousseau Espy was aghast at the toll the conflict had taken on her male kin who had been besieged at Vicksburg. She later exclaimed in her diary: "how I wish this awful war could end!"[61] Seeing malnourished loved ones return home was difficult for civilians to bear, even though they too had endured great hardship. When Confederate soldiers returned to northeast Alabama, Catherine Fennell asserted "Everyone is low spirited" that they came home "half starved."[62] By the summer of 1863, civilians' confidence in their military had weakened, and their faith in the Confederacy had declined.

The growth of African American assertiveness during the spring and summer suggests a loss of power—and possibly will—among Confederate civilians to maintain firm control over their property. The inverse relationship between sinking Confederate morale and growing optimism by African Americans would hold true for the remainder of the war. With Union soldiers raiding the region, Confederate civilians expected slaves to either attempt to flee or openly defy their masters. When rumors swirled in May that Union soldiers would soon be in Huntsville, Susanna Clay became convinced that "nearly all the negroes" in the town would leave.[63] This southern matriarch dreaded the impending loss and lamented her government's inability to protect her property: "we are in fear of the negroes all leaving or being taken & and that our poor country is willing but not able to help us."[64] Union soldiers did not reach Huntsville on this occasion, but when they returned to the region, Clay again expected "all the negroes . . . to go."[65] Slave masters' gender likely influenced how slaves interacted with them as Union soldiers drew near. Since white women did not generally wield the lash, African Americans might have been more forthright with Confederate women. This could have been why Olivia Moore O'Neal's slaves had the courage to openly tell her "they would go" as soon as the bluecoats arrived in Florence.[66] Slaves belonging to Mr. Finley chose not to openly confront him. Instead, they secretly fled from his home in northeast Alabama before he could make good on his intent to transport them out of the grasp of advancing Union soldiers.[67] By mid-spring, one Iowa soldier offered telling evidence of the determination of some African Americans to leave the region and their masters' inability to stop them. As Thomas Hoffman marched through northwest Alabama, he noticed "a great many darkies" heading toward Corinth with their hands full of possessions.[68] Susanna Clay's slaves chose to stay on the Clay property, though they had no intention of remaining subservient to their owners. Over the course of the summer, Clay witnessed a remarkable transformation among her slaves: "The negroes are worse than free. They say they *are* free. We cannot exert any authority. I beg ours to do what little is done."[69]

Whether African Americans left North Alabama or stayed in the region, they sought to engage in empowering acts of self-determination that had been largely denied to them since the 1862 occupation. When Union soldiers eventually settled into an occupation, blacks would be given additional opportunities to obtain rights they had been deprived of as slaves and to strike at the heart of secessionists' Confederate nationalism.

As raids into the region became more regular over the summer, a mutually beneficial relationship developed between Federal soldiers and local unionists. Ever since Union soldiers had left North Alabama in 1862, those loyal to the federal government had encountered considerable persecution from Confederate civilians, soldiers, and elected officials.[70] Cooperation between soldiers and unionists helped to destabilize the Confederate home front and offered unionists an opportunity to retaliate against recent attacks that left their property destroyed and men and women dead.[71] J. W. Clay likened unionists in Jackson County to a "band of traitors" who are "levying war, adhering to the enemy, and giving them aid and comfort in sundry ways."[72] News that unionists in Cherokee County were working against the Confederacy saddened Sarah Rousseau Espy. She considered the state of affairs in the county "a miserable condition for a country to be in, when a part of the inhabitants are leagued against the other part."[73] With their general knowledge of the region and its people, unionists were important contributors to the Union's pacification efforts. Some acted as spies.[74] General Grenville M. Dodge, an Iowan who commanded the Union force at Corinth, created a network of southern infiltrators stretching over portions of northern Mississippi and Alabama and parts of southern Tennessee.[75] By mid-1864, William Arnold had been paid four hundred dollars for "secret service work" performed in Pikeville, Decatur, and Tuscumbia.[76] While stationed in Huntsville, General David S. Stanley used "a respectable number" of loyalist spies to learn of enemy activities.[77] If these spies or unionists were apprehended, they faced severe punishment, if not death, for what Confederates considered treason. The prospect of retaliation or death did not stop those who were ideologically or economically motivated to seeing the Confederacy defeated. By contributing to the success of the Union's punitive policies in the region, North Alabama unionists helped undermine Confederate civilians' morale.[78]

The inability of Confederate armies to protect their civilians in the spring and summer of 1863 gave Union soldiers a free and destructive hand in North Alabama. During these months, the Union's punitive tactics and support of African Americans and unionists in the region combined with Confederate military defeats to erode Confederate civilians' once-steadfast confidence in themselves and their government. Outside of Virginia and Missouri, few populations had experienced such persistent devastation and social upheaval as North Alabama Confederates had in 1862 and 1863. This did not stop one Confederate living outside the region from accusing North Alabamians of being "bereft of their senses" when he learned some had suggested peace might be in their best interest.[79] Remarkably, there is no evidence to suggest that the majority of Confederate civilians were ready to admit defeat. They did, however, turn against Governor John Gill Shorter, a man they had overwhelmingly supported in the 1861 election.[80] In the August 8, 1863, election, Confederates who were able to vote in North Alabama threw their support behind Thomas Hill Watts. When the votes were tallied, the former Attorney General of the Confederacy handily defeated Shorter, 28,221 to 9,664 votes. Only four counties in North Alabama had more votes for Shorter than Watts.[81] In return for their support, civilians assumed Watts would work diligently to alleviate their suffering once he took office on December 1. In the meantime, Confederates in North Alabama did their best to shore up their faith in their government, military, and themselves.

After a few Confederate military setbacks in the western theater during the summer and early fall, civilians once again had reason to be confident in their chances. In early July, Union forces under Rosecrans drove Confederate Bragg and his Army of Tennessee from Middle Tennessee back to Chattanooga in what became known as the Tullahoma Campaign. Even though Rosecrans needlessly delayed a follow-up attack for weeks, he achieved another victory when he finally sent General Ambrose E. Burnside and the Army of the Ohio to attack Confederate forces at Knoxville. On September 3, Burnside entered the town unopposed. With Chattanooga now vulnerable, Bragg ordered his men to retreat south of the city. What happened next helped stabilize Confederate civilians' declining morale. On September 19, Rosecrans' Army of the Cumberland and Braggs' Army of Tennessee fought a fierce battle near Chickamauga Creek. Confederate forces won a much needed victory and forced the Union army to retreat back to Chattanooga.[82] When Catherine Fennell learned that "Confederates [had] gained a complete victory" at the Battle of Chickamauga, her vision of an independent South was bright once again.[83] Confederate civilians in and around Stevenson were confident Bragg would soon decimate the Union army that was held up in Chattanooga.[84] After enduring military setbacks for the past few months, the Army of Tennessee had achieved an important victory and appeared poised to win back a good deal of lost territory.

The elation expressed by Confederates in North Alabama was premature, as the Union forces moved quickly to break the siege. General-in-Chief Henry W. Halleck ordered General William Tecumseh Sherman to organize four divisions at Vicksburg and proceed at once to Chattanooga.[85] Around the same time, President Lincoln consolidated the departments of the Cumberland, Ohio, and Tennessee into the Military Division of the Mississippi under the command of General Ulysses S. Grant, who had been in charge of the Vicksburg Campaign. General George Thomas subsequently replaced Rosecrans as commander of the Army of the Cumberland.[86] By the end of October, a secure route into Chattanooga had been established. With Bridgeport serving as a major railhead of the "Cracker line," as the road into Chattanooga was called, Union forces would not be leaving North Alabama any time soon.[87] Henry Clay Reynolds's prediction on the eve of Chickamauga that "the Yankees will some day [sic] be in our valley" had come to fruition.[88]

In a strange twist of circumstance, the siege of Chattanooga increased rather than decreased the suffering of Confederates in North Alabama. During the ensuing weeks, Union soldiers in the region continued their confiscation of agricultural produce and livestock to supplement their diet and to help feed their comrades in Chattanooga. The amount of food needed to sustain Union soldiers was staggering. Eugene Marshall, a Union cavalry officer, estimated it would take a minimum of three thousand pounds of beef per day to feed Union soldiers in Chattanooga and North Alabama.[89] Confederates living in or nearby Huntsville were often ordered to hand over their food supplies to their enemies. Mary Chadick stated that Union soldiers "come in town every day, driving off our milk cows, yearlings, hogs, sheep and everything that they think will reduce us to starvation."[90] Susanna Clay had already run short of provisions when soldiers took "all the [cooked] food."[91] As Confederates lost provisions and continued to endure hardships, they prayed for God's intercession. After Union soldiers depleted William McDowellin's "supply of food and fuel for the winter," he asked God to "permit us all to [live] again without [fear] of being molested again by our hated northern foe."[92] The Confederacy's victory at Chickamauga and military maneuvers around Chattanooga had not brought North Alabama Confederates a reprieve from their punitive foe. At the same time that they rejoiced in their military success, they had to bear the burden of the victory.

As Union soldiers traversed North Alabama in search of provisions, their contact with African Americans increased. Military necessity and soldiers' gen-

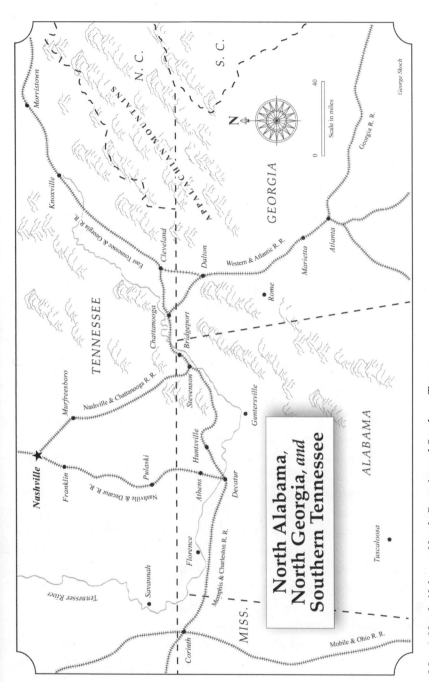

Map 4. North Alabama, North Georgia, and Southern Tennessee

eral support for the Emancipation Proclamation had created a noteworthy transformation among Union soldiers. Their daily interactions with blacks lacked the cruel treatment that occasionally marred the 1862 occupation. These soldiers still held racist attitudes toward African Americans, but they had come to accept that the defeat of the Confederacy and eradication of slavery had become intricately intertwined.[93] When soldiers were in Huntsville, they made it clear to blacks that the Emancipation Proclamation had set them free; several slaves responded by leaving their owners. Mary Chadick wrote of one instance when an impassioned speech by an "abolition preacher from Ohio . . . caused a good deal of excitement among" the black population.[94] She condemned another northerner for "doing all in his power to stir them up to rebellion by telling them that they are free *now* and *here*, that Lincoln made them so the 1st of January last." Chadick was surely aghast when she heard that the soldier had told the predominately African American audience "that the hand of God" was directly connected to the Union's arrival in North Alabama and Lincoln's Emancipation Proclamation.[95] Such talk had a profound effect among those who had known nothing but bondage. As the soldier trumpeted black freedom, a group of African American women presented him with a couple of "flags, and bouquets and a haversack." Abolitionist speeches like those held in Huntsville indicate the extent to which Confederates had lost control over the black population and their region. According to Chadick, "All the servants about town flock to hear [the speeches]. My own asked permission to go, but most of them are *too free* for this."[96] The increased interactions between Federal soldiers and black North Alabamians in the late fall portended the death of both slavery and the Confederacy. As long as Union soldiers adhered to the tenets behind the Emancipation Proclamation and hard war tactics, Confederate civilians would find it difficult to indefinitely resist their occupiers or reassert their version of Herrenvolk democracy in North Alabama.

In late November, civilians began hearing rumors of a battle between Grant's and Bragg's respective forces at Chattanooga. Mary Chadick and Sarah Rousseau Espy—despite their past and current unreciprocated sacrifices—still had faith in their soldiers and providence. Chadick assured herself "that a just God" would not allow the "enemy to triumph over us." Speaking on behalf of her fellow Confederates, she remarked that "Our faith in the justice of our cause buoys us up with the hope that all will come right in the end."[97] When Espy heard of the battle, she prayed to "the Lord [to] give the cruel enemy into our hands, without blood shed [*sic*] on our side."[98] For these two women, and likely thousands of Confederate civilians, their trust in God and Confederate soldiers was shaken when Bragg ignominiously retreated. Chadick, who rarely went more than a few days between diary entries, went an entire week between stating that a battle had begun and writing in her diary again. In her first post-defeat entry, she made no mention of the Confederacy's loss. Instead, her first words were a rare statement that Union soldiers were treating Confederate civilians with respect: "The Feds are behaving very well in town [and] are supplying the poor with fuel."[99] Espy's comments after the defeat were much more despondent. This Confederate woman acknowledged the "discouraging . . . news" in the same sentence in which she noted the one-year anniversary of her son's death. Espy was so disheartened by the loss and the general state of affairs in North Alabama that she stated, "I do not grieve that he is gone, for I cannot wish him back here."[100] Braggs' defeat, which subsequently led to his recall to Richmond, meant North Alabama would indefinitely remain under Union control.

On December 8, roughly two weeks after the Union's victory at Chattanooga, Lincoln announced his first significant Reconstruction plan.[101] Aside from high-ranking Confederate civil and military leaders, "all persons who have, directly or by implication, participated in the existing rebellion" would receive a "full pardon" upon taking an "inviolate" oath to the Union. Once ten percent of a state's citizens had taken the oath, established pro-Union government apparatuses, and included the abolition of slavery in their new state constitution, the federal government would begin the process of incorporating the state back into the Union.[102] This proclamation offered Confederates an opportunity to return to the Union on generally lenient terms. Provided they took the oath, the overwhelming majority of ex-Confederates would not be punished or charged with treason. Although they would have to acknowledge the end of slavery, Lincoln had not gone as far as to demand that the new state constitutions provide suffrage to ex-slaves or equal protection before the law as advocated by abolitionists and Radical Republicans.[103] In North Alabama, Eugene Marshall considered Lincoln's approach "the very thing needed at this juncture" because the "whole fabric of [southern] society & government [has been] destroyed" and the "great mass of the southern army . . . are tired of war & long for peace on any terms."[104] Marshall's appraisal of the condition of the Confederacy was clearly influenced by the deteriorating conditions in North Alabama and did not take into consideration Confederates in areas outside North Alabama who were still confident that the Confederacy would ultimately prevail.

Huntsville, Alabama (*Harper's Weekly Magazine*, March 19, 1864)

Still, if Marshall was correct and Lincoln's terms were accepted, the conflict would end with former Confederates likely being able to enact laws that would ensure their racial supremacy over newly freed slaves.

A small segment of Confederates in North Alabama took Lincoln up on his offer. By early February 1864, the provost marshal's office in Scottsboro had become "thronged from morning till night with a motley crowd of citizens, seeking their 'rights,' [and] taking the oath."[105] The most prominent instance of Confederates accepting Lincoln's "honorable terms" occurred at a Union meeting in Huntsville.[106] At the meeting, which Iowa soldier John Quincy Adams Campbell remarked was "rather small but very respectable," citizens claimed they had been deceived into seceding and demanded a return to "the old flag."[107] Under the leadership of David C. Humphries and Jeremiah Clemens, North Alabama's undeclared leader during the secession convention, they acknowledged "the rebellion was wrong in itself and would have been wrong even if it had been successful."[108] Having admitted their mistake, they called on all North Alabamians to cast "off their [Confederate] leaders and [act] for themselves."[109] Even though these citizens professed a readiness to return to the Union, admitting defeat was likely a somber occasion. Since their state's secession, many of these citizens had been committed to Confederate independence. Between April of 1862 and early 1864, they endured the confiscation of their resources, the destruction of their property, and for some, the loss of their slaves and loved ones, in the expectation that the Confederacy would prevail. By the spring of 1864, they no longer considered the cost of war to be worth the benefits of potential victory.

The fact that the majority of North Alabama Confederates—despite their lowered morale—rejected Lincoln's olive branch did not surprise General Sherman, who had been shifting his headquarters between southern Tennessee and North Alabama during the spring of 1864. Given his employment as a superin-

Huntsville Courthouse Square, 1864 (Huntsville Public Library)

tendent of a military academy in Louisiana during the secession crisis, Sherman considered himself well acquainted with "the temper of the South." He labeled Lincoln's recent Reconstruction proclamation "unwise" and said it would be viewed by southerners as a sign of "weakness." Northerners, Sherman asserted, could not "coax [Confederates] back into the Union"; they had to be punished and deprived of basic resources until they had no choice but surrender.[110] In January 1864, Sherman outlined his strategy on sapping the willpower of unreconstructed Confederates when he replied to General Roswell M. Sawyer's request for advice on how to subdue rebellious civilians in North Alabama. Defiant civilians would get no reprieve from Sherman. Those accused of "creat[ing] disorder" or who actively supported Confederate armies must be held accountable, even if it meant their execution.[111] When it came to civil liberties, Confederates would receive only the rights granted to them by their occupiers. According to Sherman, the "government of the United States has in North Alabama any and all rights which they choose to enforce in war—to take their lives, their homes, their lands, their everything—because [civilians] cannot deny that war exists there, and war is simply power unrestrained by constitution or compact."[112] From Sherman's perspective, Confederate civilians were to blame for their suffering. He told Sawyer, "Three years ago by a little reflection and patience they could have had a hundred years of peace and prosperity, but they preferred war; very well. Last year they could have saved their slaves, but now it is too late." The longer southerners supported the rebellion, Sherman stated, the more suffering they would cause themselves.[113] The general encouraged Sawyer to inform the local Confederate populace of his philosophy "and let them use it so as to prepare for my coming."[114]

Not surprisingly, Confederates characterized this approach as barbaric. Zillah Haynie Brandon believed that she and other self-proclaimed noncombatants should be left alone, but instead, the "enemy like an avelanch [sic] has spread over our whole country, disregarding all rights, social, religious, and political."[115] The *Charleston Mercury* and the *Daily South Carolinian* (Columbia) depicted the Union's actions in North Alabama as among the worst in the history of warfare. A correspondent for the *Mercury* considered Union soldiers' treatment of civilians in Jackson County to be the "darkest chapter in the history of this cruel war, if not in any other war," while a commentator for the *Carolinian* compared the recent devastation wrought by Union forces in North Alabama to the "utter destruction of . . . Poland by the Russian hordes."[116] Confederates condemned the Union's rough treatment of their women. When Captain D. Coleman learned that his mother's house had been "sacked and pillaged," he asked God "what creatures have we to deal with! —are they human being or are they fiends!"[117] Readers of the *Carolinian* learned that when Coleman's mother and other women begged their occupiers not to ransack the house, their pleas went unanswered as they were "violently [pushed] out of the house."[118] Incidents in which Union soldiers killed or wounded Confederates provided further evidence of the Union's callous character. J. W. Clay claimed that a Mr. Rich of Marshall County "had been taken from his bed by the enemy and cruelly murdered."[119] He wrote of another instance a few miles north of Guntersville, in which Union forces captured, lined up, and shot several men. The Yankees then "threw their bodies into the river."[120] Catherine Fennell mentioned both of these shootings in her diary, remarking that the men north of Guntersville had been taken "from their homes and shot . . . down like . . . hogs."[121] By portraying themselves as innocent victims while depicting Union soldiers as marauders intent on wreaking havoc in the region, Confederates remained convinced that the bluecoats truly were ruthless at heart.

At the same time, however, there were Confederates whose evaporating morale and disillusionment with the war led to increased fraternization with the enemy. Back in 1862, Confederate women's commitment to independence was too strong to allow for congenial relations with Union soldiers to develop. By 1864, some women were no longer able or willing to maintain such staunch defiance. Reports of Confederate women's good-natured exchanges with Union soldiers during these months indicates an evolving attitude toward the war and a conflicting view of their occupiers. Mrs. Wilson, who worked at the Female College in Huntsville, thought enough of William T. Shepherd that she encouraged him to "marry a Southern girl—perhaps one of her adopted daughters." Although this Illinois soldier was "well acquainted with two of them," he was against making any overtures because "their immense plantations, money, niggers & palefaces, have no attraction for me."[122] Dances in early 1864 were a conspicuous public confirmation of lowered female defiance; they also demonstrated a willingness among Union soldiers to momentarily put ideological differences aside. Hugh Gaston wrote of "frollicks" that were held "nearly every night" in Scottsboro. He told his wife that "there is always plenty of women to dance at every frollick [sic]," but insisted "I have not been to any of there [sic] frollicks [sic] yet nor I don't expect to go to any of them."[123] While stationed in Huntsville, Jenkins Lloyd Jones, a Wisconsin artilleryman, observed and likely participated in a competition between officers and enlisted men over who could attract more Confederate women to their respective dances. When each group held their dance on February 22, officers "failed to find but four ladies" while the "enlisted men . . . had a gay time." These women might have been more willing to attend the enlisted men's dances than the officers' because they felt that the officers had lost their gentlemanly status by ordering destructive measures against civilians. A few weeks later, Jones and his comrades held another party "to try to excel the shoulder-strap fizzle of Feb. 22." The outcome was a resounding success; forty Confederate women attended their dance.[124] When war broke out in 1861, Confederate North Alabama women fully embraced the tenets of secession. Yet their commitment to independence had its limits. Privation, military setbacks, and the inability of Confederate armies to protect them had significantly lowered their spirits by the first half of 1864. As their Confederate morale began to fade, they found Union soldiers more socially acceptable.

As Confederate commitment to disunion waned, African Americans continued to seek additional rights and responsibilities. This change was not, as one Union correspondent insinuated, solely derived from President Lincoln's "glorious Proclamation of Freedom."[125] In both 1862 and 1863, blacks had worked in

Soldiers' Ball in Huntsville (*Harper's Weekly Magazine*, April 9, 1864)

conjunction with Union soldiers to throw off the chains of bondage. Through federal policy and self-determination, North Alabama African Americans by early 1864 were engaging in numerous activities previously denied to them as slaves. The opportunity to receive an education seemed especially important. When the Union established a black school at a Huntsville church, Mary Chadick's black servant Corinna sent her son Jim, despite her mistress's commands to the contrary.[126] Corinna's son might have been one of the "bevy of [blacks] with spelling books and readers in hand on their way to school" mentioned in the *Cincinnati Gazette*.[127] Some freedmen, as blacks were beginning to be called, engaged in the free-labor enterprise. A black woman by the name of Melinda offered her and her two sons' services to Chadick for eight dollars a month. This former slave soon learned the perils of wage labor; she and her sons were dismissed after only two days.[128] African Americans also attended free and open religious services, such as the ones that were held in Athens.[129] The right to an education, paid labor, and unrestricted religious expression were just few of the newfound benefits of freedom. The transformation of these slaves into individuals with basic rights, in conjunction with the general course of the war, had a telling effect on both races. According to a Wisconsin soldier, the "negroes wear a happy look but whites look sullen and don't like to talk."[130]

First Wisconsin Brigade Band (Huntsville Public Library)

The ability of African American men to enlist in the Union army ranks as one of the most monumental developments of the entire war. Although a few black regiments had been created before the Emancipation Proclamation went into effect, large numbers of African Americans did not start enlisting until after January 1, 1863. By December, Lincoln proudly announced "one hundred thousand [former slaves] are now in the United States military service."[131] The recruitment of blacks from North Alabama picked up momentum as the Union reoccupied the region in the fall of 1863.[132] Both Federal soldiers and northern civilians, such as J. A. Spooner from the Boston Association to Promote the Enlistment of Colored Troops, served as recruiters in North Alabama.[133] Between the final months of 1863 and early 1864, General Grenville M. Dodge reported "two [black] Regiments in North Alabama" had been formed and another one was "under way."[134] While enlistment imbued black men with a newfound sense of dignity and citizenship, they encountered numerous obstacles. Virulent prejudice among white soldiers and northern whites prevented the equal treatment of black soldiers.[135] At least initially, white soldiers viewed African American men as being better suited for manual labor than for fighting battles.[136] Once enlisted, North Alabama blacks encountered additional discrimination in pay and promotions.[137] In time, North Alabama blacks and those from neighboring states proved themselves to their white comrades during skirmishes in the region and more generally as part of the occupation force.[138] With African American soldiers performing admirably in North Alabama, Eugene Marshall commented that his comrades "are now in favor of arming ne-groes."[139] As the recruitment and acceptance of African American soldiers in-creased, they became visible in occupied towns, the countryside, and along the Tennessee River.[140] In Bridgeport alone, there were over nine hundred black soldiers by January 1864.[141] Even though black soldiers from North Alabama were not treated as complete equals, they enlisted and fought to bring an end to slavery and the Confederacy.[142] In doing so, they exhibited their military worth and helped lay the groundwork for additional rights.

With African American men enlisting in the Union army, Confederates sud-denly found themselves in a situation in which black men were in a position of authority over them. Private and public denigration by Confederates was a com-mon response to the Union's use of black troops. A white Union private pre-dicted that the "Rebs [will] sware [*sic*]" when they learn that a detachment of African American soldiers were about to arrive in the region.[143] With black sol-diers stationed just north of Huntsville, a contributor to the *Memphis Daily Ap-peal* stated that "the bouquet of 'African scent'" will soon "be placed . . . over 'the loved ones'" in the city.[144] When the opportunity presented itself, Confederates often assaulted or killed black soldiers.[145] These violent tactics against blacks were born out of revenge and were meant to remind blacks that, even as sol-diers, they were vulnerable. Eugene Marshall recorded a chilling account given by an African American soldier who, along with two other black recruits, was taken captive by bushwhackers in northeast Alabama. After being "stripped . . . of everything," they were shot, leaving two dead and the one recounting the event with three bullet wounds. Such atrocities naturally elicited reprisals. Gen-eral George Crook let it be known "that no more prisoners [will] be taken amongst these guerrillas."[146] To discourage their slaves from joining the Feder-als, Confederates told potential enlistees of the dire consequences that awaited their families.[147] For those who were threatened with reprisals, joining the Union army was understandably a difficult decision. While enlistment would empower black men, it might also prompt Confederates to harass or assault—including sexually assault—the enlistees' family and friends. This dilemma might have been lost on Private James T. Ayers, a white Union recruiter. Ayers remarked that some "Pore [*sic*] ignorant Devils . . . would Rather Stay behind and geather [*sic*] up the Boxes, oald [*sic*] shoes and oald [*sic*] shirts and Pants our Boys have left than be soldiers."[148] Through the use of verbal and physical assaults on African American soldiers and their families, North Alabama Con-federates attempted to retain some resemblance of racial hierarchy. While Confederates would have claimed some success on this score, they could not fully restore their crumbling social structure. African American men from North Alabama and throughout the United States would continue to enlist and fight against the Confederacy to secure lasting freedom.[149]

The challenges that newly elected Governor Thomas H. Watts confronted in North Alabama were immense. From the moment he took office on December 1, 1863, he faced the responsibility of bringing relief to the most beleaguered region of his state. As Union soldiers appropriated Confederate property and resources and recruited blacks into the army, Watts promised to "use all the exertions in my power to provide for the families of our soldiers and for the poor in North Alabama, who have been over-run by Yankees or tories."[150] As he worked to alleviate the suffering of North Alabama Confederates, he asked them to continue "to stand firmly, to the cause of liberty and independence" and reminded them that "God is on our side."[151] As with his predecessor, Watts had limited resources at his disposal to lessen the suffering of North Alabama Confederates. At one point he commented to General Joseph E. Johnston that the "unprotected condition of N. Ala. & of N. Eastern Ala. at this time causes me great anxiety." The governor later told the general "I have the utmost confidence in your ability to drive—soon—the Yankee hordes from Georgia, and thus relieve this state from Yankee depredations."[152] Since Johnston lacked the manpower and resources to vanquish the enemy from either northern Georgia or northern Alabama, Watts continued to make public statements asking the people of North Alabama not to succumb to the enemy.

Civilians' already precarious hold on their Confederate nationalism became even more uncertain in the spring of 1864 as Confederate forces began confiscating provisions in areas not firmly under Union control. The crumbling Confederate infrastructure and the inability of the Confederate government to efficiently transport supplies and foodstuffs to soldiers in the field made such measures a military necessity. Sarah Rousseau Espy predicted "that if the Federals do not . . . ruin me . . . then our army will" after both sides had taken foodstuffs and other supplies from her property.[153] Confederate foraging parties were particularly prominent around Guntersville. Watts responded with empathy and support for those affected by the raids. The governor told A. G. Henry that he felt "deeply, for the distress of our people" of Guntersville and assured him that "something can and will be done, to protect the good citizens of N. Alabama from outrages of tories—Yankees—and our own troops."[154] The governor condemned "the lawlessness of our own troops" as an unwarranted attack on the very people they were supposed to protect.[155] Even though Watts considered these actions "inexcusable," he could not stop them from taking place.[156] If the Confederacy stood any chance of eventually beating back Union forces in North Alabama and outlying areas, soldiers and military livestock had to be fed. Still, Confederate civilians could not shake the fact that their own army was adding to their suffering.

Before the return of Union soldiers in April 1863, Confederate civilians were undeniably committed to achieving independence. Over the course of the next year, Union military victories on the national level, Union raids, and another punitive occupation peeled away several layers of their morale. John Brobst, a white Union soldier, stated that if "a continual dropping of water will wear away a rock . . . is true," he predicted "we will soon have them all worn out, for they are wearing away all the time."[157] Civilians' nationalist fervor was further weakened by the failure of two powers upholding their Confederate faith—God and the army—to protect them. While their faith in the Confederacy had not entirely dissolved, their collective morale by the end of the spring of 1864 was at its lowest level. According to Confederate soldier L. J. Morgan, demoralization was worst among the female population. Without fully committed women, Morgan wondered, "What will the country come to."[158] As spring turned to summer, embattled Confederate civilians expected a continuation of the Union's hard war policies. Sarah Rousseau Espy assumed that the worst was yet to come. She feared an angry God had handed the region to Union soldiers who "will waste us." Espy asked the Lord, if they must live under an indefinite occupation, to give the enemy "hearts of compassion."[159] Had Union soldier Alonzo A. Van Vlack known of her request, he would have told her—and all Confederate civilians—to expect no leniency from him. Van Vlack called for "death to [all] traitors and Rebels . . . fighting against the Flag of Liberty."[160]

"SECESSIONISTS HAVE HAD THEIR

RUN—THE RACE IS OVER"

By the summer of 1864, North Alabama Confederates still clung to the hope that the Confederacy would win. Even though these southerners had the opportunity to take advantage of President Lincoln's Reconstruction offers, they chose to remain committed to their cause. Their loyalty, however, was not absolute. During the latter part of 1864, the weight of Union soldiers' punitive policies began to take its toll on North Alabama Confederates. Although these Rebels did their best to regain their once redoubtable defiance, Lincoln's reelection, the continuation of hard war tactics, and Confederate military defeats quashed what remained of their willpower. When General Robert E. Lee surrendered at Appomattox in April 1865, North Alabamians acknowledged defeat, devastated that all their sacrifices were for naught. After learning that Lincoln had been assassinated and Andrew Johnson had been sworn in as president, secessionists in the region anticipated the worst from their new president.[1]

Since mid-1862, military necessity had driven Lincoln to support punitive policies against the Confederate home front. Yet, even as he relied on these hard war tactics, the president established relatively lenient conditions for reconstructing the Union. Not all Republicans agreed with this approach. During the summer of 1864, the so-called "Radicals"—ardent opponents of slavery and Confederate aristocrats—urged Lincoln to adopt a more rigorous policy. Radicals viewed Union victory as an ideal opportunity to rebuild the United States in a manner that reflected their version of American democracy: diminish the political power of southern aristocrats while providing blacks with increased political, social, and economic rights.[2] With the support of moderate Republicans, Radicals passed the Wade-Davis bill in early July. Named after Senator Benjamin Wade of Ohio and Representative Henry Winter Davis of Maryland, the bill disfranchised all men who had voluntarily taken up arms against the Union or provided Confederate soldiers with aid and comfort. Instead of starting the Reconstruction process once ten percent of a state's eligible voters took a loyalty oath, as Lincoln had outlined, the bill increased the number to fifty percent. The bill also affirmed the authority of Congress to forever abolish slavery. Wade and Davis became incensed when the president, who felt the bill would impede his current Reconstruction efforts, pocket-vetoed the bill.[3] In their subsequent "Wade-Davis Manifesto," they blasted Lincoln and branded his veto as a blatant "encroachment of the Executive on the authority of Congress."[4] Wade, Davis, and like-minded Radicals feared that without a harsh Reconstruction agenda, former Confederates would return to political power and subvert the federal government. Wade and Davis warned Lincoln of the political fallout if he ignored Congress' voice in this matter. "The President," they wrote, "must understand that our support is of a cause and not of a man; that the authority of Congress is paramount . . . and if he wishes our support, he must confine himself to his executive duties . . . and leave political reorganization to Congress."[5] With a general election only a few months away, a referendum on reconstruction was about to take place.

Lincoln won reelection, but it was not inevitable. Before and after his renomination, Radicals worked to put a man in the White House more amenable to their agenda, though they eventually realized they lacked the support to unseat Lincoln. Military stalemate and opposition from Democrats also posed a viable threat to reelection. In Virginia, Grant's Overland Campaign had turned

Abraham Lincoln (Library of Congress)

into a war of attrition. Between early May and mid-June, the Army of the Potomac suffered nearly 65,000 causalities. Even though Grant had Lee bottled up in Petersburg, Grant appeared no closer to victory than when the campaign began. During these same months, Sherman's troops suffered fewer casualties, but he had not defeated the Army of Tennessee or taken Atlanta. Without a significant military victory to suggest the war was progressing to its finale, northerners who were tired of a seemingly endless conflict might be persuaded to vote for the Democrat nominee, George B. McClellan.[6] With these challenges looming over his reelection bid, Lincoln commented that it was "exceedingly probable that this administration will not be reelected."[7] By late summer, however, Lincoln's reelection prospects began to improve. In August, the navy took control of Mobile Bay; a month later, Sherman captured Atlanta. These victories signaled to northerners that victory was indeed within reach. On election day, Lincoln won by a landslide. A group of Union soldiers skirmishing with the enemy near Florence went to extraordinary measures to cast their vote for Lincoln even as shells flew "over the ballot box." According to a Union officer, "When a regiment hat [sic] voted, [they gave] a rousing cheer for Abraham Lincoln" and returned to the fight.[8] President Lincoln's victory affirmed northerners' faith and support in his wartime measures and Reconstruction plans.[9]

In North Alabama, Confederates were not ready to concede defeat; even under dire circumstances, they refused to accept Lincoln's lenient Reconstruction overtures. When Union soldiers attempted to make southern nationalists take loyalty oaths during the second half of 1864, Confederates once again demonstrated the inherent weakness of this particular Reconstruction policy.[10] According to Octavia Wyche Otey of nearby Meridianville, this policy "has created quite a stir among the ladies," in the area, but it did not diminish their support for the Confederacy.[11] Some Rebels refused to be bullied. Even though one of Mary Chadick's male acquaintances desperately wanted a pass out of Huntsville, he "couldn't subscribe to the terms" of the loyalty oath that would have allowed him to leave.[12] Amanda Wade came to the same conclusion when told she would have to take an oath before being given a pass.[13] Even when civilians took the oath, there was a very real possibility they still considered themselves Confederate nationalists. Octavia Wyche Otey admitted to her sister Ella Burke that she took the oath but assured her sister that "I don't feel like I owe the Yankees any allegiance." Otey had simply gone along to "keep [her] family of 10 from . . . starvation" and to save her male kinsmen the indignity of taking the oath.[14] Her tone toward Burke became heated over accusations by Confederates outside the occupation zone that those who took an oath were less committed to independence. Otey made it clear to her sister, who fled the occupation, that taking the oath was a necessity and not an abandonment of the Confederate cause. This Confederate nationalist bluntly told Burke that "The people of South Ala., as any other place, where they have *laws* to *protect* them, and *plenty* to *eat*, and *wear* . . . are not competent to judge of what is right and propper [sic]." For more than a year and a half, North Alabamians had endured "*starvation* staring us in the face, [men] shot down in the midst of their families, some taken up on mere *suspicion* and thrown in to a loathsome jail." Instead of receiving the "sympathy of people farther south, who have never known the terrors of Yankee rule," Otey stated that she and her Confederate cohorts who took the oath "only [get] execration and malicious slander."[15] W. C. McClellan agreed with Otey's argument that taking the oath was not synonymous with surrender. He instructed his sister to "Tell Father to play Yankee [to] save . . . his family from . . . ruin" and not worry about potential criticism from fellow Confederates. According to McClellan, this ploy had become routine by "good Southerners . . . all over the Confederacy."[16] As a component of Reconstruction, loyalty oaths were a well-intended but flawed policy. If the Union was to crush the resolve of Confederate civilians, they would have to rely on tactics that were much harsher than loyalty oaths.

Since civilians were not yet ready to admit defeat, Union soldiers continued with a punitive style of warfare they and northerners had grown accustomed to and viewed as essential for victory.[17] The ease with which Union soldiers discussed destroying Confederate property and confiscating provisions shows a hardened indifference toward the Confederate home front. Samuel Styre's and his comrades' deep-seated hatred for Confederate civilians led them to advocate starving the enemy into submission.[18] Octavia Wyche Otey experienced firsthand soldiers' commitment to this goal. As soldiers "ripped" through her house and took "our sole dependence for something to eat this fall," they told her that "they did not care if we . . . starved."[19] Similar actions by soldiers in Athens "almost finished" a Mr. Simpson. In addition to killing all of his hogs, Union soldiers "took his beef, molasses, [and] chickens."[20] Some Athenians learned well after the fact that their crops had been taken. Henry Nurse, an Illinois soldier who enlisted in 1862, stated that he and his men "went and dug and carried off and ate all of [the] sweet potatoes and did not say anything to [civilians] about it." According to Nurse, "This is the way we gather crops in the army."[21] General William Tecumseh Sherman, who spent time in North Alabama during the fall of 1864, was impressed by the severity and thoroughness of his men. He told his wife that "I am practicing [my soldiers] in the art of foraging" and they "take to it like Ducks to water. They like pigs, sheep, chickens, calves, and Sweet potatoes better than Rations."[22] With a commanding officer and northern populace supporting harsh measures toward the Confederate home front, Union soldiers could target the enemy population with near impunity.[23]

General Sherman and the men he took with him on his invasion of Georgia

General William Tecumseh Sherman (Library of Congress)

and his March to the Sea continued their "practicing" while marching toward the Georgia line. When they stopped at Gaylesville to replenish their supplies, Confederate civilians in the area witnessed the destructive capabilities of Sherman and his men. Zillah Haynie Brandon, a pious Methodist who lost two of her four sons who fought for the Confederacy, accused Union soldiers of stealing over "two thousand dollars worth" of food. Among the provisions taken were "two or three hundred pounds of bacon [and] two or three hundred pounds of salt." Soldiers even grabbed the honey and "left the bees to starve."[24] When Brandon's daughter questioned Sherman on his right to take their food, he replied that "God had authorized him to do what he did." The elder Brandon privately fumed that the general's power was more likely "received from the beast . . . from the bottomless pit."[25] Illinois soldier Henry Nurse described an incident in which a Confederate townsman who objected to handing "three barrels of molasses" over to Union soldiers almost suffered an even worse fate. A comrade of Nurse told the argumentative Rebel that if he did not "keep his mouth shut," they would set fire to his house. When it came to soldiers taking what they needed—or what they wanted—Nurse remarked that they "don't allow a citizen to have anything to say about such matters."[26] The countryside around Gaylesville offered soldiers an abundance of foodstuffs.[27] With Union soldiers intending "to live [off] the country a little more than [they were] in the habit of doing," Confederates residing in the outlying farms felt the full weight of the Union's hard war civil-military measures.[28] William Pepper, a Union soldier from Illinois, stated that soldiers were "helping themselves" to the region's crops and livestock.[29] Within days of the Union's foraging forays, farms became barren. At one point, Pepper "rode some ten or twelve miles and never got a thing." He saw neither "a hog or chicken" on his ride, and concluded there was not "a potato [within] twenty miles" of the town.[30] Pepper's appraisal of the situation appeared to confirm a promise Sherman made after Zillah Haynie Brandon's daughter asked that he spare the local mill her parents co-owned. The general told the young woman that not only would he burn the mill, but upon leaving the area, "I will not leave enough for a grasshopper to subsist on."[31] By the time Sherman and his men crossed over into Georgia, they were well trained in living off the resources available in Confederate towns and farms.[32]

While the state of affairs for North Alabama Confederates looked grim, all was not yet lost. Between September and mid-December, Confederate cavalry units from the Army of Tennessee made forays into northern Alabama and southern Tennessee to disrupt Union supply and communication lines. Confederate civilians hoped that these attacks would lessen their distress and dislodge the enemy from the region. The most successful Confederate assault on Union soldiers came at the end of September, when General Nathan Bedford Forrest surprised Union soldiers at Athens. Aside from taking nearly 2,000 white and black Union soldiers prisoner, the cavalrymen captured an assortment of weapons and livestock, commandeered a Union train, and damaged railroad

Union Soldiers in front of Thomas McCalley Home, 1864 (Huntsville Public Library)

tracks leading into the town.[33] A Union correspondent for Philadelphia's *Christian Recorder* blasted Colonel Wallace Campbell for surrendering the town "after [fighting] only long enough to disable thirty of the enemy."[34] Confederate residents in and around Athens were undoubtedly disappointed when Forrest and his men left the town and headed east with the intention of making a similar attack on Huntsville. Unlike Colonel Campbell, General R. S. Granger refused to surrender Huntsville to the former slave trader. When Forrest learned of Granger's rebuff, he warned the general that "I expect to attack you tomorrow morning from every rock houses trees & shrubs in the vicinity & feeling confident of [my] ability to succeed . . . prepare yourself for the fury."[35] Forrest's "fury" never materialized; he and his men retreated to Tennessee.[36] Several thousand Union soldiers were subsequently sent to Huntsville to protect the city from a future attack. Over the next few months, Confederate cavalry units sporadically returned to the region and harassed Union soldiers, though they never took long-term control of any strategically important locations. Unbeknownst to these Confederate civilians, any potential large-scale attack on Union forces in the region or the liberation of North Alabama from enemy control ended when General George H. Thomas defeated John Bell Hood's Army of Tennessee at the Battle of Nashville in mid-December.[37]

With Union forces in the western theater continuing their assault on the Confederate home front and Grant tightening his grip around Lee and the Army of Northern Virginia at Petersburg, Congress and President Lincoln continued to debate the constitutional and civil rights of African Americans.[38] Senator Charles Sumner of Massachusetts was among the most prominent Radical Republicans who pushed for greater citizenship rights for African Americans. During a speech to Massachusetts Republicans, Sumner stated that the North had taken important strides to ending slavery, but he stressed that the "work of liberation is not yet completed . . . until the equal rights of every person, once claimed as a slave, are placed under the safeguard of irreversible guarantees." For Sumner, Reconstruction had to entail more than punishing disloyal southern whites: "you must also lift up the slave."[39] To achieve this goal and to create a strong Republican foothold in the post-war South, the Massachusetts senator joined other Radicals in calling for African American suffrage.[40] Lincoln, who was no stranger to disagreeing with Radicals, was not yet willing to publicly commit to a suffrage amendment for black men. He did, however, recognize the need for a constitutional amendment that abolished slavery. In early December, he asked House Democrats for their support and vote in favor of the Thirteenth Amendment, which the Senate had already passed.[41] With Republican gains in the November election guaranteeing the amendment's passage once the new Congress convened, Lincoln told Democrats that it "is only a question of *time*" before the amendment would be in the hands of state legislators.[42] To help sway Democrats, Lincoln made promises of future patronage in return for their support. The president's argument and enticements carried the day, and on January 31, 1865, the House ratified the Thirteenth Amendment 119–56.[43] By early February, John C. Norton, a Union surgeon in North Alabama, calmly remarked in his diary that "several states" had ratified the amendment.[44] Even though the president, members of Congress, and northerners in general had not initially gone to war to eradicate slavery, military and moral necessity ultimately pushed them to demand an end to nearly two hundred and fifty years of race-based slavery in America.

While the Thirteenth Amendment signaled a revolutionary reconfiguration of post-war America, it did not erase white Union soldiers' ingrained prejudice toward African Americans. White soldiers supported the military and moral rationale behind the Thirteenth Amendment, but they were not ready to treat blacks as their equals.[45] In North Alabama, white soldiers were able to separate the need for the Thirteenth Amendment from their racist attitudes just as soldiers had done in 1862 when they retained their racial assumptions while working with blacks to break the master-slave bond. William Tecumseh Sherman did not hide his belief that racism in the North would not be going away anytime soon. Before crossing over into Georgia, he told the secretary of war that he preferred "to keep negros, yet for some time to come, in a subordinate State, for our prejudice, yours as well as mine are not yet schooled for absolute Equality."[46] John C. Norton wholeheartedly supported letting "slavery [perish] from the earth it [has] cursed so long," but he agreed with his commanders' stance that African Americans should not be given full citizenship until they were ready for such a privilege. Norton bluntly stated that whites should treat African Americans "as an equal when [they] become such."[47] Even with all the contributions and sacrifices North Alabama blacks had made in support of the Union, white Union soldiers in North Alabama generally refused to accept African Americans as their equals.

The racist attitudes of Union soldiers paled in comparison to the opinions and actions of North Alabama Confederates. With the probability of Confederate defeat increasing, southern nationalists turned to intimidation, assault, and murder in an effort to maintain racial supremacy. African American soldiers in North Alabama were among the most conspicuous targets.[48] These soldiers embodied the advances and opportunities black men had gained during the war and what Confederates felt they had lost in the process. A black soldier taken prisoner by roaming Confederate forces, partisans, or civilians likely faced harsher treatment than captured white soldiers. When Confederate cavalrymen under General Forrest captured Joseph Howard, a private in the One Hundred and Tenth Regiment, U.S. Colored Infantry, they robbed him of his personal items and sent him, along with other captured black soldiers, to work on fortifications near Mobile. As captured black soldiers toiled under slave-like conditions, those who "lagged or faltered" while working "were whipped and abused." Howard claimed that some of these whippings were carried out by fellow black soldiers "detailed to whip the others."[49] Private Howard eventually escaped his captors and made his way to a U.S. gunboat in Mobile Bay. Rather than take African American soldiers prisoner, some Confederates preferred to execute them. Near Athens, an African American woman told a correspondent for the *Liberator* that a black soldier had been ambushed and mutilated by Confederates. In addition to being shot in the head, "His mouth [was] smashed and his nose broken by a heavy blow from the butt of a musket."[50] An Iowa newspaper claimed that Forrest "butchered all the negroes" when he liberated Athens, but there is no corroboratory evidence of this massacre.[51] African Americans who tried to protect themselves by following Union soldiers became vulnerable to clandestine Confederate attacks. One such attack occurred between Huntsville and Stevenson when more than three thousand blacks were following Union soldiers. According to Colonel William Penn Lyon of Wisconsin, the African Americans were "bushwhacked" by Confederates. In the ensuing panic, Lyon stated "a great many young children and infants were abandoned by their mothers."[52] Confederate attacks on African Americans in late 1864 and early 1865 suggested an ominous future for African Americans in North Alabama. Even though North Alabama Confederates' commitment to independence was weakening, they continued to terrorize the region's black population.

As the Confederate home front in North Alabama began to crumble, parts of the region resembled a wasteland of barren fields, ruined property, and shattered dreams. For a region where no major battle had occurred, the Confederate people, towns, and countryside had suffered greatly. In January 1865, Union soldier John S. McGraw reflected on the physical changes from when he arrived in 1862 as part of General Mitchel's occupation force. He recalled a moment during that occupation when he was awestruck by the "beautiful scenery" of Huntsville and its outlying areas. When McGraw returned to the same area in early 1865, it had "been desolated a great deal."[53] Adolph Gaes made a similar statement about Decatur. Initially, Decatur "was a beautiful town," but the Union occupation left the town "totally destroyed."[54] Having endured immense destruction and privation, Confederate civilians were starting to wonder if the end of the Confederacy was at hand. On January 1, 1865, Mary Chadick recalled the last New Year's Day "before the advent of this miserable war!" On that 1860 day, the Chadick house was filled with optimism and joy as they sang "to each other, 'I wish you a Happy New Year!'"[55] There would be no singing on this New Year's Day, as Chadick was recovering from one of her "nervous attacks, which are becoming more frequent of late." With each day bringing only "terrible and startling events," she began to lose hope in Confederate independence.[56] Since the 1862 occupation, the battle between Confederate civilians and Federal soldiers had become a test of perseverance and willpower. At first, Confederates had willed themselves to remain confident that their military would protect them and that the South would win the war. By late 1864 and early 1865, the cracks in the foundation of their Confederate nationalism were beginning to widen.

Several factors influenced the collapse of the Confederate home front in North Alabama. Union soldiers' unremitting policy of confiscating foodstuffs played a decisive role in breaking down civilians' morale and resistance. According to Octavia Wyche Otey, 1864 "has been a year of trouble to our family, and also to the whole country. Anxiety about *something to eat* something to wear, and anxiety about *everything*. . . . *God only* knows what will become of us."[57] As Otey continued to live "in constant expectation of every thing [*sic*] we have being taken from us," her journal entries revealed a sense of helplessness.[58] This was especially the case after soldiers raided her house, leaving her "poor children [with] nothing [to eat] but a little piece of fried middling, and bread and water."[59] Confederates like the Otey family, who had no choice but to hand over what remained in their cupboards and smokehouses or watch as Federal soldiers seized fall harvests, were often in desperate straits. Mary Chadick remarked that it had become "difficult" for families in Huntsville "to procure provisions." Even if they were allowed to travel beyond city limits, it was unlikely they would find anything to eat: "Everything in the country [has] been taken, and the country people have not enough for themselves."[60] Conditions were just as bad in Limestone County, where Mary Fielding and her neighbors did not have enough food, "especially corn," to eat. "I . . . never thought I'd starve," Fielding confessed, "but I don't know where the bread is to come from now."[61] She later learned that Dick Newby was selling his excess supply of corn before it fell into the hands of the enemy. However, by the time she arrived at Newby's farm "he had sold all that he had to spare."[62] Occasionally, Confederates opened their homes to Union boarders in return for access to their stores.[63] The severe food shortage in North Alabama left civilians with a decision to make: remain committed to their defiant ways, even if it meant starvation, or seek the aid of their occupiers. In the end, they chose not to become martyrs to what appeared to be an unwinnable war. Before receiving victuals, Confederate civilians likely needed to give at least a tacit indication to their occupiers that they would behave. Private Elisha A. Peterson of Ohio remarked that extra supplies were brought up the Tennessee River for "citizens as there are a great many suffering now especially the poorer classes."[64] According to one Midwestern correspondent, there was a "great scarcity" of victuals "except where the people have been able to obtain food from our abundant storehouses."[65] After nearly two years of occupation and raids, the Union's confiscation of foodstuffs helped bring North Alabama Confederates to their knees. While receiving rations from the enemy was surely a humbling experience for these once-proud secessionists, they had reached the point where they were no longer willing to needlessly sacrifice for the Confederacy.

Union soldiers' unremitting use of punitive policies, along with their improved ability to locate guerrillas, further undermined the Confederate war effort in North Alabama. By early 1865, the anti-Union violence that plagued the region had dramatically decreased. Northern readers of the *Cincinnati Gazette* learned that the "difficulty of holding secure the lines of communications [in North Alabama] is not near as great as it has been." The correspondent commented, "Those who were engaged in the business of firing into trains, [and] pulling up rails . . . appear to be convinced of the folly and danger of their attempts and are abandoning such a calling."[66] With the prospect of defeat looming, a number of formerly defiant Confederates no longer viewed armed resistance as a practical method of defiance, especially since it would result in swift reprisals. Union soldiers' growing familiarity with their surroundings and information gleaned from unionists, blacks, and disheartened Confederates helped them hunt down those who continued to engage in armed resistance. When Union personnel learned a "notorious guerrilla named McWilliams" was hiding out near Larkinsville, a unit of black and white soldiers under the command of Colonel Prince Salm set out and soon apprehended the Rebel at his own wedding reception. What followed might have given the bridegroom pause over his choice of a wife. Since the "women and children" in attendance were certain Union soldiers would eventually execute McWilliams, they "begged piteously that he might be killed right there, so that they could bury him decently." Rather than give in to their pleas, soldiers collected information from McWilliams on the whereabouts of other guerrilla fighters before taking him to Bridgeport.[67] When Illinois soldier William Titze learned that his comrades had captured a notorious rebel by the name of S. Moore forty miles west of Athens, he wished he could have been there to help remove the man's "pistols, spurs & powder flask."[68] Less than two weeks before General Lee's surrender, a Wisconsin officer shot down "Whitecorn," one of the region's most notorious guerrillas. According to a Union correspondent, Whitecorn had "boasted that he had killed twenty-seven men . . . when Gen. Mitchell [*sic*] was here." This correspondent thought such men deserved no leniency "except that which may be found when they are dangling from the end of a rope; or, as they catch the sound of a dozen rifles, each one of which is sending a bullet into their miserable carcasses."[69] Few tasks had been more daunting for Union soldiers than bringing an end to violent Confederate resistance in North Alabama. The eventual pacification of North Alabama was a lengthy process that depended heavily on the continual use of punitive and retaliatory tactics to discourage civilian resistance and capture violent partisans. With the Union firmly in control of North Alabama, once-rebellious civilians in the region awaited word that the war was over.

Southerners' attempt at nationhood ended in the spring of 1865 as their home front collapsed and Confederate military forces either disintegrated or surrendered. With North Alabama largely pacified, 13,000 cavalrymen under the command of General James H. Wilson began their advance into the interior of Alabama. Confederates along their path experienced what had become routine for North Alabama secessionists. Wisconsin cavalryman Stephen Vaughn Shipman asserted that cavalrymen out ahead of his unit crossed the line of acceptable conduct while they were in Jasper (Walker County). When this officer and his men arrived in the town, they "found all sorts of books and papers scattered about the streets, showing that our men . . . had been playing the vandal." As a soldier who held a minority opinion, he felt nothing could be done, especially since his commanding general supported soldiers' use of harsh civil-military policies. "I am grieved to see it but one mans [sic] voice is not heard in such a mass of roughness," Shipman wrote.[70] Julius C. Greene, a resident of Jefferson County, recalled that as "Wilson's army [came] through . . . they destroyed everything in the country." Upon arriving at Robert H. Greene's farm, soldiers "took all his sweet potatoes." Soldiers continued their merciless tactics the next morning when "they emptied all the feather beds and pillows on the parlor floor, then poured two barrels of molasses and all the lard on the feathers, stirred them up until they were thoroughly mixed." When soldiers became hungry, their search for breakfast was aided by a newly freed black man who told them "where [his] old master hid his meat."[71] Wilson and his men reached the outskirts of Selma in early April, where they routed an enemy force under the command of General Forrest. After destroying the city's arsenal and depot, soldiers turned their attention to taking Montgomery. With rumors swirling that Wilson was en route to the Confederacy's first capital, Governor Watts called out the militia to defend the city while he and other state officials fled to Eufaula; when Wilson and his men entered the city on April 12, they encountered no resistance. By that time, Lee had already surrendered his Army of Northern Virginia to Ulysses Grant. A few days later, General Joseph E. Johnston surrendered to Sherman near Durham, North Carolina. The war had ended.[72]

Confederate women in North Alabama were devastated by military defeat, even as they welcomed an end to the war.[73] Only days before Lee surrendered, the women of Huntsville seemed to sense that defeat lay at hand. According to Mary Chadick, "Several ladies [had] to go to bed [as a] consequence," of the impending defeat.[74] Others lashed out at Confederate soldiers. When Mary Fielding learned that soldiers from Athens were surrendering and taking loyalty oaths to Union forces, she questioned their masculinity. This southerner could not believe that the very men she and other North Alabama women looked to for victory had "no more patriotism, or sense of honor, or sense of duty, than to give up in that way."[75] Fielding stopped writing in her diary for nearly four months after she learned that the Confederacy had lost. When she took her pen up again, Fielding remarked: "The Surrender! How it hurts me to write that." Time had not abated this woman's sorrow over the sacrifices she and other civilians had made during the conflict. She lamented "that after all we have endured, lives lost, the untold suffering of thousands of widows & orphans, that it all should be for nothing, worse than nothing, 'tis almost unendurable."[76] Catherine Fennell shared Fielding's despondency. She wrote that "the people must submit but it is hard, after all the blood has been spilled, to go back to submit to Yankee Government."[77] Over in Cherokee County, Sarah Rousseau Espy had been waiting for the war to end. Like so many other North Alabama women, she had lost loved ones—in her case, a cousin—and helplessly watched Union soldiers take her property and food. By late March, Espy exclaimed "O! that this cruel war was over. And all could be at peace at home."[78] Persistent rain in Cherokee County prevented news of "the downfall of the Confederacy" from reaching her until early May. Espy tried to remain optimistic that a return to the Union "will be well for us."[79] As Confederate women came to terms with defeat, they eagerly awaited the return of their men. According to one observer, mothers in northwest Alabama were growing "white-headed wearying for news of their sons."[80] In Madison County, the "poor mothers and wives are waiting, watching, anxiously, for their husbands or sons return."[81] For the Confederate women and children who lost husbands, fathers, and brothers in the war, the consequences of disunion persisted long after their houses had been repaired and crops planted. An empathetic Huntsville man asked "God [to] pity the poor widows and orphans who are . . . in a destitute condition to battle their way through this [cruel] world."[82] As Confederate nationalists, women in North Alabama had made innumerable sacrifices in an effort to achieve independence. For these defeated Confederates, acknowledging defeat was a complex process. Even though their support for the war had already collapsed, they agonized over the implications of surrendering and becoming, once again, part of the United States.

Confederate men—soldiers and civilians—varied in their responses toward defeat. For Confederate soldiers who were war-weary, hungry, or answering the pleas from their families to come home, the Union's lenient terms of surrender presented them with a welcome opportunity to return home with few restrictions. By the end of April, Confederate soldiers were arriving in Huntsville on a daily basis to surrender and take a loyalty oath to the Union.[83] When men under General Phillip Roddey reached the city, Alonzo Palmer noted how they "looked bad being diseased & very poorly dressed and [had] no money."[84] Not all Confederate soldiers were ready to admit defeat or accept a return to the Union. Florence native James B. Irvine had been languishing in Fort Delaware since December 1864, and for several days after Lee's surrender, he had rejected an offer to be released in exchange for an oath to the Union. When told by a Union soldier that he would indefinitely remain in prison until he took the oath, Irvine changed his mind and agreed to the conditions necessary for his release. He rationalized his reversal by claiming he was needed back home to protect his family from Union soldiers: "It may be that [my] Wife Children Mother Sister are suffering insult [and] oppression . . . all of which I might by my presence advert from them."[85] Eppie Fielding shared his sister's misery and almost wished "he had been killed" in battle. This southerner had no intention of repatriating himself to the Union. As of early August 1865, Mary Fielding reported that her brother "has never" taken an oath and "says he don't care ever to vote again."[86] When news reached Joshua Burns Moore that the war had ended, the often melancholic Confederate succinctly stated, "The secessionists have had their run—The race is over."[87] During the conflict, Moore had been one of North Alabama's most vocal critics of the Confederacy, and he continued this trend in the days following defeat. The former planter considered the conflict the "most disgraceful war ever inaugurated and the most causeless" and accused Confederate leaders to "have in a shorter time done more injury—caused more suffering and the lives of more men, than was ever before done by the same number."[88] The reaction of North Alabama men to military defeat was shaped by their wartime experiences, responsibility to their families, and any remaining fidelity to their defunct nation. Having lost their struggle for independence, North Alabama men, like their womenfolk, began rebuilding their region while awaiting the terms of reunion.

Northern jubilation over the restoration of the Union was soon silenced by news that on April 14, President Lincoln had been shot while he and Mary Todd Lincoln attended a play at Ford's Theater. The assassination had been part of an elaborate scheme by pro-Confederate actor John Wilkes Booth and his accomplices to kill Lincoln, Vice President Andrew Johnson, and Secretary of State William H. Seward, who was confined to his bed from a recent carriage accident. Had General Grant and his wife accepted Lincoln's invitation to attend the play, he too would have been targeted. Co-conspirators George A. Atzerodt and Lewis Paine were given the responsibility of killing Johnson and Seward. Atzerodt's attack on Johnson never came to pass; Paine repeatedly stabbed but did not kill Seward.[89] Once inside Ford's Theater, Booth had little difficulty reaching the president's box. After shooting Lincoln in the back of the head, the assassin jumped from the balcony and yelled "*Sic semper tyrannis*" [thus always to tyrants]. Despite breaking his leg in the jump, Booth managed to escape. With Lincoln too weak to survive a carriage ride to the White House, doctors had him carried to a house across the street. For the next several hours the unconscious president struggled to breathe while lying diagonally across a bed that barely accommodated his 6'4" body. As news of the shooting spread, his son Robert, cabinet members, and congressional leaders rushed to be by his side. At one point, a distraught Mary Todd Lincoln had to be temporarily removed from her husband's room. At 7:22 the following morning, doctors announced that Lincoln had died. According to Edwin Stanton, Lincoln "now . . . belongs to the ages."[90]

In North Alabama, ex-Confederates hardly grieved over Lincoln's death, but they did fear what would happen under his successor. As president, Lincoln had commanded an army that brought ruin, suffering, and racial upheaval to North Alabama. Ex-Confederates likely viewed Lincoln's death as punishment for his soldiers' misdeeds. When Union officers in Huntsville ordered "every house [to] put [black] crape on their front door-knobs" as a sign of mourning, Laura Wharton Plummer stated that a few "did, but many did not." One southern man ignored this order and attached "a great big Negro doll . . . to his door-knob" as a sign of his hatred for Lincoln, blacks, and the Union. Federal soldiers "promptly put [him] behind . . . bars" after learning of his defiance.[91] A furious General R. S. Granger warned that civilians caught "exalting" over the death of Lincoln "shall be summarily punished." Mary Chadick wrote that Granger was determined that "treason shall have no HOME in The District of Northern Alabama."[92] Ella Scruggs and Edmonia Toney were two young women who ig-

Andrew Johnson (Library of Congress)

nored Granger's threat and continued to express joy over Lincoln's death. Instead of charging Scruggs and Toney with a crime, the general gave the women a stern lecture and sent them home.[93] Even though Lincoln offered a lenient Reconstruction agenda, ex-Confederates displayed minimal empathy over his death; they simply could not mourn for a man who had defeated their armies and sanctioned the use of harsh civil-military policies against them.[94]

When ex-Confederates expressed concern over the assassination, they most worried that Andrew Johnson would implement a harsh peace. Southern nationalists had reason to fear the new president. Back in 1862, Johnson told Stanton,

"The rebels must be made to feel the weight and ravages of the war they have brought upon the country. Treason must be made odious and traitors impoverished."[95] Soon after Lincoln's assassination, Senator Charles Sumner spoke with Johnson about Reconstruction and came away convinced that the president still believed "treason was a crime" and that pro-Confederate southerners would be dealt with accordingly.[96] With Congress not convening until early December, North Alabamians feared Johnson would make good on his previous comments. Mary Chadick "felt in [her] heart" that having Johnson as president "must be bad news for the South."[97] James B. Irvine was still at Fort Delaware when he learned that Johnson had become president. This southerner did not lament "Pres. Lincolns [sic] death," but he could not see anything good coming from it, either. According to Irvine, "Lincoln was . . . to accord us honorable terms. . . . I fear [Johnson's] policy will not be such as Lincolns [sic] would have been."[98] Writing from his farm in Lauderdale County, Joshua Burns Moore predicted Johnson would surely "arrest, try, convict and hang" those responsible for starting the war.[99] Given Moore's often cantankerous nature, he probably supported such an action. With Johnson as president, Sarah Rousseau Espy looked "to the future with dread for I think we have every [reason] to fear if we are subjected as I suppose we are."[100] By all accounts, Johnson did not appear to support his predecessor's lenient Reconstruction philosophy. Instead, he seemed ready to carry the Union's harsh wartime policies into Reconstruction.

After four years of war and over 600,000 lives lost, southerners had lost their bid for independence. In North Alabama, Confederates' dogged determination to resist their occupiers for most of the conflict brought ruin to the region: Confederates were arrested, abused, and occasionally executed, houses and personal belongings were destroyed, crops were confiscated, and their slaves were set free. This devastation and social upheaval resulted from their refusal to be conciliated or give their allegiance to a Republican president. Civilians' initial efforts to surmount their enemy's punitive policies proved successful as their faith in their Confederate armies and divine intervention remained strong. As Union soldiers continued to pursue their hard war tactics in North Alabama, they gradually wore down Confederates' faith and willpower to support independence. The Confederacy's defeat and President Lincoln's assassination, however, did not mark the end of the conflict: the vanquished still had to be reconstructed back into the Union.

Epilogue: "It Is All Nonsense to Talk about Equalizing a Negro with a White Man"

When the Confederacy collapsed in the spring of 1865, secessionists in North Alabama entered a new stage in the conflict. Having lost a bitter struggle for independence, they were now expected to accept a return to the Union and acknowledge still-undefined civil liberties for African Americans. The political, economic, and social turmoil caused by the war and occupations convinced a small segment of the formerly Confederate population to work with northern officials and even attend various unionist meetings that cropped up across North Alabama during the spring and summer. Cultivating an amicable relationship with Union personnel or voicing pro-Union sentiments gave presumably repentant whites an opportunity to help guide their state back into the Union fold and potentially influence post-war politics.

The more common response among former Confederates, however, was to reject a harmonious reunion with their northern brethren; their Confederate nationalism had been broken, but their southern nationalism remained firmly intact. This was particularly the case for women who regained their defiant mentality toward the North during the immediate post-war period. For ex-Confederate men, circumventing the Thirteenth Amendment and regaining political power without acquiescing to Union expectations became primary goals. Southern nationalists' initial efforts to seize control of the Reconstruction process was largely successful and was aided by the rapid demobilization of the Union army in North Alabama and President Andrew Johnson's indulgent Reconstruction policies. Johnson's refusal to call Congress into a special session or to require white southerners to extend basic rights to blacks beyond the Thirteenth Amendment allowed southern whites to coerce African Americans back into quasi-slavery status and elect former Confederate leaders to local, state, and national political positions. The leniency that permeated early Reconstruction efforts in North Alabama even enticed individuals who had been attending unionist meetings to return to their disobedient ways. When Congress finally convened in December and endeavored to take control of the Reconstruction process from former Confederates and President Johnson, southern nationalists in North Alabama had already returned to power and taken steps they considered necessary to ensure control over blacks *sans* slavery.[1]

The joint gatherings of ex-Confederates and unionists in support of Alabama's return to the United States were not clandestine affairs, nor were they held only in unionist areas south of the Tennessee River. Pro-Union meetings were held throughout North Alabama and were "largely attended" by individuals who had been loyal throughout the war and those hoping to reclaim their American citizenship rights.[2] The frequency of pro-Union gatherings in North Alabama led Ben C. Truman, a noted Union correspondent, to tell President Johnson that "Nine-tenths of the people in North Alabama . . . are strictly loyal and devoted to the United States Government and its laws."[3] Although Truman's claim of ninety-percent was most likely a gross overstatement, it nevertheless suggests that a number of former Confederates believed that working alongside unionists and northerners would prove beneficial. Some likely attended pro-Union meetings hoping it would help insulate them from potential post-war retaliation from the president and unionists. Individuals who felt they had been deceived into supporting the war and men who held post-war political aspirations also attended. Joshua Burns Moore was both. Moore, who would eventually be elected as a delegate to Alabama's 1865 constitutional convention, argued that North Alabamians had never really endorsed secession despite their commitment to defying their former occupiers. Moore asserted that pro-Union meetings in North Alabama offered citizens "the first occasion since the war commenced [to] have . . . an opportunity to express their real sentiments."[4] Former Confederates hoped that their attendance at these meetings would hasten the restoration of citizenship rights. At one gathering in Marshall County, they stated it was their "earnest wish . . . to resume their former relations to the Government of the United States, and to have the protection of its laws and armies."[5] For weeks after the collapse of the Confederacy, contrite and politically ambitious ex-Confederates called for the resumption of constitutional ties between the people of Alabama and the federal government.[6] Their motivations for attending these meetings varied, but they shared common ground in the belief that supporting a return to the Union was in their best interest.

Ex-Confederates who sought reconciliation with the North did not comprise the majority of defeated Confederates in North Alabama. After all of the destruction, punitive occupation policies, and diminished authority over blacks, most former Confederates still refused to accept a harmonious return to the Union. These individuals understood they had lost the war and that continued physical resistance would not change the outcome, but they remained ideologically defiant. When Congress convened in December 1865, one of their first actions was to create a special committee to examine President Johnson's Reconstruction policies and to assess the attitudes of ex-Confederates toward the federal government. The men who offered testimony about North Alabama to the Joint Committee on Reconstruction depicted the area as being rife with anti-Union sentiment. Union General Clinton B. Fisk came away from his time in the region convinced that the "old slaveholding population in northern Alabama are a rebellious spirit as ever."[7] D. C. Humphreys, a former Confederate officer turned Union supporter, stated that there "is a feeling of hostility to the union in the minds of a large portion of the people; that is, a hatred of the idea of submitting to the laws of the United States."[8] Union General Edward Hatch concurred with Humphreys' assessment that time had not lessened the abhorrence these ex-Confederates had for the Union. According to this Iowa native, "The bitterness [of North Alabamians] towards the government, for some months after the surrender was so great that it is difficult to say whether there is any good feeling towards it."[9] Northern correspondents covering the Reconstruction process routinely came into contact with unruly ex-Confederates. In one instance, a paroled Confederate soldier told a correspondent that he did not "intend to submit" and assured the northerner that he was "just as good a rebel as ever."[10] This parolee was soon arrested for his remark, as was a former Confederate officer who "talked so much rebel language" that Union soldiers were forced to "put him in the guard house."[11] These and other cases of temporary detention did little to change the loathing ex-Confederates had for the Union. The pervasiveness of anti-Union sentiment among civilians and former Confederate soldiers led the correspondent to conclude that "the *strength* but not the spirit of the rebellion is broken" in North Alabama.[12]

This "spirit" of defiance was particularly strong among ex-Confederate women. In spite of all they endured during the Union occupations and war, these women were still committed to the ideals behind secession. Catherine Fennell dreaded reunification so much that she claimed she "would almost wish to die, rather than live to see our beloved South trampled under the foot of the triumphant Northerner."[13] Zillah Haynie Brandon stated that the Confederacy did not lose the war because of any ideological weakness, but rather because of "overwhelming [Union] numbers." Brandon considered secessionists to have embodied the ideals of their revolutionary ancestors and that the "grand patriotism of 76 is [still] burning as if it had been of this hours [*sic*] kindling."[14] When women realized that they could once again verbally assault the enemy without fear of punishment, they had few qualms about letting northerners know of their feelings. In Bridgeport, one woman told a correspondent for the *Cincinnati Gazette* that "the people of the South will live under your Government; live under it because we can't help ourselves [but] we will always hate it and hate you!" This correspondent received another tongue-lashing in Huntsville, where a woman said she would "never . . . surrender" and informed him that from the moment "Mitchel occupied this city in 1862," she refused to respect Union soldiers or even allow them to escort her down the street. The intense disdain this woman felt led her to give an ominous prediction. According to this southerner, *"there is a broad line of demarkation* [sic] *between the North and South, over which neither time nor love nor politics can ever hope to pass."*[15] The Confederacy had been thoroughly defeated, but ex-Confederates in North Alabama rejected a cordial return to the Union. As these men and women went about rebuilding their homes and communities, they publically and privately indicated their determination to resist Union-led Reconstruction efforts. To have done otherwise would have entailed tacit acknowledgment of the illegitimacy of secession and agreeing to increased rights for African Americans.

Ex-Confederates began laying the groundwork for taking control of the Reconstruction process and maintaining white supremacy soon after military defeat. In post-war North Alabama, whites understood that slavery as it had previously existed could not be resurrected and that delegates at their state's upcoming constitutional convention had to ratify the Thirteenth Amendment before Alabama would be allowed back into the Union. Since ratification of the Thirteenth Amendment was non-negotiable, North Alabama whites convinced themselves and attempted to assure others that they were pleased to see slavery end. As former Confederates went about rebuilding their region, some felt that the Thirteenth Amendment would lessen their post-war burdens.[16] Catherine Fennell, for instance, was "not . . . sorry" to see her family's slaves set free "for they were so much trouble. . . . [N]ow we will not feel the responsibility for their comfort."[17] The cantankerous tone Joshua Burns Moore often took in describing Confederate officials' management of the war carried over into his thoughts on losing thousands of dollars in property: "Well slavery is at an end—Let it go. . . . I have made nothing with them and never would." This ex-planter even suggested that the peculiar institution had made him a slave since his ownership of human property obligated him to "keep them fed and clothed."[18] In the town of Stevenson, ex-Confederates who had fought a war to protect the institution of slavery now asserted that "abolition will prove a blessing to both races."[19]

While these whites applauded the benefits of freeing their slaves, they remained committed to the belief that individuals of African descent were inherently inferior and that any post-war effort to improve the lives of newly freed blacks would jeopardize their once unquestioned authority. Joshua Burns Moore argued that increased African American civil rights would be degrading to whites and make it impossible for "a white man [to] live amongst them."[20] Under sworn testimony, D. C. Humphreys told members of the Joint Committee on Reconstruction that in North Alabama "There is dread, an apprehension in the minds of some narrow-minded people, that if the negro is given any rights, he will" subvert the power of whites.[21] Former Confederates found the efforts by northerners to educate African Americans particularly disconcerting. When Massachusetts native Wilmer Walton first arrived in Stevenson to help educate ex-slaves, whites treated him "with coolness and indifference." Ex-Confederates were so opposed to black education that they even threatened this white northerner. While these ex-Confederates eventually warmed up to Walton, they were still convinced that he was "wasting [his] time" and tried to dissuade him from educating blacks.[22] Walton was among a number of northern teachers or agents of the Freedmen's Bureau—a federal agency established in March 1865 to oversee blacks' transition from slavery to freedom—who came into contact with ex-Confederates opposed to educating African Americans. General Clinton B. Fisk stated that in Huntsville, "There is hardly a family . . . who would permit a teacher of colored children to board with them." Without government intervention, Fisk was certain teachers would be unable to "obtain a building to teach in."[23] Aside from attempting to obstruct the education of blacks, whites also interfered with Union efforts to extend economic rights to African Americans in North Alabama by colluding to keep wages artificially low, and in some cases, refusing to hire black workers.[24] Ex-Confederates' determination to resist the policies and programs designed to help tens of thousands of North Alabama blacks suggests the limits of the Thirteenth Amendment and Union victory in post-war North Alabama. The Confederacy's defeat guaranteed the permanent abolition of slavery and the reunification of the North and South, but it had not convinced these former Confederates to abandon their southern nationalist ideology or belief in the inherent inferiority of African Americans.

The efforts by ex-Confederates to stifle racial progress in North Alabama were aided by important developments that occurred soon after Appomattox: demobilization and President Johnson's Reconstruction policies. Once the war ended, the Union Army underwent rapid demobilization; between May and November roughly 800,000 soldiers were mustered out of the army. Of the approximately 35,000 soldiers stationed in Alabama at the end of the war, as few as 7,000 might have been in the state by the fall.[25] The presence of Freedmen's Bureau agents in post-war Alabama was even more anemic; there were never more than twenty agents assigned to the state at any one time. With an inadequate number of Union personnel to oversee Reconstruction efforts and safeguard the rights of blacks, the door was opened for ex-Confederates to shape the meaning of defeat. Once southern nationalists realized Johnson would adhere to a lenient Reconstruction agenda, their intent to keep African Americans relegated to second-class citizenship took on a sense of certainty.[26] In many respects, the president became a friend to those who had supported disunion. Johnson's general amnesty of May 1865 restored citizenship rights to thousands of former Confederates in North Alabama.[27] His choice for provisional governor also contributed to ex-Confederates' return to power. Instead of following the requests by unionists to appoint one of their own as provisional governor, the president picked Lewis Parsons, who had supported the South's struggle for independence, in an effort to create a loyal following among ex-Confederates.[28] President Johnson shared white southerners' aversion to racial equality and, aside from ratifying the Thirteenth Amendment, felt that the citizens within the southern states should be in charge of managing their own race relations.[29] This policy sat well with Joshua Burns Moore: "It is all nonsense to talk about equalizing a negro with a white man and I am glad Johnson had the boldness to stem this torrent of fanaticism, and lay down the broad doctrine that the states are to settle it for themselves."[30] Unionists and Federal officers condemned Johnson for his complicity in bringing ex-Confederates back to power in North Alabama. J. J. Giers considered President Johnson a personal friend, but assailed his "mistaken policy" of leniency.[31] Before the amnesty proclamation, Giers stated that ex-Confederates "would have accepted any terms and every term" of Reconstruction. With their rights restored, there was no longer an incentive for them to repent.[32] General Hatch offered an equally blistering assessment of Johnson's policy in North Alabama: "immediately after the surrender" ex-Confederates "were certainly penitent enough" to accept any condition for returning to the Union, but the president made them "feel safe again."[33] While Giers and Hatch might have overstated whites' willingness to accept all requirements for reunion, they do demonstrate the influence President Johnson had on the resurgence of southern nationalism in North Alabama. By the summer of 1865, his lenient approach toward reunification and a meager Union occupation force in North Alabama created ideal conditions for ex-Confederates to regain their political power and racial supremacy over blacks.

With their citizenship and voting rights reinstated, former Confederates in North Alabama consolidated their power. Until local elections were scheduled, Governor Lewis Parsons reinstated civic officials who had had their authority taken away during the military occupations.[34] When election day arrived, voters in some communities banded together to elect former Confederate soldiers or men who had led anti-Union resistance efforts during the occupations. The most noteworthy instance occurred in Madison County, where voters elected Frank Gurley—who had killed General Robert L. McCook in 1862—as county sheriff.[35] The appointment of such individuals to positions of local power encouraged ex-Confederates to resist or obstruct the Reconstruction efforts of Union soldiers, Freedmen's Bureau agents, and members of northern benevolent societies. These elections also ensured that statewide laws restricting the rights and privileges of African Americans would be implemented. The catalyst behind these "Black Codes," as they came to be called, originated at Alabama's constitutional convention held in September. Southern nationalists dominated the convention.[36] Joshua Burns Moore, who represented Franklin County, stated a few months before the convention that delegates would "have the power to pass stringent laws to govern the negroes." According to this ex-Confederate, "We will refuse to let them vote or hold office or to testify against a white person."[37] Moore considered such measures a vital tool in the struggle against "a great many northern men who through fanaticism or from mistaken sympathy or because of ignorance" sought to uplift blacks. Moore argued that if northern whites had only lived amongst African Americans as white southerners had, they would understand the need to maintain a Herrenvolk democracy. "Those who know the negro, his dullness—his stupidity—his mendacity, will know that these measures are absolutely necessary for the security in person and property of the whites," Moore wrote.[38] When the constitutional convention ended in late September, delegates had outlawed slavery, as required for readmittance to the Union, but requested that members of Alabama's incoming legislative assembly "enact such laws as will protect the freedmen of this State . . . and guard them and the State against any evils that may arise from their sudden emancipation."[39] When the session convened, legislators made sure African Americans remained second-class citizens by disfranchising black men, passing vagrancy laws, and restricting African Americans' ability to choose their employer.[40] Legislators also gave employers broad discretion in reprimanding black workers. Acceptable forms of punishment included "the use of chain-gangs, putting in stocks . . . to prevent escapes," and any other reasonable "correction as a parent may inflict upon a stubborn, refractory child."[41] Ex-Confederates continued to strengthen their hold over the state in the final weeks of 1865. In the November elections, voters elected as governor Robert M. Patton, who had supported the war and had financial ties to the Confederacy.[42] Lewis Parsons and George S. Houston of Athens were elected to represent Alabama in the U.S. Senate. Houston was no stranger to Congress; he had served eight terms as a member of the House of Representatives before resigning after Alabama left the Union in 1861. Based on a comment he made to Colonel Milton M. Bane, it appears that this North Alabamian embodied his constituents' defiant mentality. After his election to the Senate, Houston reportedly told Bane that Abraham Lincoln was a "worse traitor" than Jefferson Davis.[43] Within eight months of the collapse of the Confederacy, southern nationalists had returned to power in North Alabama without having to compromise their devotion to racial hegemony or their belief in the legitimacy of secession.

When Congress reconvened in early December, they quickly moved to reverse what they considered an appalling start to Reconstruction. The Republican-controlled Congress accepted ex-Confederate states' ratification of the Thirteenth Amendment, but they refused to seat representatives from those states. Led by Thaddeus Stevens, members of Congress created the Joint Committee on Reconstruction to examine the state of affairs in the South. The consensus among those who spoke before the committee was to increase federal presence in North Alabama. Otherwise, the future would continue to be bleak for an African American population that had aided Union soldiers during the occupations and helped bring the war to an end in the region. According to General George E. Spencer, a unionist who fought for the First Alabama Cavalry (U.S.), "the general disposition" of whites in North Alabama "is to mistreat [blacks] in every possible manner." Spencer feared that without federal intervention, ex-Confederates "would reduce [blacks] to some state approaching slavery or peonage."[44] J. J. Giers echoed Spencer's comments: "There is a kind of innate feeling, a lingering hope among many in the south, that slavery will be regalvanized [*sic*] in some shape or other."[45] The continuation of the Freedmen's Bureau beyond its one-year lifespan was a vital concern for General Hatch. He stated that if Congress did not extend the life of the Freedmen's Bureau, there would be "no inclination" among ex-Confederates in North Alabama to educate blacks. Without government protection, Hatch envisioned a situation in which African Americans would be in a worse condition than they had been in under slavery.[46] D. C. Humphreys foresaw prolonged "turmoil" for North Alabama blacks, unionists, and the country as a whole if Congress failed to act.[47] Congress responded to the extensive testimony on former Confederates' dogged defiance toward reunion and increased rights for blacks by presenting President Johnson with two Reconstruction bills in early 1866. One extended the life of the Freedmen's Bureau. The other was a comprehensive civil rights bill that would nullify the Black Codes and extend fundamental American rights to blacks that had been denied to them during slavery and the initial months of Reconstruction.

From the moment Congress convened and sought to rein in Johnson's leniency and southerners' resurgent defiance, a struggle commenced over the meaning of the war and the legacy of defeat. For the previous several months, ex-Confederates in North Alabama had successfully worked to regain the political and social power they had lost during the military occupations. Their transition from being defeated Confederates to consolidating their authority had been made possible by an undermanned Federal presence after Appomattox and a president who allowed pardoned disunionists the freedom to reconcile with the North on their own terms. In some respects, Johnson's policy in North Alabama during the summer and fall of 1865 had come full circle with General Buell's conciliatory approach in 1862. In both instances, Confederates were allowed to be ideologically opposed to the Union while still being treated as American citizens. The near-complete control ex-Confederates had in North Alabama came to an end in December when Congress denied white Alabamians' claim, and the claims by southerners in other states, that they had been properly reconstructed. At that moment, it remained unclear whether Congress would be able to convince former Confederates to accept improved race relations. What is known is that the crucial moments after the collapse of the Confederate home front that could have been used to begin mending the sectional discord and put the South on the path to increased racial toleration had passed. As it stood, ex-Confederates in North Alabama had retained their ideological opposition to the Union. The fact that these individuals were able to endure over two years of military rule and survive the conflict still committed to the tenets behind secession and white supremacy should have sent an ominous sign to Congress concerning the resiliency of southern nationalism in post-war North Alabama.

Notes

Introduction

1. Address to Special Session of Congress, July 4, 1861. Roy P. Basler, ed., *The Collected Works of Abraham Lincoln* (New Brunswick: Rutgers University Press, 1953), vol. IV, 437; Mark Grimsley, *The Hard Hand of War: Union Military Policy Toward Southern Civilians, 1861–1865* (New York: Cambridge University Press, 1995), 8–9.

2. First Inaugural Address, March 4, 1861. Basler, ed., *Collected Works of Abraham Lincoln*, vol. IV, 250.

3. David Herbert Donald, *Lincoln* (New York: Simon & Schuster, 1995), 167; Phillip Shaw Paludan, *The Presidency of Abraham Lincoln* (Lawrence: University Press of Kansas, 1994), 17; Orville Vernon Burton, *The Age of Lincoln* (New York: Hill and Wang), 63. For other examinations of Lincoln's attitude toward slavery see Herman Belz, *Abraham Lincoln, Constitutionalism, and Equal Rights in the Civil War Era* (New York: Fordham University Press, 1998); Mark E. Neely, Jr., *The Fate of Liberty: Abraham Lincoln and Civil Liberties* (New York: Oxford University Press, 1991).

4. Stephen D. Engle, *Don Carlos Buell: Most Promising of All* (Chapel Hill: University of North Carolina Press, 1999), 185.

5. Stephen V. Ash, *When the Yankees Came: Conflict and Chaos in the Occupied South, 1861–1865* (Chapel Hill: University of North Carolina Press, 1995), 8–10; Anne Sarah Rubin, *A Shattered Nation: The Rise and Fall of the Confederacy, 1861–1868* (Chapel Hill: University of North Carolina Press, 2005), 14–15; Margaret M. Storey, *Loyalty and Loss: Alabama Unionists in the Civil War and Reconstruction* (Baton Rouge: Louisiana State University Press, 2004), 21. Also see Michael F. Holt, *The Fate of Their Country: Politicians, Slavery Extension, and the Coming of the Civil War* (New York: Hill and Wang, 2004); Michael A. Morrison, *Slavery and the American West: The Eclipse of Manifest Destiny and the Coming of the Civil War* (Chapel Hill: University of North Carolina Press, 1997).

6. More generally, historians tend to focus on the presence of unionism in the area. There is merit to this. In all of Alabama, unionists were most prominent in the northern counties, comprising roughly ten to fifteen percent of the region's population. Outside of the Appalachian Mountains, North Alabama likely had one of the most concentrated pockets of unionism during the war years. The strength and prevalence of unionism in the region defies simple explanation. Unionists came from diverse economic backgrounds and held wide-ranging views and attachments toward slavery. According to Margaret M. Storey, who offers the seminal account of unionism in North Alabama, their common belief that the Union should remain intact "may be the only 'interest' [they] shared" (Storey, *Loyalty and Loss*), 12–13, 15–16, 20. Counties in the Tennessee Valley include Jackson, Franklin, Lauderdale, Limestone, Lawrence, Madison, and

Morgan. The Hill counties include Blount, DeKalb, Cherokee, Marion, Fayette, Marshall, Walker, St. Clair, and Winston (Storey, *Loyalty and Loss*), 7–8.

7. See Drew Gilpin Faust, *The Creation of Confederate Nationalism: Ideology and Identity in the Civil War South* (Baton Rouge: Louisiana State University Press, 1988); Gary W. Gallagher, *The Confederate War: How Popular Will, Nationalism, and Military Strategy Could Not Stave Off Defeat* (Cambridge, Mass.: Harvard University Press, 1997); George C. Rable, *Civil Wars: Women and the Crisis of Southern Nationalism* (Urbana: University of Illinois Press, 1991); George C. Rable, *God's Almost Chosen Peoples: A Religious History of the American Civil War* (Chapel Hill: University of North Carolina Press, 2010); Rubin, *A Shattered Nation*, 14–15, 34.

Chapter 1. "I Am for Alabama under Any and All Circumstances"

1. Paludan, *The Presidency of Abraham Lincoln*, 5, 28, 58; Grimsley, *Hard Hand of War*, 8–9.

2. Elizabeth R. Varon, *Disunion!: The Coming of the American Civil War, 1789–1859* (Chapel Hill: University of North Carolina Press, 2008), 337.

3. *Milwaukee Daily Sentinel*, November 17, 1860.

4. Malcolm McMillan, *The Disintegration of a Confederate State: Three Governors and Alabama's Wartime Home Front, 1861–1865* (Macon, Ga.: Mercer University Press, 1986), 2; William Warren Rogers, Sr., Robert David Ward, Leah Rawls Atkins, Wayne Flynt, *Alabama: The History of a Deep South State* (Tuscaloosa: University of Alabama Press, 1994), 179; Joseph W. Danielson, "'Twill be Done Again': The Union Occupation of North Alabama, April through August, 1862" (M. A. thesis: University of Alabama, 2004), 20.

5. 1850 and 1860 census, Historical Census Browser, University of Virginia, Geospatial and Statistical Data Center: http://fisher.lib.virginia.edu/collections/stats/histcensus/index .html. Calculations made by the author. In 1850 there were 6,192 farms located in the seven Tennessee Valley counties, while 6,045 farms were in the Hill counties. A decade later, the Hill counties had 8,257 farms compared to 6,159 in the Tennessee Valley.

6. 1850 and 1860 census, Historical Census Browser, University of Virginia, Geospatial and Statistical Data Center http://fisher.lib.virginia.edu/collections/stats/histcensus/index.html. Calculations made by the author.

7. In Jackson County, the cash value of farms more than tripled over the decade, jumping from roughly $952,000 to $3.12 million. Farm values in Madison County, which neighbors Jackson to the west, increased from approximately $3.27 million in 1850 to over $6 million in 1860. In Limestone County, farm value increased from $2 million to $3.6 million, while the cash value of farms in Lauderdale County nearly tripled in value from about $1.6 million to over $4.5 million between 1850 and 1860. The value of farmland in the four counties on the southern banks of the Tennessee River also experienced impressive growth. During the 1850s, the cash value of farms in Franklin County went from about $2.2 million to nearly $4.1 million. A similar change took place in Lawrence County, where the collective value of farms rose from roughly $1.6 million to about $3 million. Farmers in Morgan County experienced a total increase from roughly $900,000 to $1.44 million in the value of their farms during the decade, while the farm values in Marshall County nearly tripled from about $416,000 to over $1.37 million during the same span (1850 and 1860 census, Historical Census Browser, University of Virginia, Geospatial and Statistical Data Center: http://fisher.lib.virginia.edu/collections/stats/histcensus/index .html. Calculations made by the author).

8. 1850 and 1860 census, Historical Census Browser, University of Virginia, Geospatial and Statistical Data Center: http://fisher.lib.virginia.edu/collections/stats/histcensus/index.html. Calculations made by the author.

9. 1850 and 1860 census, Historical Census Browser, University of Virginia, Geospatial and Statistical Data Center: http://fisher.lib.virginia.edu/collections/stats/histcensus/index.html. Calculations made by the author.

10. Historian J. Mills Thornton notes that cooperationists' aversion to immediate secession "was not a vote for continued union." Rather, Thornton argues that "their primary fear was simply that an independent republic of Alabama would not be economically viable." J. Mills Thornton, *Politics and Power in a Slave Society: Alabama, 1800–1860* (Baton Rouge: Louisiana State University Press, 1978), 347.

11. *Semi-Weekly Mississippian* (Jackson), December 7, 1860.

12. Jeremiah Clemens to S. A. M. Wood, November 26, 1860, S. A. M. Wood Papers, Alabama Department of Archives and History (hereafter cited as ADAH).

13. Historian William L. Barney asserts that North Alabamians were "part of an environment and life-style not as intimately involved with slavery as the Black Belt society. Since these areas did not feel as directly threatened by the Republicans, they could support a more openly cooperationist movemen." William L. Barney, *The Secessionist Impulse: Alabama and Mississippi in 1860* (Tuscaloosa: University of Alabama Press, 1974), 280.

14. 1860 census, Historical Census Browser, University of Virginia, Geospatial and Statistical Data Center: http://fisher.lib.virginia.edu/collections/stats/histcensus/index.html. Calculations made by author. Slaves accounted for 11.5 percent of the population in Marion, 6.1 percent in Blount, 6.5 percent in Walker, and 7.9 percent in De Kalb.

15. 1860 census, Historical Census Browser, University of Virginia, Geospatial and Statistical Data Center: http://fisher.lib.virginia.edu/collections/stats/histcensus/index.html. Calculations made by author. As of 1860, there were 69,234 whites, 51,789 slaves, and 368 free blacks.

16. 1860 census, Historical Census Browser, University of Virginia, Geospatial and Statistical Data Center: http://fisher.lib.virginia.edu/collections/stats/histcensus/index.html. Calculations made by author. In Morgan County, whites outnumbered slaves 7,592 to 3,706, while Lauderdale's population included 10,639 white residents and 6,737 slaves. In Franklin County, whites numbered 10,119 to 8,495 slaves.

17. 1860 census, Historical Census Browser, University of Virginia, Geospatial and Statistical Data Center: http://fisher.lib.virginia.edu/collections/stats/histcensus/index.html. Calculations made by author. Limestone (22), Lauderdale (28), Franklin (29), Jackson (32); Lawrence and Morgan tied for thirty-seventh.

18. 1860 census, Historical Census Browser, University of Virginia, Geospatial and Statistical Data Center: http://fisher.lib.virginia.edu/collections/stats/histcensus/index.html. Calculations made by author. The percentage of planters in some of the Black Belt counties is as follows: Wilcox (25.1 percent), Autauga (25 percent), Montgomery (24.25 percent), and Barbour (20.5 percent).

19. McMillan, *Disintegration of a Confederate State*, 13.

20. McMillan, *Disintegration of a Confederate State*, 14; Malcolm McMillan, *Constitutional Development in Alabama, 1798–1901: A Study in Politics, the Negro, and Sectionalism* (Chapel Hill: University of North Carolina Press, 1955), 76; Joseph Hodgson, *Cradle of the Confederacy, Or the Times of Troup, Quitman and Yancey: A Sketch of Southwestern Political History from the Formation of the Federal Government to A.D. 1861* (Spartanburg, South Carolina: The Reprint Company, 1876), 492; Storey, *Loyalty and Loss*, 30–31. In Winston County, Christopher C.

Sheats was elected on a cooperationist ticket even though he was a committed unionist (Storey, *Loyalty and Loss*), 34.

21. Wallace Hettle, *The Peculiar Democracy: Southern Democrats in Peace and Civil War* (Athens: University of Georgia Press, 2001), 122, 126. Clemens' final novel, *Tobias Wilson*, published posthumously in 1865, chronicled guerrilla warfare in the mountains of northern Alabama during the Civil War.

22. Jeremiah Clemens to S. A. M. Wood, November 26, 1860, S. A. M. Wood Papers, ADAH.

23. Jeremiah Clemens to S. A. M. Wood, November 26, 1860, S. A. M. Wood Papers, ADAH. Gibbets were metal devices attached to a pole to hold the dead bodies of convicted criminals, which served as a warning to other potential criminals.

24. Jeremiah Clemens to S. A. M. Wood, November 26, 1860, S. A. M. Wood Papers, ADAH.

25. Thomas J. McClellan to wife, January 6, 1861, Thomas J. McClellan Letters, ADAH.

26. James S. Clark Speech, 1861, ADAH.

27. Davis P. Lewis (Lawrence County), William Winston (DeKalb County), R. S. Watkins (Franklin County), and Robert Jemison (Tuscaloosa County) also contributed to writing the Minority Report.

28. The Crittenden Compromise would have restored the Missouri Compromise of 1820, prohibiting the abolition of slavery on federal property and in the District of Columbia, outlawing congressional interference with the interstate slave trade, and providing federal compensation to southerners who could not recover fugitive slaves. None of these amendments could be overturned in the future. See James M. McPherson, *Battle Cry of Freedom: The Civil War Era* (New York: Oxford University Press, 1988), 252–254.

29. Thomas J. McClellan to John McClellan, January 13, 1861, Robert Anderson McClellan Papers, Manuscript Department, William R. Perkins Library, Duke University (hereafter, Duke University).

30. *The Ripley Bee* (Ohio), January 24, 1861. Also see *The Beaver Dam Argus* (Wisc.), February 1, 1861.

31. William Henry Mitchell to wife, January 11, 1861, William Henry Mitchell Papers, ADAH.

32. William R. Smith, *The History and Debates of the Convention of the People of Alabama, Begun and Held in the City of Montgomery, on the Seventh Day of January, 1861* (Spartanburg, South Carolina: The Reprint Company, 1975), 77–80.

33. *Fayetteville Observer* (NC), January 24, 1861.

34. John W. Inzer Recollections, ADAH.

35. William Henry Mitchell to wife, January 11, 1861, William Henry Mitchell Papers, ADAH.

36. John W. Inzer Recollections, ADAH.

37. *Fayetteville Observer* (NC), January 24, 1861.

38. John W. Inzer Recollections, ADAH.

39. Storey, *Loyalty and Loss*, 32.

40. Smith, *History and Debates of the Convention*, 117–118.

41. Lawrence Ripley Davis to John B. McClellan, January 13, 1861, Robert Anderson McClellan Papers, Duke University.

42. A few of the North Alabama delegates sent to Montgomery as cooperationists were aligned more closely with unionism and therefore refused to support the Confederate war effort (Storey, *Loyalty and Loss*), 34.

43. Storey, *Loyalty and Loss*, 32.

44. Smith, *History and Debates of the Convention*, 96.

45. John W. Inzer Recollections, ADAH.

46. Thomas J. McClellan to wife, January 14, 1861, Thomas J. McClellan Letters, ADAH.

47. Lawrence Ripley Davis to John B. McClellan, January 13, 1861, Robert Anderson McClellan Papers, Duke University.

48. *The Agitator* (Wellsboro, Penn.), January 23, 1861.

49. Storey, *Loyalty and Loss*, 32.

50. *Coshocton County Democrat* (Ohio), January 2, 1861.

51. January 11, 1861, Catherine Fennell Diary, Huntsville/Madison County Public Library (hereafter cited as HMCPL).

52. *New York Times*, January 26, 1861.

53. Rogers, Sr., et al., *Alabama: History of a Deep South State*, 189.

54. The *Columbus Daily Enquirer* (Ga.) reported that the citizens of Huntsville voted against a proposed resolution urging the United States to permanently protect slavery in return for reunion, April 4, 1861.

55. *Columbus Daily Enquirer* (Ga.), April 22, 1861.

56. *Columbus Daily Enquirer* (Ga.), April 22, 1861.

57. April 20, 1861, Catherine Fennell Diary, HMCPL.

58. April 26, 1861, Catherine Fennell Diary, HMCPL. A week later, Fennell wrote that she "attended a barbecue at Warrenton today given to the Volunteers" (May 4, 1861, Catherine Fennell Diary, HMCPL).

59. May 29, 1861, Catherine Fennell Diary, HMCPL.

60. Thomas R. Lightfoot to Henrietta S. Cody, May 2, 1861, in Edmund Cody Burnett, ed., *Letters of Three Lightfoot Brothers, 1861–1865* (Savannah, Ga.: privately published, 1942), 56.

61. May 9, 1861, Catherine Fennell Diary, HMCPL.

62. John Gill Shorter to George W. Randolph, April 5, 1862, *War of the Rebellion: A Compilation of the Official Records of the Union and Confederate Armies*, 127 Volumes (Washington, D.C.: Government Printing Office, 1880–1901), series I, volume, VI, 871 (hereafter cited as *OR*).

63. *Charleston Mercury*, November 25, 1861.

Chapter 2. "Lincoln's Hordes"

1. The Third Division included three brigades. The Eighth Brigade consisted of the Nineteenth Illinois Volunteers, Twenty-Fourth Illinois Volunteers, Thirty-Seventh Indiana Volunteers, and the Eighteenth Ohio Volunteers. The Second Ohio Volunteers, Twenty-First Ohio Volunteers, Thirty-Third Ohio Volunteers, and Tenth Wisconsin Volunteers were part of the Ninth Brigade. The Seventeenth Brigade consisted of the Forty-Second Indiana Volunteers, Fifteenth Kentucky Volunteers, Third Ohio Volunteers, and the Tenth Ohio Volunteers. In addition to these brigades there were also several unattached regiments: the First Michigan Engineers, Fourth Ohio Cavalry, First Ohio Battery, First Michigan Battery, and Fifth Indiana Battery. Civil-military policies toward Confederates were policies devised by Union personnel to convince secessionists to accept a return to the Union.

2. Gerald J. Prokopowicz, *All for The Regiment: The Army of the Ohio, 1861–1862* (Chapel Hill: University of North Carolina Press, 2001), 62.

3. Prokopowicz, *All for the Regiment*, 66–67.

4. Prokopowicz, *All for the Regiment*, 92.

5. Engle, *Most Promising of All*, 205; Prokopowicz, *All for the Regiment*, 95.

6. Leroy Pope Walker to Daniel Ruggles, March 8, 1862, *OR*, ser. I, vol. X/II, 304. Bear Creek is located in northwest Alabama.

7. *Cincinnati Gazette*, April 14, 1862.

8. April 11, 1862, Nancy M. Rohr, ed., *Incidents of the War: The Civil War Journal of Mary Jane Chadick* (Huntsville, Ala.: Silver Threads Publishing, 2005), 30.

9. Ormsby M. Mitchel to James Fry, April 11, 1862, *OR*, ser. I., vol. X/I, 641–642. Mitchel issued a similar statement to General Lorenzo Thomas: "The city was taken completely by surprise, no one having considered the march practicable at the time. . . . we have at length succeeded in cutting the great artery of Railway communication between the Southern states" (Ormsby M. Mitchel to Lorenzo Thomas, April 12, 1862, Abraham Lincoln Papers at the Library of Congress, American Memory, www.loc.gov). Union soldier Martin Moor remarked that "the 8th Brigade took Huntsville at a right shoulder shift just at day light. Got Twelve or fifteen locomotives and freight cars in proportion and some prisoners" (Martin Moor Diaries, April 11, 1862, Indiana Historical Society [hereafter cited as IHS]).

10. *Louisville Daily Journal*, May 6, 1862.

11. Ormsby M. Mitchel to Don Carlos Buell, April 11, 1862, *OR*, ser. I, vol. X/I, 641–642.

12. Ormsby M. Mitchel to James Fry,April 11, 1862, *OR*, ser. I., vol. X/I, 641. The confidence Mitchel displayed after taking North Alabama has caused historians to depict him as a vain, arrogant, glory-seeking officer. Stephen Engle argues that although sending Mitchel's Third Division into North Alabama decreased the numerical strength of the Army of the Ohio for the eventual Battle at Shiloh, "it was perhaps justified by the fact that it meant sending the army's second most winded, conceited, and vainglorious commander along with it. Only [William] Nelson rivaled Mitchel when it came to arrogance" (Engle, *Most Promising of All*), 212. Gerald J. Prokopowicz also has a low opinion of the general: "Mitchel's private correspondence with the secretary of war, his boastful dispatches, and his attempts to wriggle from under Buell's authority and operate his division as a separate entity all supported Buell's description of him as 'ambitious in an ostentatious way' and unsuited for independent command" (Prokopowicz, *All for the Regiment*), 118.

13. Engle, *Most Promising of All*, 243.

14. *Journal of the Executive Proceedings of the Senate of the United States of America, 1861–1862*, May 1, 1862, Library of Congress, American Memory, www.loc.gov.

15. Robert H. Caldwell to Mother, April 26, 1862, Robert H. Caldwell Papers, Center for Archival Collection, Bowling Green University (hereafter cited as CAC).

16. John Beatty, *The Citizen-Soldier: The Memoirs of a Civil War Volunteer* (Lincoln: University of Nebraska Press, 1998), April 21, 1862, 133.

17. *Louisville Daily Journal*, April 30, 1862.

18. Early May 1862, Charles Dahlmer Letters, Abraham Lincoln Presidential Library, Springfield, Illinois (hereafter cited as Lincoln Library).

19. Robert H. Caldwell to Father, April 12, 1862, Robert H. Caldwell Papers, CAC. An anonymous southerner shared Caldwell's assertion: the Union invasion had "cut the great artery of . . . communication [and supplies] between [the] Southern states" (Unknown author, April 11, 1862, Clay Collection, Duke University).

20. Mansfield Lovell to George Randolph, April 17, 1862, *OR*, ser. I, vol. VI, 878.

21. *Frank Leslie's Illustrated Newspaper*, April 26, 1862. A correspondent for the *Cincinnati Gazette* wrote that the Third Division's recent accomplishments had broken "communication between the rebel armies" in the west and east (*Cincinnati Gazette*, April 17, 1862).

22. Edward Norphlet Brown Sr. to Fannie Brown, April 18, 1862, Edward Norphlet Brown Sr. Letters, ADAH.

23. *Daily National Intelligencer* (Washington, D.C.), April 14, 1862.

24. John Withers Clay to Clement Claiborne Clay, Jr., May 15, 1862, Clay Collection, Duke University.

25. April 13–25, 1862, Journal of Miss Sarah Lowe, ADAH. William Cooper, a resident of Florence, noted that the Union's advance to the west of Huntsville created "much excitement" among the civilian population. April 12, 1862, William Cooper Diaries, Southern Historical Collection, University of North Carolina at Chapel Hill (hereafter cited as SHC).

26. April 12, 1862, Joshua Burns Moore Diary, ADAH.

27. Clement Claiborne Clay, Jr. to Virginia Clay, April 12, 1862, Clay Collection, Duke University.

28. April 24, 1862, Catherine Fennell Diary, HMCPL.

29. Smith, *History and Debates of the Convention*, 117–118.

30. Ash, *When the Yankees Came*, 18.

31. See John Withers Clay to Clement Claiborne Clay, Jr., May 15, 1862, Clay Collection, Duke University.

32. John Withers Clay to Clement Claiborne Clay, Jr., May 15, 1862, Clay Collection, Duke University; Rohr, ed., *Incidents of the War*, April 11, 1862, 30.

33. "Unnamed diary of a young man, donated by Mr. John M. Doyle from Huntsville," no date, Uncatalogued manuscript collection, ADAH.

34. William C. Scott, Jr., ed., "Marshall C. Wilson's Memories of the Civil War," *Journal of Muscle Shoals History* 9 (1981): 33.

35. April 18, 1862, Catherine Fennell Diary, HMCPL.

36. April 19, 1862, Joshua Burns Moore Diary, ADAH.

37. April 26, 1862, Joshua Burns Moore Diary, ADAH.

38. C. Wilder Watts, ed., "Civil War Journal of Thomas Washington Peebles," *Journal of Muscle Shoals History* 6 (1978): April 12, 1862, 68.

39. Rowena Webster Memoir, HMCPL.

40. Laura Wharton Plummer, *Memoirs of Laura Wharton Plummer: A Brief Sketch of My Life during the Civil War; Written Exclusively for and dedicated to her children and grandchildren* (unknown publisher, 1910), 7–8, Ralph Brown Draughon Library, Auburn University (hereafter cited as RBD Library).

41. *Daily Cleveland Herald*, May 8, 1862.

42. *Daily Cleveland Herald*, May 8, 1862.

43. Ormsby M. Mitchel to Salmon P. Chase, April 21, 1862, *OR*, ser. I, vol. X/II, 115.

44. Ormsby M. Mitchel to Edwin Stanton, May 28, 1862, *OR*, ser. I, vol. X/II, 222.

45. Edwin Stanton to Ormsby M. Mitchel, May 28, 1862, *OR*, ser. I, vol. X/II, 222.

46. Grimsley, *Hard Hand of War*, 61–62, 66.

47. Grimsley, *Hard Hand of War*, 63–64. According to Stephen Engle, "Buell sincerely hoped to convince errant southerners that his army was not representative of an allegedly wicked northern society that many in the South feared. Instead, he wanted to prove that his soldiers represented the best of democracy, which meant they would uphold constitutional guarantees of private citizens in war" (Engle, *Most Promising of All*), 185.

48. Grimsley, *Hard Hand of War*, 66.

49. General Orders 13a, February 20, 1862, Original Broadside, HMCPL.

50. Engle, *Most Promising of All*, 185; Grimsley, *Hard Hand of War*, 63–64.

51. Mitchel graduated in 1829 along with future Confederate generals Robert E. Lee and Joseph E. Johnston.

52. General Orders 81, March 15, 1862, Original Broadside, HMCPL.

53. General Orders 85, March 23, 1862, Original Broadside, HMCPL.

54. Grimsley, *Hard Hand of War*, 65.

55. *New York Herald*, April 18, 1862.

56. Rohr, ed., *Incidents of the War*, April 28, 1862, 39.

57. E. Kirby Smith to P. G. T. Beauregard, April 13, 1862, *OR*, ser. I, vol. X/II, 417.

58. Faye Acton Axford, ed., *"To Lochaber Na Mair": Southerners View the War* (Athens, Ala.: Athens Publishing Company, 1986), April 25, 1862, 41 (hereafter cited as Mary Fielding Diary).

59. May 6, 1862, Catherine Fennell Diary, HMCPL.

60. April 25, 1862, Joshua Burns Moore Diary, ADAH.

61. May 6, 1862, Catherine Fennell Diary, HMCPL.

62. May 20, 1862, Sarah Rousseau Espy Diary, ADAH.

63. June 8, 1862, Rebecca Vasser Journal, Duke University.

64. April 11, 1862, Joshua Burns Moore Diary, ADAH.

65. Ormsby M. Mitchel to Don Carlos Buell, May 2, 1862, *OR*, ser. I, vol. XVI/I, 777. Mitchel remarked to Stanton that Rebel civilians would "cut the telegraph wires, attack the guards of bridges, [and] cut off and destroy my couriers" (Ormsby M. Mitchel to Edwin Stanton, May 5, 1862, *OR*, ser. I, vol. X/II), 165–166.

66. *Cincinnati Gazette*, July 22, 1862.

67. Ormsby M. Mitchel to Edwin Stanton, May 4, 1862, *OR*, ser. I, vol. X/II, 161; *Cincinnati Gazette*, May 6, 1862.

68. Ormsby M. Mitchel to Edwin Stanton, May 5, 1862, *OR*, ser. I, vol. X/II, 165–166.

69. "The Late Reverend James Monroe Mason, D.D.: An Account of some of the Activities of Confederate Forces in and around Huntsville, Alabama," ADAH Pamphlet Collection, 4, 7.

70. Lillie Bibb Greet, the granddaughter of former Alabama governor Thomas Bibb, recalled that "The climax of my war experience was reached when I went with [men] to burn a railroad bridge near my home. . . . The burning of this bridge detained the supplies for a whole division of the Yankees." Greet does not state if her participation took place during the 1862 occupation or one of the subsequent occupations (Lillie Bibb Greet, "Personal Reminiscences of Civil War Times in Huntsville," HMCPL).

71. Ormsby M. Mitchel to Edwin Stanton, May 5, 1862, *OR*, ser. I, vol. X/II, 165–166.

72. Robert H. Caldwell to Parents, May 4, 1862, Robert H. Caldwell Papers, CAC; Beatty, *Citizen-Soldier*, May 2, 1862, 137–138; May 10, 1862, Catherine Fennell Diary, HMCPL.

73. *Cincinnati Gazette*, June 12, 1862.

74. May 21, 1862, Robert S. Dilworth Journal, CAC.

75. June 14, 1862, Robert S. Dilworth Journal, CAC.

76. *Daily Morning News* (Savannah, Ga.), May 29, 1862.

77. August 12, 1862, William M. Austin Diary, Lincoln Library.

78. April 13, 1862, Robert S. Dilworth Journal, CAC.

79. *Cincinnati Gazette*, May 2, 1862.

80. Rohr, ed., *Incidents of the War*, June 9, 1862, 51.

81. April 13, 1862, Robert S. Dilworth Journal, CAC.

82. *Cincinnati Gazette*, July 10, 1862.

83. *Cincinnati Gazette*, May 28, 1862.

84. *Cincinnati Gazette*, July 11, 1862.

85. Drew Gilpin Faust, *Mothers of Invention: Women of the Slaveholding South in the American Civil War* (New York: Vintage Books, 1996), 59.

86. Axford, ed., Mary Fielding Diary, April 27, 1862, 41.

87. *Charleston Mercury*, May 21, 1862. This statement was originally printed in the *Cincinnati Gazette*.

88. Beatty, *Citizen-Soldier*, May 23, 1862, 144–145.

89. Henry Ackerman Smith to Wife, May 6, 1862, Henry Ackerman Smith Papers, Duke University. Also see Brian Hogan, ed., "My Very Dear Wife: The Letters of a Union Corporal, Part I," *The Huntsville Historical Review*, 28, no. 1 (Summer–Fall 2002): 16–67.

90. Rohr, ed., *Incidents of the War*, May 10, 1862, 42.

91. Rowena Webster Memoir, HMCPL.

92. April 24, 1862, Robert S. Dilworth Journal, CAC.

93. *Cincinnati Gazette*, July 7, 1862.

94. *Charleston Mercury*, May 21, 1862. Thomas Small wrote while stationed near Tuscumbia: "The girls say they don't like the Blue Belley Yankees" (Thomas Small Diary, June 30, 1862, Thomas Small Diary, IHS).

95. Rowena Webster Memoir, HMCPL.

96. Faust, *Mothers of Invention*, 199.

97. Henry Ackerman Smith to Wife, May 6, 1862, Henry Ackerman Smith Papers, Duke University. Ohio brothers Alfred and Addison Searles acknowledged that "We have so many fals [*sic*] alarms that we are brocken [*sic*] every night of our rest" (Alfred and Addison Searles to Parents, August 5, 1862, Rachel Stanton/Searles Family Papers, CAC).

98. John Withers Clay to Clement Claiborne Clay, Jr., May 15, 1862, Clay Collection, Duke University. If Mrs. Burton had been a man, Union soldiers probably would have responded differently. Toward the end of the occupation, Mary Fielding remarked that a man by the name of Dink Thach got drunk one night and "hurrahed" for Jeff Davis, the southern Confederacy, etc., while the soldiers were on dress parade. "Once the soldiers were dismissed they ran after him & beat, kicked, & knocked him about considerably" (Axford, ed., Mary Fielding Diary), August 12, 1862, 79.

99. James Thomson to unknown person, April 13, 1862, "Letters from a Union Soldier," *Limestone Legacy*, 4 (1988): 129.

100. Laura Wharton Plummer, *Memoirs of Laura Wharton Plummer*, 7, RDB Library.

101. Robert H. Caldwell to Parents, May 7, 1862, Robert H. Caldwell Papers, CAC.

102. Rohr, ed., *Incidents of the War*, June 9, 1862, 51.

103. Rowena Webster Memoir, HMCPL.

104. Rohr, ed., *Incidents of the War*, June 20, 1862, 59.

Chapter 3. "In the Service of Jeff Davis"

1. Ormsby M. Mitchel to Don Carlos Buell, May 2, 1862, *OR*, ser. I, vol. XVI/I, 777.

2. Ormsby M. Mitchel, "Proclamation to the Citizens of Alabama North of the Tennessee River," May 2, 1862, HMCPL.

3. Grimsley, *Hard Hand of War*, 39.

4. *Cincinnati Gazette*, July 22, 1862.

5. Liberty Warner to Dear Friends, May 30, 1862, Liberty Warner Papers, CAC.

6. *Cincinnati Gazette*, July 25, 1862.

7. James A. Garfield to Austin Garfield, June 25, 1862, Frederick D. Williams, ed., *The Wild Life of the Army: Civil War Letters of James A. Garfield* (East Lansing: Michigan State University Press, 1964), 116–117.

8. Rohr, ed., *Incidents of the War*, April 21, 1862, 37. Around this same time, she noted that two men who had been arrested escaped by donning Union uniforms. According to Chadick, Union soldiers subsequently "hurried off" an unknown number of detained men to Camp Chase, Ohio, before it could happen again (ibid.).

9. May 13, 1862, Catherine Fennell Diary, HMCPL. While in jail, the man saw a cousin of Fennell's father, who claimed that he "did not know why he was arrested nor what they were going to do with him" (ibid.).

10. Clement Claiborne Clay, Jr., to Huey Lawson Clay, May 29, 1862, Clay Collection, Duke University.

11. *Cincinnati Gazette*, May 15, 1862.

12. John Withers Clay to Clement Claiborne Clay, Jr., May 17, 1862, Clay Collection, Duke University.

13. John Withers Clay to Huey Lawson Clay, May 18, 1862, Clay Collection, Duke University.

14. Rohr, ed., *Incidents of the War*, 39; *Daily Morning News*, May 28, 1862; Bishop Henry C. Lay Diary, May 2, 1862, Henry C. Lay Papers, SHC.

15. Bishop Henry C. Lay Diary, May 2, 1862, Henry C. Lay Papers, SHC. After Junius Newport Bragg read in the *Huntsville Democrat* that Lay had been arrested and "placed in close confinement," he wrote to his wife that "This is rather hard on your minister but I had rather it was himself than me!" Junius Newport Bragg to Anna Josephine Goddard Bragg, June 3, 1862, Helen Bragg Gaughan, ed., *Letters of a Confederate Surgeon, 1861–1865* (Camden, Ark.: The Hurley Company, 1960), 68.

16. Bishop Henry C. Lay Diary, May 4, 1862, Henry C. Lay Papers, SHC.

17. Ibid.

18. Ibid.

19. Ormsby M. Mitchel to Edwin Stanton, May 8, 1862, *OR*, ser. I, vol. X/II, 174.

20. Bishop Henry C. Lay Diary, May 6, 1862, Henry C. Lay Papers, SHC.

21. Rohr, ed., *Incidents of the War*, May 10, 1862, 41.

22. Bishop Henry C. Lay Diary, May 12, 1862, Henry C. Lay Papers, SHC.

23. Bishop Henry C. Lay Diary, May 13, 1862, Henry C. Lay Papers, SHC.

24. Rohr, ed., *Incidents of the War*, May 18, 1862, 45. Since Dr. Fearn had been released from jail, he was either compelled to sign the document with the other men or Chadick made a mathematical mistake.

25. John Withers Clay to Huey Lawson Clay, May 18, 1862, Clay Collection, HMCPL, Duke University.

26. *Mobile Register*, May 4, 1862.

27. *Daily Morning News* (Savannah, Ga.), June 9, 1862.

28. Rohr, ed., *Incidents of the War*, June 25, 1862, 62.

29. Ibid., 62.

30. *Daily Morning News* (Savannah, Ga.), May 29, 1862.

31. June 24, 1862, Catherine Fennell Diary, HMCPL.

32. April 20, 1862, William Cooper Diaries, SHC.

33. Jason M. Neibling to James Fry, August 11, 1862, *OR*, ser. I, vol. XVI/II, 311.

34. August 14, 1862, Joshua Burns Moore Diary, ADAH.

35. James Fry to Robert L. McCook, July 10, 1862, *OR*, ser. I, vol. XVI/I, 117.

36. Henry Ackerman Smith to Wife, April 15, 1862, Henry Ackerman Smith Papers, Duke University.

37. *Cincinnati Gazette*, July 22, 1862.

38. Harold M. Hyman, *Era of the Oath: Northern Loyalty Tests During the Civil War and Reconstruction* (Philadelphia: University of Pennsylvania Press, 1954), 151.

39. *Daily Morning News* (Savannah, Ga.), May 29, 1862.

40. Axford, ed., Mary Fielding Diary, August 8, 1862, 77.

41. Rohr, ed., *Incidents of the War*, June 9, 1862, 51–52.

42. May 4, 1862, Joshua Burns Moore Diary, ADAH.

43. Rohr, ed., *Incidents of the War*, June 20, 1862, 59.

44. Axford, ed., Mary Fielding Diary, May 10, 1862, 49.

45. June 8, 1862, Rebecca Vasser Journal, Duke University.

46. John Withers Clay to Clement Claiborne Clay, Jr., May 17, 1862, Clay Collection, HMCPL, Duke University.

47. John Withers Clay to Huey Lawson Clay, May 29, 1862, Clay Collection, Duke University.

48. Edward D. Tracy to Clement Claiborne Clay, Jr., April 27, Clay Collection, Duke University.

49. Robert Bliss to Mother, August 5, 1862, Robert Bliss Papers, ADAH.

50. Robert Bliss to Mother, August 25, 1862, Robert Bliss Papers, ADAH.

51. June 8, 1862, Rebecca Vasser Journal, Duke University.

52. Rohr, ed., *Incidents of the War*, June 19, 1862, 58.

53. Rohr, ed., *Incidents of the War*, July 5, 1862, 68.

54. Rohr, ed., *Incidents of the War*, July 6, 1862, 71.

55. June 26, 1862, Joshua Burns Moore Diary, ADAH.

56. June 11, 1862, Rebecca Vasser Journal, Duke University.

57. May 20, 1862, Sarah Rousseau Espy Diary, ADAH.

58. May 6, 1862, Catherine Fennell Diary, HMCPL.

59. John Withers Clay to Clement Claiborne Clay, Jr., June 6, 1862, Clay Collection, Duke University.

60. Faust, *Mothers of Invention*, 179–180.

61. Ada Sterling, ed., *A Belle of the Fifties; Memoirs of Mrs. Clay of Alabama, Covering Social and Political Life in Washington and the South, 1853–1866. Put into Narrative Form by Ada Sterling* (New York: Da Capo Press, 1969), 183.

62. Axford, ed., Mary Fielding Diary, April 27, 1862, 41–42.

63. Axford, ed., Mary Fielding Diary, May 25, 1862, 54.

64. Frederick A. Ross, born in December 1796, was the son of a Virginia merchant. His father left Ross a large inheritance, but he squandered it in the cotton trade. In the early 1850s, Ross was appointed minister at the First Presbyterian Church in Huntsville. See *Autobiography of Rev. F. A. Ross, D.D., In Letters to a Lady of Knoxville, Tennessee* (no publication) date, 1, 9.

65. April 27, 1862, Robert S. Dilworth Journal, CAC.

66. *Cincinnati Gazette*, July 26, 1862.

67. *Cincinnati Gazette*, July 29, 1862; Rohr, ed., *Incidents of the War*, July 19, 1862, 76.

68. *Louisville Daily Journal*, July 5, 1862. A.C.S. most likely stands for *American Confederate States*.

69. *Louisville Daily Journal*, August 5, 1862.

70. Stephen D. Engle suggests that Mitchel became involved in the sale of cotton because he

had nothing better to do and faced no threat from Confederates. According to Engle, "It was unlikely that [Mitchel] would see much difficulty from the enemy—so unlikely that [he] became involved in the sale of contraband cotton" (Engle, *Most Promising of All*), 243. Also see Prokopowicz, *All for the Regiment*, 117–118.

71. Ormsby M. Mitchel to Edwin Stanton, May 8, 1862, *OR*, ser. I, vol. X/II, 174.

72. Mitchel's statement to Buell was included in a telegram Mitchel sent to Stanton in mid-July. See Ormsby M. Mitchel to Edwin Stanton, July 19, 1862, *OR*, ser. I, vol. X/II, 293.

73. *New York Evening Post*, July 1, 1862.

74. Axford, ed., Mary Fielding Diary, August 4, 1862, 76.

75. *Cincinnati Gazette*, July 7, 1862.

76. Ormsby M. Mitchel to Edwin Stanton, May 13, 1862, *OR*, ser. I, vol. X/II, 188.

77. *Louisville Daily Journal*, May 24, 1862.

78. *Southern Confederacy* (Atlanta), June 1, 1862.

79. June 3, 1862, Catherine Fennell Diary, HMCPL.

80. *Cincinnati Gazette*, July 28, 1862.

81. Axford, ed., Mary Fielding Diary, July 20, 1862, 69. Mary Chadick also recorded instances of her government destroying cotton. See Rohr, ed., *Incidents of the War*, July 9, 1862, 72.

82. *Cincinnati Gazette*, July 7, 1862.

83. June 22, 1862, Catherine Fennell Diary, HMCPL.

84. June 23–24, 1862, Catherine Fennell Diary, HMCPL.

85. August 17, 1862, Joshua Burns Moore Diary, ADAH.

86. *Cincinnati Gazette*, July 24, 1862; *Charleston Mercury*, July 25, 1862. No known record of Norton's testimony exists.

87. Ormsby M. Mitchel to Edwin Stanton, July 19, 1862, *OR*, ser. I, vol. X/II, 291.

88. *Louisville Daily Journal*, August 2, 1862.

89. General Orders 28, June 30, 1862, *OR*, ser. I, vol. XVI/I, 80.

90. Axford, ed., Mary Fielding Diary, May 5, 1862, 46.

91. Axford, ed., Mary Fielding Diary, June 10, 1862, 60.

Chapter 4. "'Twill Be Done Again All over the South"

1. Rowena Webster Memoir, HMCPL.

2. *Louisville Daily Journal*, May 22, 1862.

3. Beatty, *Citizen-Soldier*, July 18, 1862, 155.

4. The confiscation of slaves will be addressed in the following chapter.

5. Beatty, *Citizen-Soldier*, May 17, 1862, 143.

6. *Daily Morning News* (Savannah, Ga.), May 29, 1862.

7. *Daily Morning News* (Savannah, Ga.), May 28, 1862.

8. Axford, ed., Mary Fielding Diary, June 4, 1862, 59.

9. In northwestern Alabama, soldiers promised to reimburse Dr. Rand for the forty hams they had commandeered, though he likely had to take a loyalty oath before receiving a voucher (April 19, 1862, Joshua Burns Moore Diary, ADAH). On one occasion, Mitchel lessened the economic suffering of the residents of Huntsville, even if it was not his main objective. About a month into the occupation he told Bob Coltart, the mayor of Huntsville, that his men were in need of food, possibly because Union supply lines had been severed. In a show of dom-

inance over Coltart and Confederate civic authorities, the general gave the mayor an ultimatum of paying civilians for the provisions and then turning the food over to him or letting Union soldiers rummage through the cupboards and smokehouses of residents on their own. The mayor decided to shield his people from further economic harm and purchase "at city expense $500 worth of bacon, flour, [and] meat" (John Withers Clay to Clement Claiborne Clay, Jr., May 15, 1862, Clay Collection, Duke University; *Daily Morning News*, May 29, 1862).

10. *Charleston Mercury*, May 30, 1862.

11. Axford, ed., Mary Fielding Diary, July 13, 1862, 68.

12. July 31, 1862, Martin Moor Diary, IHS.

13. Liberty Warner to Friends, April 19, 1862, Liberty Warner Papers, CAC.

14. Liberty Warner to Friends, May 30, 1862, Liberty Warner Papers, CAC.

15. July 21, 1862, Robert S. Dilworth Journal, CAC.

16. Robert H. Caldwell to Father, June 1, 1862, Robert H. Caldwell Papers, CAC.

17. *Charleston Mercury*, May 24, 1862.

18. June 10, 1862, Catherine Fennell Diary, HMCPL.

19. Nimrod William Ezekiel Long to unknown person, October 4, 1862, Nimrod William Ezekiel Long Letters, Emory University.

20. George Morgan Kirkpatrick, *The Experiences of a Private Soldier of the Civil War* (Indianapolis, Ind.: The Hoosier Bookshop, 1973), 42.

21. William M. Austin Diary, September 5, 1862, Lincoln Library.

22. Henry Ackerman Smith to Wife, May 27, 1862, Henry Ackerman Smith Papers, Duke University.

23. Mary Jane McDaniel, ed., "Civil War Memories of Mrs. Josephine Thompson Bryan," *The Journal of Muscle Shoals History* 7 (1979): 69.

24. Martin Moor Diary, May 7, 1862, IHS.

25. Scott, Jr., ed., "Marshall C. Wilson's Memories of the Civil War," *Journal of Muscle Shoals History* 9 (1981): 34.

26. Some historians have argued that Confederate civilians in other occupied areas called for the end of guerrilla warfare because of Federal soldiers' retaliation against Confederate communities. See Daniel E. Sutherland, *A Savage Conflict: The Decisive Role of Guerrillas in the American Civil War* (Chapel Hill: University of North Carolina Press, 2009).

27. Rohr, ed., *Incidents of the War*, July 30, 1862, 83.

28. Beatty, *Citizen-Soldier*, May 2, 1862, 138–139; Grimsley, *Hard Hand of War*, 80.

29. Beatty, *Citizen-Soldier*, May 5, 1862, 139; Grimsley, *Hard Hand of War*, 80.

30. John Withers Clay to Clement Claiborne Clay, Jr., May 17, 1862, Clay Collection, Duke University.

31. June 10, 1862, Catherine Fennell Diary, HMCPL.

32. Rohr, ed., *Incidents of the War*, July 27, 1862, 82.

33. Frank Gurley Diary, No date, Frank Gurley Papers, HMCPL.

34. Rohr, ed., *Incidents of the War*, June 9, 1862, 51.

35. Rohr, ed., *Incidents of the War*, August 8, 1862, 88.

36. September 1, 1862, Catherine Fennell Diary, HMCPL.

37. June 24, 1862, Catherine Fennell Diary, HMCPL.

38. Rohr, ed., *Incidents of the War*, July 28, 1862, 83.

39. Rowena Webster Memoir, HMCPL.

40. George H. Thomas to Don Carlos Buell, August 7, 1862, *OR*, ser. I, vol. XVI/I, 839.

41. *Charleston Mercury*, August 29, 1862.

42. Axford, ed., Mary Fielding Diary, August 11, 1862, 78–79.

43. The Late Reverend James Monroe Mason, DD: An Account of Some of the Activities of Confederate Forces in and around Huntsville, Alabama, ADAH Pamphlet Collection.

44. Prokopowicz, *All for the Regiment*, 133.

45. *Cincinnati Gazette*, August 8, 1862.

46. *Daily Morning News* (Savannah, Ga.), May 28, 1862.

47. *Charleston Mercury*, August 16, 1862. A few weeks later, the *Mercury* claimed that Union soldiers' inhumane tactics resulted in the entire area "between Huntsville and Stevenson [being] desolated and deserted, Jackson County having been left almost entirely without inhabitants or signs of animal life. . . . Blackened ruins is all that remain" (*Charleston Mercury*, September 20, 1862).

48. *Fayetteville Observer* (N. C.) June 12, 1862.

49. *Charleston Courier, Tri-Weekly*, June 14, 1862.

50. The Eighth Brigade consisted of the Eighteenth Ohio Volunteers, Nineteenth and Twenty-Fourth Illinois Volunteers, and Thirty-Seventh Indiana Volunteers.

51. James Thomson to unknown person, April 13, 1862, "Letters from a Union Soldier," *Limestone Legacy* 1 (1989): 19. Thomson, a Union soldier from Ohio, started the letter on April 13, but it apparently took him a few weeks to finish the letter.

52. T. M. Eddy, *The Patriotism of Illinois: A Record of the Civil and Military History of the State in the War for the Union, with a History of the Campaigns in Which Illinois Soldiers Have Been Conspicuous, Sketches of Distinguished Officers, the Roll of the Illustrious Dead, Movements of the Sanitary and Christian Commissions* (Chicago: Clarke & Co., 1865), 335.

53. James Thomson to unknown person, April 13, 1862, "Letters from a Union Soldier," *Limestone Legacy* 1 (1989): 19.

54. T. M. Eddy, *The Patriotism of Illinois*, 335.

55. Axford, ed., Mary Fielding Diary, May 4, 1862, 43.

56. May 10, 1862, Robert S. Dilworth Journal, CAC.

57. Spillard F. Horrall, *History of the 42nd Indiana Volunteer Infantry* (Chicago: Donohue, Henneberry Printers, 1892), 127–128.

58. Rowena Webster Memoir, HMCPL.

59. Axford, ed., Mary Fielding Diary, May 11, 1862, 49.

60. *Newark Advocate* (Ohio), July 18, 1862.

61. Axford, ed., Mary Fielding Diary, May 4, 1862, 42.

62. May 6, 1862, Catherine Fennell Diary, HMCPL.

63. Rowena Webster Memoir, HMCPL.

64. *Newark Advocate* (Ohio), July 18, 1862.

65. Axford, ed., Mary Fielding Diary, May 27, 1862, 55.

66. *Newark Advocate* (Ohio), July 18, 1862.

67. Court-Martial of John Basil Turchin, August 6, 1862, *OR*, ser. I, vol. XVI/II, 275.

68. Axford, ed., Mary Fielding Diary, May 19, 1862, 53.

69. May 19, 1862, Martin Moor Diary, IHS.

70. Ormsby M. Mitchel to George S. Hunter and others, May 24, 1862, *OR*, ser. I, vol. X/II, 212-213; Prokopowicz, *All for the Regiment*, 122; Grimsley, *Hard Hand of War*, 81–82.

71. Ormsby M. Mitchel to Edwin Stanton, July 19, 1862, *OR*, ser. I, vol. X/II, 291.

72. When Buell arrived in Huntsville, he had 40,000 men under his command, though nearly 14,000 were "absent without permission" and the enlistment terms for thousands of others were about to expire (Engle, *Most Promising of All*), 263.

73. John Otto, *History of the 11th Indiana Battery; Connected with an Outline History of the Army of the Cumberland during the War of the Rebellion, 1861–1865* (Auburn, Ind.: 1891), 16.

74. Wisconsin officer to Wife, July 25, 1862, The Abraham Lincoln Papers at the Library of Congress, American Memory, www.loc.gov.

75. Robert H. Caldwell to Father, July 27, 1862, Robert H. Caldwell Papers, CAC.

76. At the time of his comments, Mihalotzy was on trial for his role in the Sack of Athens (*U.S. v Geza Mihalotzy*, Geza Mihalotzy Papers, Lincoln Library).

77. Mary E. Kellogg, ed., *Army Life of an Illinois Soldier: Including a Day by Day Record of Sherman's March to the Sea: Letters and Diary of the Late Charles W. Willis, Private and Sergeant 8th Illinois Infantry, Lieutenant and Battalion Adjutant 7th Illinois Cavalry, Captain, Major, and Lieutenant Colonel 103rd Illinois Infantry* (Washington D.C.: Globe Printing Company, 1906), Early August, 1862, 121.

78. Horrall, *History of the 42nd Indiana Volunteer Infantry*, 127.

79. James A. Garfield to Austin Garfield, June 25, 1862, Williams, ed., *Wild Life of the Army*, 116–117.

80. Robert H. Caldwell to Father, July 27, 1862, Robert H. Caldwell Papers, CAC.

81. Horrall, *History of the 42nd Indiana Volunteer Infantry*, 136.

82. Ormsby M. Mitchel to Edwin Stanton, May 28, 1862, *OR*, ser. I, vol. X/II, 222; Edwin Stanton to Ormsby M. Mitchel, May 28, 1862, *OR*, ser. I, vol. X/II, 222. Salmon P. Chase disagreed with Stanton and the president's decision. The secretary of the treasury communicated to Mitchel that "I wish you were in a position where your abilities and energies could be utilized more properly. You have done so much; you ought to be permitted to do more. If I could decide the question you would come here at once, and be put where you could do most." Frederick A. Mitchel, *Ormsby MacKnight Mitchel: Astronomer and General* (New York: Houghton, Mifflin, and Company, 1887), 338.

83. Edwin Stanton to Ormsby M. Mitchel, June 21,1862, *OR*, ser. I, vol. XVI/I, 44.

84. Engle, *Most Promising of All*, 264; Mitchel, *Mitchel*, 339.

85. Rohr, ed., *Incidents of the War*, July 1, 1862, 67.

86. Axford, ed., Mary Fielding Diary, July 1, 1862, 66.

87. Axford, ed., Mary Fielding Diary, July 1, 1862, 66; Rohr, ed., *Incidents of the War*, July 1, 1862, 67.

88. Mr. Bradley to Governor John Gill Shorter, July 9, 1862, John Gill Shorter Papers, ADAH.

89. August 5, 1862, Robert S. Dilworth Journal, CAC.

90. July 27, 1862, Robert S. Dilworth Journal, CAC.

91. *Cincinnati Gazette*, July 16, 1862.

92. *New York Times*, July 13, 1862.

93. *The Daily Cleveland Herald*, July 9, 1862.

94. Michael Burlingame, ed., *Lincoln's Journalist: John Hay's Anonymous Writings for the Press, 1860–1864* (Carbondale: Southern Illinois University Press, 1998), 286.

95. John Niven, ed., *The Salmon P. Chase Papers: Volume I, Journals, 1829–1872* (Kent, Ohio: Kent State University Press, 1993), 352–353. There is no known document detailing Mitchel's discussion with Lincoln.

96. Mitchel, *Mitchel*, 352–353.

97. See *Daily Cleveland Herald*, July 9, 1862; *Wisconsin State Register* (Portage, Wisc.), July 12, 1862. The *Boston Daily Advertiser* succinctly stated that "General Mitchel is shortly to be assigned an important command" (*Boston Daily Advertiser*, July 30, 1862).

98. Proceedings of the Cincinnati Astronomical Society in Commemoration of Prof. Ormsby

M. Mitchel, Late Director of the Cincinnati Observatory (Cincinnati: Bradley & Webb, Steam Printers and Stationers, 1862), 3–4.

99. *New York Times*, November 5, 1862.

100. *Daily Cleveland Herald*, November 5, 1862.

101. *The Weekly Mississippian* (Jackson, Miss.), November 19, 1862.

102. *Huntsville Confederate*, November 12, 1862.

103. Special Orders 99, July 11, 1862, *OR*, ser. I, vol. XVI/II, 127.

104. *Vermont Chronicle* (Bellow Falls, Vt.), July 15, 1862. After Rousseau assumed command, a correspondent for the *Cincinnati Gazette* commented that "all our prayers now are directed to these two ends. First that General Rousseau may continue unflinchingly to pursue the firm and manly course which he has commenced; and second, that he may not be overruled by the authority of superiors, who do not sympathize with him in his detestation of rebels and his desire for a vigorous prosecution of the war" (*Cincinnati Gazette*, July 29, 1862).

105. *Cincinnati Gazette*, July 25, 1862.

106. Beatty, *Citizen-Soldier*, July 19, 1862, 155.

107. *Cincinnati Gazette*, July 28, 1862.

108. August 15, 1862, Sarah Rousseau Espy Diary, ADAH.

109. Special Orders 90, July 2, 1862, *OR*, ser. I, vol. XVI/II, 92.

110. For a detailed analysis of Turchin's court-martial, see George C. Bradley and Richard L. Dahlen, *From Conciliation to Conquest: The Sack of Athens and the Court-Martial of Colonel John B. Turchin* (Tuscaloosa: University of Alabama Press, 2006).

111. The jury consisted of a Colonel Johns, a Colonel Sedgewick, Colonel Jacob Ammen, Colonel Curren Pope, Colonel Marc Mundy, Colonel John Beatty, and General James A. Garfield (Beatty, *Citizen-Soldier*, July 7, 1862), 151.

112. Beatty, *Citizen-Soldier*, July 21, 1862, 155.

113. General Orders 39, August 6, 1862, *OR*, ser. I, vol. XVI/II, 274. According to a male Confederate, "Turchin's brigade robbed him of twelve hundred dollars worth of silver plates" (Beatty, *Citizen-Soldier*, July 14, 1862), 152.

114. General Orders 39, August 6, 1862, *OR*, ser. I, vol. XVI/II, 273–274.

115. General Orders 39, August 6, 1862, *OR*, ser. I, vol. XVI/II, 275. When Colonel Jesse Norton testified before the Committee on the Conduct of the War, he accused his fellow soldiers of stealing "rings from ladies' fingers," as well as "cutting bacon upon parlor carpets, [and] piling meat upon pianos" (*Cincinnati Gazette*, July 24, 1862).

116. General Orders 39, August 6, 1862, *OR*, ser. I, vol. XVI/II, 274.

117. Ibid., 275.

118. General Orders 39, August 6, 1862, *OR*, ser. I, vol. XVI/II, 273–274.

119. Ibid., 274–275.

120. *Cincinnati Gazette*, July 24, 1862.

121. July 17, 1862, Robert S. Dilworth Journal, CAC.

122. *Cincinnati Gazette*, August 7, 1862.

123. Ibid.

124. James Fenton Diary, No date, Lincoln Library.

125. James A. Garfield to Harry Garfield, July 17, 1862, Williams, ed., *Wild Life of the Army*, 121; Grimsley, *Hard Hand of War*, 83.

126. James A. Garfield to Wife, July 17, 1862, Williams, ed., *Wild Life of the Army*, 123.

127. Beatty, *Citizen-Soldier*, July 14, 1862, 152.

128. Ibid., 152; Grimsley, *Hard Hand of War*, 83–84.

129. Beatty, *Citizen-Soldier*, July 14, 1862, 153.

130. Grimsley, *Hard Hand of War*, 83.

131. General Orders 39, August 6, 1862, *OR*, ser. I, vol. XVI/II, 277; Grimsley, *Hard Hand of War*, 84.

132. General Orders 39, August 6, 1862, *OR*, ser. I, vol. XVI/II, 277; Grimsley, *Hard Hand of War*, 84.

133. Don Carlos Buell to Edwin Stanton, June 29, 1862, *OR*, ser. I, vol. XVI/II, 71.

134. The *Cincinnati Gazette* reported that, "The confirmation of Col. Turchin as Brigadier-General . . . places him beyond the reach of the general court-martial which has been so busily engaged in trying him for the last week" (*Cincinnati Gazette*, July 29, 1862).

135. Grimsley, *Hard Hand of War*, 85.

136. *Daily Cleveland Herald*, June 30, 1862.

137. *Ripon Weekly Times* (Ripon, Wisc.), July 11, 1862.

138. *Cincinnati Gazette*, July 11, 1862.

139. *Cincinnati Gazette*, August 23, 1862.

140. Grimsley, *Hard Hand of War*, 63–64.

141. P. H. Watson to Ormsby M. Mitchel, May 11, 1862, *OR*, ser. I, vol. X/II, 181.

142. General Orders 7, July 10, 1862, *OR*, ser. I, vol. XVI/I, 51.

143. July 30, 1862, Robert S. Dilworth Journal, CAC.

144. Axford, ed., Mary Fielding Diary, August 4, 1862, 76.

145. *Cincinnati Gazette*, July 17, 1862.

146. Beatty, *Citizen-Soldier*, July 24, 1862, 157.

147. *Cincinnati Gazette*, August 9, 1862.

148. August 3, 1862, Joshua Burns Moore Diary, ADAH.

149. Axford, ed., Mary Fielding Diary, August 4, 1862, 76.

150. *Charleston Mercury*, September 20, 1862.

151. Andrew W. Johnson to Miss Julia, August 8, 1862, Andrew W. Johnson Papers, Lincoln Library.

152. Kellogg, ed., *Army Life of an Illinois Soldier*, Early August, 1862, 121.

Chapter 5. "We All Ready to Fall into Abraham's Bosom"

1. With so many of the men away at war, Confederate women had to take on unaccustomed tasks. However, they were hesitant to discipline unruly slaves because pre-occupation gender roles dictated that this was primarily a man's responsibility (Faust, *Mothers of Invention*), 63.

2. Rohr, ed., *Incidents of the War*, August 15, 1862, 93. Chadick's slaves included "Old" Tom, Vienna, Corinna, and Corinna's two young boys, Jim and John (Rohr, ed., *Incidents of the War*), 28.

3. Rohr, ed., *Incidents of the War*, August 17, 1862, 94.

4. Faust, *Mothers of Invention*, 77.

5. Rohr, ed., *Incidents of the War*, August 29, 1862, 101.

6. Calculations by author, 1860 census, Historical Census Browser, University of Virginia, Geospatial and Statistical Data Center: http://fisher.lib.virginia.edu/collections/stats/histcensus .html.

7. 1860 census, Historical Census Browser, University of Virginia, Geospatial and Statistical Data Center: http://fisher.lib.virginia.edu/collections/stats/histcensus/index.html. Calculations done by author. As of 1860, there were 69,234 whites, 51,789 slaves, and 368 free blacks.

8. Robert H. Caldwell to Parents, April 14, 1862, Robert H. Caldwell Papers, CAC.

9. James A. Garfield to Lucretia Garfield, June 14, 1862, Williams, ed., *Wild Life of the Army*, 114.

10. Robert G. Athearn, ed., *Soldiers in the West: The Civil War Letters of Alfred Lacey Hough* (Philadelphia: University of Pennsylvania Press, 1957), 77.

11. *Cincinnati Gazette*, April 23, 1862.

12. *Cincinnati Gazette*, April 23, 1862.

13. Rowena Webster Memoir, HMCPL.

14. "Unnamed diary of a young man, donated by Mr. John M. Doyle from Huntsville," no date, ADAH (Uncatalogued manuscript collection).

15. George P. Rawick, ed., *The American Slave: A Composite Autobiography;* volume 6, *Alabama and Indiana Narratives* (Westport, Conn.: Greenwood Publishing Company, 1941), 420.

16. James Wilson Davidson to Wife, June 14, 1862, James Wilson Davidson Papers, CAC.

17. James A. Garfield to Lucretia Garfield, June 14, 1862, Williams, ed., *Wild Life of the Army*, 114.

18. April 18, 1862, Catherine Fennell Diary, HMCPL.

19. April 25, 1862, Catherine Fennell Diary, HMCPL.

20. Hugh Lawson Clay to Clement Claiborne Clay, Jr., August 6, 1862, Clay Collection, Duke University.

21. Rohr, ed., *Incidents of the War*, June 19, 1862, 58.

22. April 26, 1862, Joshua Burns Moore Diary, ADAH.

23. April 30, 1862, Joshua Burns Moore Diary, ADAH; Ash, *When the Yankees Came*, 149.

24. Sterling, ed., *A Belle of the Fifties*, 182.

25. April 30, 1862, Joshua Burns Moore Diary, ADAH; Ash, *When the Yankees Came*, 149.

26. Chandra Manning, *What This Cruel War Was Over: Soldiers, Slavery, and the Civil War* (New York: Alfred A. Knopf, 2007), 50.

27. June 30, 1862, Joshua Burns Moore Diary, ADAH.

28. Axford, ed., Mary Fielding Diary, May 27, 1862, 55. In Tuscumbia, a female slave who feared capture disguised herself in male attire and boarded a Union train bound for Nashville to escape her owner (*Louisville Daily Journal*, July 9, 1862).

29. June 28, 1862, Catherine Fennell Diary, HMCPL.

30. July 21, 1862, Joshua Burns Moore Diary, ADAH.

31. *Jacksonville Republican* (Jackson County, Ala.), July 3, 1862.

32. Scott, Jr., ed., "Marshall C. Wilson's Memories of the Civil War," 34.

33. *Charleston Mercury*, August 16, 1862.

34. Guy Morgan to Henry Hill, June 8, 1862, Hill/Morgan Family Collection, CAC.

35. Beatty, *Citizen-Soldier*, May 10, 1862, 140.

36. *Cincinnati Gazette*, May 1, 1862.

37. August 26, 1862, William M. Austin Diary, Lincoln Library.

38. James Thomson to Folks at Home, May 23, 1862, "Letters from a Union Soldier," *Limestone Legacy* 4 (1990): 125.

39. James Thomson to the Folks at Home, May 6, 1862, "Letters from a Union Soldier," *Limestone Legacy* 3 (1989): 93–94.

40. *Cincinnati Gazette*, July 22, 1862.

41. Beatty, *Citizen-Soldier*, August 10, 1862, 171.

42. Rohr, ed., *Incidents of the War*, April 12, 1862, 34.

43. Rohr, ed., *Incidents of the War*, August 17, 1862, 94.

44. Rohr, ed., *Incidents of the War*, August 19, 1862, 94–95.

45. *Cincinnati Gazette*, June 7, 1862.

46. Beatty, *Citizen-Soldier*, April 20, 1862, 132.

47. General Orders 27, March 21, 1862, *OR*, ser. III, vol. I, 937–938.

48. Beatty, *Citizen-Soldier*, April 20, 1862, 132.

49. Ormsby M. Mitchel to Edwin Stanton, May 4, 1862, *OR*, ser. I, vol. X/II, 162–163.

50. Ormsby M. Mitchel to Edwin Stanton, May 4, 1862, *OR*, ser. I, vol. X/II, 163.

51. Edwin Stanton to Ormsby M. Mitchel, May 5, 1862, *OR*, ser. I, vol. X/II, 165.

52. Ormsby M. Mitchel to Edwin Stanton, May 5, 1862, *OR*, ser. I, vol. X/II, 166.

53. See Thomas D. Morris, *Southern Slavery and the Law, 1619–1860* (Chapel Hill: University of North Carolina Press, 1996), 229–249; Melvin Patrick Ely, *Israel on The Appomattox: A Southern Experiment In Black Freedom From The 1790s Through The Civil War* (New York: Alfred A. Knopf, 2004), 43.

54. Edwin Stanton to Ormsby M. Mitchel, May 22, 1862, *OR*, ser I, vol. X/II, 210.

55. John C. Fremont, proclamation declaring martial law and freeing all slaves owned by Confederates in the state of Missouri, August 30, 1861, *OR*, ser. I, vol. III, 467.

56. Burrus M. Carnahan, *Act of Justice: Lincoln's Emancipation Proclamation and the Law of War* (Lexington: University Press of Kentucky, 2007), 73.

57. General Orders 11, May 9, 1862, *OR*, ser. I, vol. XIV, 341; *Cincinnati Gazette*, May 17, 1862.

58. Carl Schurz to Abraham Lincoln, May 16, 1862, Frederic Bancroft, ed., *Speeches, Correspondence, and Political Papers of Carl Schurz, volume I* (New York: G. P. Putnam's Sons, 1913), 206–207.

59. Salmon P. Chase to David Hunter, May 20, 1862, Niven, ed., *Salmon P. Chase Papers, vol. III, Correspondence, 1858–March 1863.* (Kent, Ohio: Kent State University Press, 1993), 202.

60. John Hay, Lincoln's personal secretary, noted that "From the first moment that [Lincoln] heard of [Hunter's] order, his mind was determined [to] nullify the order" (Burlingame, *Lincoln's Journalist*), 163–164.

61. Edwin Stanton to Ormsby M. Mitchel, May 28, 1862, *OR*, ser. I, vol. X/II, 222.

62. *Vermont Chronicle* (Bellow Falls), August 12, 1862.

63. Ormsby M. Mitchel to Edwin Stanton, July 26, 1862, *OR*, ser. I, vol. XVI/II, 584.

64. E. D. Townsend to Don Carlos Buell, July 28, 1862, *OR*, ser. I, vol. XVI/II, 583.

65. Don Carlos Buell to Lorenzo Thomas, August 15, 1862, *OR*, ser. I, vol. XVI/II, 584.

66. W. S. Smith to James Fry, August 6, 1862, *OR*, ser. I, vol. XVI/II, 585.

67. Lovell Rousseau to James Fry, August 7, 1862, *OR*, ser. I, vol. XVI/II, 585.

68. Mitchel, *Mitchel*, 317–318.

69. Unknown Aide-de-Camp and Acting Assistant Adjuant-General to Robert L. McCook, June 21, 1862, *OR*, ser. I, vol. XVI/II, 44.

70. James Fry to Lovell Rousseau, July 28, 1862, *OR*, ser. I, vol. XVI/II, 222.

71. *Cincinnati Gazette*, July 11, 1862.

72. Don Carlos Buell to C. O. Harker, August 10, 1862, *OR*, ser. I, vol. XVI/II, 303.

73. *Cincinnati Gazette*, July 24, 1862.

74. *Cincinnati Gazette*, August 7, 1862.

75. *Cincinnati Gazette*, July 11, 1862.

76. James A. Garfield to Austin Garfield, June 25, 1862, Williams, ed., *Wild Life of the Army*, 117.

77. *Cincinnati Gazette*, July 28, 1862.

78. John Sherman to William Tecumseh Sherman, May 19, 1862, Rachel Sherman Thorn-

dike, ed., *The Sherman Letters: Correspondence between General and Senator Sherman, 1837–1891* (New York: De Capo Press, 1969), 151.

79. *Cincinnati Gazette*, July 17, 1862; Sivana R. Siddali, *From Property to Person: Slavery and the Confiscation Acts, 1861–1862* (Baton Rouge; Louisiana State University Press, 2005), 260–261.

80. Basler, ed., *Collected Works of Abraham Lincoln*, vol. V, 328–329.

81. Beatty, *Citizen-Soldier*, July 24, 1862, 157–158.

82. *Cincinnati Gazette*, July 28, 1862.

83. *Charleston Mercury*, August 11, 1862.

84. Rohr, ed., *Incidents of the War*, August 4, 1862, 86.

85. For analyses of whites' racial attitudes toward blacks, see George M. Fredrickson, *The Black Image in the White Mind: The Debate on Afro-American Character and Destiny, 1817–1914* (Hanover, Conn.: Wesleyan University Press, 1971); Winthrop Jordan, *White Over Black: American Attitudes Toward the Negro, 1550–1812* (Chapel Hill: University of North Carolina Press, 1968); Edmund S. Morgan, *American Slavery, American Freedom: The Ordeal of Colonial Virginia*, (New York: W. W. Norton & Company, 1975).

86. James Thomson to the Folks at Home, May 6, 1862, "Letters from a Union Soldier," *Limestone Legacy* 3 (1989): 94.

87. Liberty Warner to Friends, July 14, 1862, Liberty Warner Papers, CAC.

88. Kellogg, ed., *Army Life of an Illinois Soldier*, 122–123.

89. James Thomson to the Folks at Home, May 6, 1862, "Letters from a Union Soldier," *Limestone Legacy* 3 (1989): 94.

90. August 3, 1862, Robert S. Dilworth Journal, CAC.

91. *New York Evening Post*, August 26, 1862.

92. Beatty, *Citizen-Soldier*, May 23, 1862, 145.

93. Chandra Manning argues that soldiers' "hostility to slavery did not necessarily mean support for racial equality. In fact, white Union soldiers strove mightily to keep the issues of slavery and black rights separate" (Manning, *What This Cruel War Was Over*), 50.

94. Kellogg, ed., *Army Life of an Illinois Soldier*, 123.

95. Liberty Warner to Friends, July 14, 1862, Liberty Warner Papers, CAC.

96. Beatty, *Citizen-Soldier*, July 3, 1862, 149.

97. Kirkpatrick, *Experiences of a Private Solider*, 9.

98. Manning, *What This Cruel War Was Over*, 50.

99. William Nazareth Mitchell to Rachel Caroline Roberts Mitchell, August 23, 1862, Civil War Letters of William Nazareth Mitchell, W. S. Hoole Special Collections Library, University of Alabama (hereafter, Hoole Library).

100. *Cincinnati Gazette*, July 5, 1862.

101. See *Cincinnati Gazette*, July 24, 1862; General Orders 39, August 6, 1862, *OR*, ser. I, vol. XVI/I, 273–275.

102. *Cincinnati Gazette*, July 4, 1862; June 14, 1862, Robert S. Dilworth Journal, CAC. Lieutenant Dilworth wrote that he and his men "left Huntsville at 6 this morning and came as far as Athens and stopped to see 2 negroes hanged. They had been taken, tried and condemned to be hanged for committing an insult on the person of their mistress" (June 25, 1862, Robert S. Dilworth Journal, CAC).

103. April 30, 1862, Joshua Burns Moore Diary, ADAH.

104. Journal of Miss Sarah Lowe, September 7, 1862, HMCPL. Lowe further stated that the "Noble Confederates have taken the place of Yankees and everyone has unfurled the Stars and Bars" (ibid).

105. September 5, 1862, Rebecca Vasser Journal, Duke University.

106. Frank Gurley Diary, No date, Frank Gurley Papers, HMCPL.

107. September 15, 1862, Joshua Burns Moore Diary, ADAH.

108. *Charleston Mercury*, September 20, 1862.

109. September 1, 1862, Catherine Fennell Diary, HMCPL.

110. Nimrod William Ezekiel Long to unknown person, October 3, 1862, William Ezekiel Long Letters, Emory University.

111. August 24, 1862, William M. Austin Diary, Lincoln Library.

112. Kellogg, ed., *Army Life of an Illinois Soldier*, August 19, 1862, 127.

113. William Nazareth Mitchell to Rachel Caroline Roberts Mitchell, August 23, 1862, Civil War Letters of William Nazareth Mitchell, Hoole Library.

114. Don E. Fehrenbacher and Virginia Fehrenbacher, eds., *Recollected Words of Abraham Lincoln* (Palo Alto, Calif.: Stanford University Press, 1996), 469; Carnahan, *Act of Justice*, 96.

115. Horrall, *History of the 42nd Indiana Volunteer Infantry*, 133.

116. Basler, ed., *Collected Works of Lincoln*, vol. V, 433, vol. VI, 30; Carnahan, *Act of Justice*, 165–166, 171.

117. James A. Garfield to Lucretia Garfield, September 27, 1862, Williams, ed., *Wild Life of the Army*, 145.

118. Ormsby M. Mitchel to Salmon P. Chase, September 22, 1862, Niven, ed., *Salmon P. Chase Papers*, vol. III, 279; *Cincinnati Gazette*, January 3, 1863. The editor for the *Cincinnati Gazette* asserted that "the President grounds his proclamation on its necessity as a war measure. . . . War permitted the recognition of but two classes of persons—friends and enemies. We must either have the blacks as friends and allies, or as enemies and the base of supplies for the rebellion" (*Cincinnati Gazette*, January 3, 1862).

119. Historians have offered conflicting views on the extent to which soldiers supported the Emancipation Proclamation. Chandra Manning argues that "when the preliminary and final proclamation came, many soldiers regarded them less as unwelcome surprises than as evidence that a tardy government was finally catching up to what soldiers had known for more than a year" (Manning, *What This Cruel War Was Over*), 89. James McPherson states that a "large minority" of Union soldiers, especially those who were Democrats or from border states, were strongly against emancipating slaves. James M. McPherson, *For Cause and Comrades: Why Men Fought in the Civil War* (New York: Oxford University Press, 1997), 120–121.

120. James B. Fry, *Operations of the Army under Buell from June 10th to October 20th, 1862* (New York: D. Van Nostrand, 1884), 123; Engle, *Most Promising of All*, 336.

Chapter 6. "A Continual Dropping of Water Will Wear Away a Rock"

1. Catherine Fennell remarked in late October that civilians were short of "salt to cure their meat" and that "nearly all of the ladies" were wearing "homespun" due to high prices (October 26, 1862, Catherine Fennell Diary, HMCPL). An article in the *Louisville Daily Journal* stated that a "refugee from Georgia arrived at Murfreesboro yesterday, and reports terrible destitution in North Alabama" (*Louisville Daily Journal*, February 17, 1863).

2. *Daily Southern Crisis* (Jackson, Miss.), January 31, 1863.

3. D. P. Lewis to Thomas Hill Watts, February 9, 1863, *Old Lawrence Reminiscences* 8 (1994): 20.

4. Sir Arthur James Lyon Fremantle, *Three Months in the Southern States: April–June, 1863* (Edinburgh: William Blackwood & Son, 1863), 144.

5. Charles Royster, *The Destructive War: William Tecumseh Sherman, Stonewall Jackson, and the Americans* (New York: Random House, 1993), 79.

6. Grimsley, *Hard Hand of War*, 133–134, 138.

7. Grimsley, *Hard Hand of War*, 92; Storey, *Loyalty and Loss*, 112.

8. Rawick, ed., *The American Slave*, vol. six, 389; Grimsley, *Hard Hand of War*, 135–141.

9. Three slaves belonging to Basil Manly, a prominent Baptist preacher from Tuscaloosa, who presided over Jefferson Davis's inauguration, were caught attempting to reach Union soldiers rumored to be in northern Alabama and northern Mississippi (Basil Manly Diary, January 18, 1863, Manly Family Papers, Hoole Library).

10. L. Lynn Hogue, "Lieber's Military Code and Its Legacy," in Charles R. Mack and Henry H. Lesesne, eds., *Francis Lieber and the Culture of the Mind* (Columbia: University of South Carolina Press, 2005), 51.

11. Article Sixteen, "General Orders No. 100, Instructions for the Government of Armies of the United States in the Field," April 24, 1862 (The Avalon Project at Yale Law School, www.yale.edu/lawweb/avalon); Grimsley, *Hard Hand of War*, 150.

12. Article Fourteen, "General Orders No. 100," The Avalon Project; Grimsley, *Hard Hand of War*, 150.

13. Articles Fourteen, Twenty-One, and One-Hundred-Two, "General Orders No. 100," The Avalon Project; Grimsley, *Hard Hand of War*, 150.

14. Article One-Hundred-Two, Article Seventeen, "General Orders No. 100," The Avalon Project.

15. Article Twenty-Nine, "General Orders No. 100," The Avalon Project.

16. See Gregory A. Raymond, "Lieber and the International Laws of War," in Mack and Lesesner, eds., *Francis Lieber and the Culture of the Mind*; Grimsley, *Hard Hand of War*, 149, 151.

17. Abel D. Streight to William D. Whipple, December 10, 1864, *OR*, ser. I, vol. XXIII/I, 285; Rogers, Sr., et al., *Alabama: History of a Deep South State*, 210. The Army of the Ohio was renamed the Army of the Cumberland when General William Rosecrans took command in October 1862.

18. April 18, 1863, Joshua Burns Moore Diary, ADAH.

19. Thomas Hoffman Diary, late April 1863, Thomas Hoffman Diaries, State Historical Society of Iowa (hereafter cited as SHSI).

20. Thomas Hoffman Diary, April 24, 1863, Thomas Hoffman Diaries, SHSI.

21. Olivia Moore O'Neal to Edward Asbury O'Neal, April 23, 1863, Edward Asbury O'Neal Papers, SHC.

22. Olivia Moore O'Neal to Edward Asbury O'Neal, April 23, 1863, Edward Asbury O'Neal Papers, SHC.

23. Thomas Hoffman Diary, April 24, 1863, Thomas Hoffman Diaries, SHSI.

24. Abel D. Streight to William D. Whipple, December 10, 1864, *OR*, ser. I, vol. XXIII/I, 292.

25. May 3, 1863, D. Coleman Diary, SHC.

26. Zillah Haynie Brandon Diary, May 13, 1863, Zillah Haynie Brandon Diaries, ADAH.

27. Abel D. Streight to William D. Whipple, December 10, 1864, *OR*, ser. I, vol. XXIII/I, 292.

28. February 26, 1863, Joshua Burns Moore Diary, ADAH.

29. David S. Stanley to William S. Rosecrans, July 22, 1863, *OR*, ser. I, vol. XXIII/I, 825.

30. Susanna Claiborne Withers Clay to one of her sons, July 24, 1863, Clay Collection, Duke University.

31. Susanna Claiborne Withers Clay to one of her sons, August 11, 1863, Clay Collection, Duke University.

32. Rohr, ed., *Incidents of the War*, mid-July, 1863, 109–110.

33. May 9, 1863, Catherine Fennell Diary, HMCPL.

34. Kinnion S. Lee to Wife, August 5, 1863, Kinnion S. Lee Civil War Letters, ADAH.

35. Susanna Claiborne Withers Clay to Clement Claiborne Clay, Jr., September 5, 1863, Clay Collection, Duke University.

36. Royster, *Destructive War*, 181.

37. D. Lieb Ambrose, *From Shiloh to Savannah: The Seventh Illinois Infantry in the Civil War* (De Kalb: Northern Illinois University Press, 2003), April 23, 1863, 23.

38. Rohr, ed., *Incidents of the War*, mid-July, 1863, 109–110.

39. Mary Jane McDaniel, ed., "Reminiscences of Mrs. N. C. Cunningham," *Journal of Muscle Shoals History* 6 (1978): April 1863, 72.

40. Ellen Virginia Saunders, "War Time Journal of a Little Rebel," *Old Lawrence Reminiscences* 20 (March 2006): 13.

41. May 2, 1863, Joshua Burns Moore Diary, ADAH.

42. Olivia Moore O'Neal to Edward Asbury O'Neal, May 29, 1863, Edward Asbury O'Neal Papers, SHC. A correspondent for the *Louisville Daily Journal* reported "An engagement took place near Florence. The [enemy] was badly whipped. The Federals took the town of Florence, captured one hundred prisoners and eight commissioned officers" (*Louisville Daily Journal*, June 2, 1863).

43. Olivia Moore O'Neal to Edward Asbury O'Neal, June 5, 1863, Edward Asbury O'Neal Papers, SHC.

44. *Cincinnati Gazette*, September 7, 1863.

45. Susanna Claiborne Withers Clay to one of her sons, August 24, 1863, Clay Collection, Duke University.

46. July 17, 1863, Sarah Rousseau Espy Diary, ADAH. The previous month, Espy hoped "the Lord [would] strike confusion into the hearts of the our enemies" (June 3, 1863, Sarah Rousseau Espy Diary, ADAH).

47. *Cincinnati Gazette*, May 7, 1863.

48. Susanna Claiborne Withers Clay to one of her sons, July 25, 1863, Clay Collection, Duke University.

49. July 14, 1863, Catherine Fennell Diary, HMCPL.

50. Rohr, ed., *Incidents of the War*, July 1863, 108.

51. Robert Anderson McClellan to J. M. Moore, August 1863, Robert Anderson McClellan Papers, Duke University.

52. Olivia Moore O'Neal to Edward Asbury O'Neal, June 5, 1863, Edward Asbury O'Neal Papers, SHC.

53. Olivia Moore O'Neal to Edward Asbury O'Neal, June 11, 1863, Edward Asbury O'Neal Papers, SHC.

54. Rohr, ed., *Incidents of the War*, July 1863, 108.

55. September 3, 1863, Sarah Rousseau Espy Diary, ADAH.

56. May 5, 1863, Sarah Rousseau Espy Diary, ADAH. A few months later, Espy remarked she "[f]inished getting in our wheat. I helped pack it away; it is impossible to hire help now, men are so scarce" (July 9, 1863, Sarah Rousseau Espy Diary, ADAH). Near Stevenson, Eugene Marshall, a Union cavalry officer from Caledonia, Minnesota, remarked that there are "no young or middle aged men anywhere in the country . . . they are all gone to the war. . . . Old

men, children & women are all that are left" (Eugene Marshall to Sister, October 23, 1863, Eugene Marshall Papers, Duke University).

57. Olivia Moore O'Neal to Edward Asbury O'Neal, June 5, 1863, Edward Asbury O'Neal Papers, SHC.

58. McMillan, *Disintegration of a Confederate State*, 59.

59. Athearn, ed., *Civil War Letters of Alfred Lacey Hough,* Alfred Lacey Hough to Mary Hough, August 26, 1862, 132.

60. Bessie Martin, *A Rich Man's War, a Poor Man's Fight: Desertion of Alabama Troops from the Confederate Army* (Tuscaloosa: University of Alabama Press, 2003), 45. Forcing these men back into the Confederate ranks would not be a simple task. General Stephen A. Hurlbut reported to President Lincoln that "Heavy bodies of [Confederate] deserters with their arms hold the mountains of North Alabama and defy [Confederate] Conscription" (Stephen A. Hurlbut to Abraham Lincoln, August 11, 1863, Abraham Lincoln Papers, American Memory, loc.gov).

61. July 25, 1863, Sarah Rousseau Espy Dairy, ADAH.

62. July 14, 1863, Catherine Fennell Diary, HMCPL.

63. Susanna Claiborne Withers Clay to one of her sons, May [no specific date], 1863, Clay Collection, Duke University.

64. Susanna Claiborne Withers Clay to one of her sons, August 11, 1863, Clay Collection, Duke University.

65. Susanna Claiborne Withers Clay to Clement Claiborne Clay, Jr., September 5, 1863, Clay Collection, Duke University.

66. Olivia Moore O'Neal to Edward Asbury O'Neal, April 23, 1863, Edward Asbury O'Neal Papers, SHC.

67. September 12, 1863, Sarah Rousseau Espy Diary, ADAH.

68. May 1, 1863, Thomas Hoffman Diary, SHSI.

69. Susanna Claiborne Withers Clay to Clement Claiborne Clay, Jr., September 5, 1863, Clay Collection, Duke University.

70. Storey, *Loyalty and Loss*, 60–62, 82; Ash, *When the Yankees Came*, 121–124.

71. The *New Hampshire Statesmen* (Concord) asserted a "number of Unionists have been shot and hung, and their houses burned" during the winter of 1862 and early spring of 1863 (*New Hampshire Statesmen*, March 13, 1863). A Confederate woman urged General Nathan Bedford Forrest to execute a captured unionist relative to "atone for the disgrace inflicted upon a poor but honest family" (*Cincinnati Gazette*, July 16, 1863). At the same time that Confederates were decrying the Union's treatment of Confederate women, some Confederates tortured and intimidated female unionists. One northern correspondent reported "Two women . . . were torn to pieces by blood hounds" in Tuscumbia (*New Hampshire Statesmen*, March 13, 1863). Colonel Hans Christian Heg, a Wisconsin soldier, learned of a few instances in northeast Alabama where unionist "women have been hung till they were compelled to tell where their husbands were." Heg also wrote of an incident when a woman "nearly dead with consumption" told him Confederates had taken "her husband right before her eys [*sic*] and tied him with a rope, and then shot him." Theodore C. Blegen, ed., *The Civil War Letters of Colonel Hans Christian Heg* (Northfield, Minnesota: Norwegian-American Historical Association, 1936), Colonel Hans Christian Heg to Wife, September 6, 1863, 241–243; Also see Storey, *Loyalty and Loss*, 133–134.

72. *Louisville Daily Journal*, September 5, 1863.

73. September 8, 1863, Sarah Rousseau Espy Diary, ADAH; Storey, *Loyalty and Loss*, 151–154.

74. Storey, *Loyalty and Loss*, 154–159.

75. Storey, *Loyalty and Loss*, 154.

76. Grenville M. Dodge Papers: Secret Service Records Box 63, Volume 148, File 2, SHSI.

77. David S. Stanley to William S. Rosecrans, July 22, 1863, *OR*, ser. I, vol. XXIII/II, 548.

78. Storey, *Loyalty and Loss*, 135.

79. *Cincinnati Gazette*, August 14, 1863.

80. McMillan, *Disintegration of a Confederate State*, 32–33.

81. *Louisville Daily Journal*, August 29, 1863. Malcolm McMillan argues that the "rigors of civil war in [North Alabama] and Shorter's inability to drive out the enemy turned his Democratic constituency against him" (McMillan, *Disintegration of a Confederate State*), 68; George C. Rable, *The Confederate Republic: A Revolution Against Politics* (Chapel Hill: University of North Carolina Press, 1994), 220–221.

82. McPherson, *Battle Cry of Freedom*, 670–672.

83. September 25, 1863, Catherine Fennell Diary, HMCPL.

84. See Eugene Marshall to Sister, October 23, 1863, Eugene Marshall Papers, Duke University.

85. McPherson, *Battle Cry of Freedom*, 675.

86. General Orders 337, October 16, 1863, *OR*, ser. I, vol. XXX/IV, 404.

87. McPherson, *Battle Cry of Freedom*, 679.

88. Henry Clay Reynolds to Mary Jane Reynolds, September 18, 1863, H. C. Reynolds Papers, ADAH.

89. Eugene Marshall to Sister, November 15, 1863, Eugene Marshall Papers, Duke University.

90. Rohr, ed., *Incidents of the War*, late October/early November, 1863, 122.

91. Susanna Claiborne Withers Clay to Clement Claiborne Clay, Jr., September 5, 1863, Clay Collection, Duke University. Clay dated the letter September 5, but wrote of events through October 22, 1863.

92. William McDowellin to Daughter, November 12, 1863, William McDowellin Civil War Letters, ADAH; also see *Memphis Daily Appeal*, October 28, 1863.

93. Ash, *When the Yankees Came*, 151–152.

94. Rohr, ed., *Incidents of the War*, November 17, 1863, 123.

95. Rohr, ed., *Incidents of the War*, November 22, 1863, 124.

96. Rohr, ed., *Incidents of the War*, November 24, 1863, 124.

97. Rohr, ed., *Incidents of the War*, November 27, 1863, 125.

98. November 28, 1863, Sara Rousseau Espy Diary, ADAH.

99. Rohr, ed., *Incidents of the War*, November 27, 1863, 125–126.

100. November 28, 1863, Sara Rousseau Espy Diary, ADAH.

101. Foner, *Reconstruction*, 35.

102. Proclamation of Amnesty and Reconstruction, December 8, 1863, Michael P. Johnson, ed., *Abraham Lincoln, Slavery, and the Civil War: Selected Writings and Speeches* (Boston: Bedford/St. Martin's, 2001), 276–277; Foner, *Reconstruction*, 35.

103. Foner, *Reconstruction*, 36.

104. Eugene Marshall to Sister, December 21, 1863, Eugene Marshall Papers, Duke University.

105. *Cincinnati Gazette*, February 1, 1864.

106. *Daily National Intelligencer* (Washington D.C.), March 14, 1864.

107. Mark Grimsley and Todd D. Miller, eds., *Union Must Stand: The Civil War Diary of John*

Quincy Adams Campbell, Fifth Iowa Volunteer Infantry (Knoxville: University of Tennessee Press, 2000), March 12, 1864, 151; *Chicago Times*, March 12, 1864; *Ripley Bee* (Ohio), March 24, 1864.

108. Grimsley and Miller, eds., *Diary of John Quincy Adams Campbell*, March 14, 1864, 227–228.

109. *Dakotian* (Yankton, S. D.), March 29, 1864. Also see *Ripley Bee* (Ohio), March 24, 1864.

110. William Tecumseh Sherman to John Sherman, December 29, 1863, Thorndike, ed., *The Sherman Letters*, 216–219.

111. William Tecumseh Sherman to Roswell M. Sawyer, January 31, 1864, Thorndike, ed., *The Sherman Letters*, 279.

112. Ibid., 280.

113. Ibid., 280–281. A Wisconsin soldier shared Sherman's sentiments. According to John Brobst, "Wherever the army goes, they leave nothing behind. . . . the longer the rebs hold out the worse it is for them." John Brobst to Mary Englesby, April 1864, Margaret Brobst Roth, ed., *Well Mary, Civil War Letters of a Wisconsin Volunteer* (Madison: University of Wisconsin Press, 1960), 47.

114. William Tecumseh Sherman to Roswell M. Sawyer, January 31, 1864, Thorndike, ed., *The Sherman Letters*, 281.

115. Zillah Haynie Brandon Diary, May 29, 1864, Zillah Haynie Brandon Diaries, ADAH.

116. *Charleston Mercury*, April 14, 1864; *Daily South Carolinian* (Columbia), April 14, 1864.

117. February 2, 1864, D. Coleman Diary, SHC.

118. *Daily South Carolinian* (Columbia), April 14, 1864.

119. John Withers Clay to Clement Claiborne Clay, Jr., January 7, 1864, Clay Collection, Duke University.

120. John Withers Clay to Clement Claiborne Clay, Jr., January 7, 1864, Clay Collection, Duke University. Jim Hardcastle was the only man to survive the shooting.

121. December 25, 1863, Catherine Fennell Diary, HMCPL.

122. Kurt H. Hackemer, ed., *To Rescue My Native Land: The Civil War Letters of William T. Shepherd, First Illinois Light Artillery* (Knoxville: University of Tennessee Press, 2005), March 28, 1864, 302.

123. Hugh Gaston to Catharine Gaston, January 23, 1864, Hugh Gaston Civil War Letters, IHS.

124. Jenkins Lloyd Jones, *An Artilleryman's Diary* (Madison: Wisconsin History Commission, 1914), February 22, 1864, March 9, 1864, 178, 183; also see entry for January 2, 1864, 160.

125. *Cincinnati Gazette*, May 7, 1864.

126. Rohr, ed., *Incidents of the War*, February 8, 1864, 138.

127. *Cincinnati Gazette*, May 7, 1864.

128. Rohr, ed., *Incidents of the War*, April 9, April 11, 1864, 150.

129. George Hovey Cadman to Wife, March 9, 1864, George Hovey Cadman Papers, SHC.

130. Chauncey Herbert Cooke, *Soldier Boy's Letters to His Father and Mother, 1861–5* (New York: News Office, 1915), Chauncey Herbert Cooke to Parents, April 12, 1864, 62.

131. President Abraham Lincoln's Annual Message to Congress, December 8, 1863, Johnson, ed., *Abraham Lincoln, Slavery and the Civil War*, 273.

132. Ira Berlin, Steven F. Miller, Joseph P. Reidy, and Leslie S. Rowland, eds., *Freedom: A Documentary History of Emancipation, 1861–1867, series I, volume II* (New York: Cambridge University Press, 1993), 63. According to Margaret M. Storey, roughly 5,000 blacks from Alabama enlisted in the Union army during the war (Storey, *Loyalty and Loss*), 114–115.

133. *Cincinnati Gazette*, April 23, 1864.

134. Grenville M. Dodge to Lorenzo Thomas, January 19, 1864, Berlin, et al., *Freedom, ser. I, vol. II,* 424.

135. Joseph T. Glatthaar, *Forged in Battle: The Civil War Alliance of Black Soldiers and White Officers* (New York: The Free Press, 1990), 12.

136. Eugene Marshall Diary, November 11, 1863, Eugene Marshall Papers, Duke University; Glatthaar, *Forged in Battle*, 79.

137. Glatthaar, *Forged in Battle*, 36, 170.

138. Glatthaar, *Forged in Battle*, 32. Fred A. Starky, one of a handful of free North Alabama blacks before the war, was "wounded in the head" while fighting the Confederates near Bridgeport (Berlin, et al., eds., *Freedom,* ser. I, vol. II), 406. The pride some black soldiers took in their role as Union soldiers translated into high standards of military conduct from themselves and their white comrades. When a few African American soldiers stationed in North Alabama came across two inebriated white soldiers, the white soldiers were arrested for drunkenness (June 18, 1864, Diary of E. P. Burton [Des Moines, Iowa: The Historical Records Survey, 1939], 18, SHSI).

139. Eugene Marshall to Sister, December 21, 1863, Eugene Marshall Papers, Duke University.

140. Storey, *Loyalty and Loss*, 115.

141. *Chicago Times*, January 13, 1864.

142. Glatthaar, *Forged in Battle*, 61.

143. John Hope Franklin, ed., *The Diary of James T. Ayers, Civil War Recruiter* (Springfield: Illinois State Historical Society, 1947), May 1, 1864, 6.

144. *Memphis Daily Appeal*, March 14, 1864.

145. Glatthaar, *Forged in Battle*, 69–70.

146. Eugene Marshall Diary, November 7, 1863, Eugene Marshall Papers, Duke University.

147. Glatthaar, *Forged in Battle*, 70.

148. Franklin, ed., *The Diary of James T. Ayers,* April 30, 1864, 5.

149. Glatthaar, *Forged in Battle*, 2.

150. Thomas Hill Watts to M. Davenport, April 21, 1864, Governor Thomas Hill Watts Correspondence, 1863–1865, ADAH.

151. Thomas Hill Watts to I. S. Sheffield, April 25, 1864, Governor Thomas Hill Watts Correspondence, 1863–1865, ADAH.

152. Thomas Hill Watts to Joseph E. Johnston, May 25, 1864, Governor Thomas Hill Watts Correspondence, 1863–1865, ADAH.

153. June 25, 1864, Sarah Rousseau Espy Diary, ADAH.

154. Thomas Hill Watts to A. G. Henry, April 26, 1864, Governor Thomas Hill Watts Correspondence, 1863–1865, ADAH.

155. Thomas Hill Watts to A. C. Beard, A. G. Henry, A. S. Harris, Wm. McGriffin, and I. L. Sheffield, May 24, 1864, Governor Thomas Hill Watts Correspondence, 1863–1865, ADAH.

156. Thomas Hill Watts to I. S. Sheffield, April 25, 1864, Governor Thomas Hill Watts Correspondence, 1863–1865, ADAH.

157. John Brobst to Mary Englesby, April 1864, Roth, ed., *Well Mary*, 44.

158. L. J. Morgan to Sister, June 8, 1862, L. J. Morgan Letter, ADAH.

159. July 15, 1864, Sarah Rousseau Espy Diary, ADAH.

160. Alonzo A. Van Vlack to Parents, July 28, 1864, Alonzo A. Van Vlack Letters, ADAH.

Chapter 7. "Secessionists Have Had Their Run—The Race Is Over"

1. Ash, *When the Yankees Came*, 228.

2. Michael Les Benedict, *A Compromise of Principle: Congressional Republicans and Reconstruction, 1863–1869* (New York: W. W. Norton and Company, 1974), 59; Hans L. Trefousse, *The Radical Republicans: Lincoln's Vanguard for Racial Justice* (New York: Alfred A. Knoff Press, 1969), 267; Foner, *Reconstruction*, 36.

3. Trefousse, *Radical Republicans*, 287, 293. After vetoing the bill, Lincoln argued that the bill would have "set aside" the reconstruction process that had already started in Louisiana ("Proclamation Concerning Reconstruction," July 8, 1864, Basler, ed., *Collected Works, vol. VII*), 433.

4. *New York Times*, August 9, 1864.

5. At the top of their list were Salmon P. Chase, Benjamin Butler, John C. Fremont, and Ulysses S. Grant (*New York Times*, August 9, 1864).

6. Long, "Ballots over Bullets," in Holzer et al., *Lincoln and Freedom*, 145, 148, 155.

7. John Nicolay and John Hay, *Abraham Lincoln: A History, Ten Volumes* (New York: Century, 1886), vol. ix, 251.

8. *The Liberator* (Boston), December 9, 1864.

9. Manning, *What This Cruel War Was Over*, 183, 186.

10. Rohr, ed., *Incidents of the War*, September 22, 1864, 196.

11. Mickey Maroney, ed., "Civil War Journal of Octavia Wyche Otey," *Huntsville Historical Review* 1 (1991): September 23, 1864, 9; Rohr, ed., *Incidents of the War*, 196–197.

12. Rohr, ed., *Incidents of the War*, September 22, 1864, 196.

13. Maroney, ed., "Civil War Journal of Octavia Wyche Otey," September 27, 1864.

14. Octavia Wyche Otey to Miss Ella Burke, December 12, 1864, Wyche-Otey Papers, SHC.

15. Octavia Wyche Otey to Miss Ella Burke, December 12, 1864, Wyche-Otey Papers, SHC.

16. W. C. McClellan to Matilda McClellan, October [no day] 1864, Buchanan-McClellan Family Papers, SHC.

17. Royster, *Destructive War*, 321.

18. Samuel Styre to Parents, October 21, 1864, Samuel Styre Papers, Duke University.

19. Maroney, ed., "Civil War Journal of Octavia Wyche Otey," September 16, 1864, 5.

20. Axford, ed., Mary Fielding Diary, November 1, 1864, 147.

21. Henry Nurse to Father, October 13, 1864, Henry Nurse Letters, Lincoln Library.

22. William Tecumseh Sherman to Ellen Sherman, October 21, 1864, Brooks D. Simpson and Jean V. Berlin, eds., *Sherman's Civil War: Selected Correspondence of William T. Sherman, 1860–1865* (Chapel Hill: University of North Carolina Press, 1999), 744.

23. There were limits to soldiers' destructiveness. Union officer Stephen Vaughn Shipman participated in several military trials near Waterloo in Franklin County. In one trial, the jury convicted James Malone of the Sixth Kentucky Cavalry of murder. Malone did not face execution, though he was sentenced to "loss of all pay and allowances and imprisoned [for] twelve years" (March 16, 1865, S. V. Shipman Diary, ADAH).

24. October 29, 1864, Zillah Haynie Brandon Diaries, ADAH.

25. October 30, 1864, Zillah Haynie Brandon Diaries, ADAH.

26. Henry Nurse to Folks back home, October 23, 1864, Henry Nurse Letters, Lincoln Library.

27. Abiel Barker to Mr. Newell Brown, October 22, 1864, Abiel Barker Letters, Lincoln Library.

28. Henry Nurse to Folks back home, October 23, 1864, Henry Nurse Letters, Lincoln Library.

29. October 21, 1864, William Pepper Diary, Lincoln Library.

30. October 25, 1864, William Pepper Diary, Lincoln Library.

31. December 9, 1864, Zillah Haynie Brandon Diaries, ADAH. Since Sherman was nearing Savannah when Brandon wrote this, she most likely was reflecting on earlier interactions between her daughter and Sherman.

32. Aside from giving his men additional experience living off the land, Sherman was confident that the severity of confiscation at Gaylesville would make it difficult for enemy soldiers to follow their route. Sherman told Secretary of War Edwin Stanton, "We have foraged close, and Guerillas & Armies wont follow this Road. That was one object of my coming" (William Tecumseh Sherman to Edwin Stanton, October 25, 1864, Simpson and Berlin, eds., *Sherman's Civil War*), 744.

33. Rohr, ed., *Incidents of the War*, September 25, 1864, 197; *Council Bluffs Bugle*, October 6, 1864.

34. *Christian Recorder* (Philadelphia), October 8, 1864.

35. General Nathan Bedford Forrest to General R. S. Granger, September 30, 1864, Edward F. Reid Papers, IHS; Rohr, ed., *Incidents of the War*, 202.

36. Rohr, ed., *Incidents of the War*, 202.

37. Grimsley, *Hard Hand of War*, 169.

38. Foner, *Reconstruction*, 60.

39. *Daily Picayune* (New Orleans), September 27, 1864.

40. Foner, *Reconstruction*, 60.

41. Manning, *What This Cruel War Was Over*, 189.

42. Annual Message to Congress, December 6, 1864, Basler, *Collected Works of Lincoln,* vol. VIII, 149.

43. McPherson, *Battle Cry of Freedom*, 839.

44. February 4, 1865, John C. Norton Diary, Lincoln Library.

45. Manning, *What This Cruel War Was Over*, 190–191.

46. William Tecumseh Sherman to Edwin Stanton, October 25, 1864, Simpson and Berlin, eds., *Sherman's Civil War*, 740.

47. January 14, 1865, John C. Norton Diary, Lincoln Library.

48. Berlin, et al., eds., *Freedom,* ser. I, vol. II, 125.

49. Affidavit by an Alabama Black Soldier: Statement of Private Joseph Howard, January 30, 1865, Berlin, et al., eds., *Freedom,* ser. I, vol. II, 591–592.

50. *Liberator* (Boston), October 7, 1864.

51. *Council Bluffs Bugle*, October 6, 1864.

52. William Penn Lyon to Adelia Caroline Lyon, December 4, 1864, William Penn Lyon, *Reminiscences of the Civil War* (San Jose: Muirsen and Wright, 1907), 183. Some sought refuge in contraband camps created to house African Americans, but these barracks offered poor sanitation and living conditions. The contraband camp erected in Huntsville could house over 220 African Americans, while a camp near Decatur was home for nearly 2,600 (Berlin, et al., eds., *Freedom,* ser. I, vol. II, 383–384).

53. John S. McGraw to Wife, January 18, 1865, John S. McGraw Letters, Hoole Library.

54. Adolph Gaes to Sister, January 9, 1865, Adolph and Robert Gaes Papers, Lincoln Library.

55. Rohr, ed., *Incidents of the War*, January 1, 1865, 246.

56. Rohr, ed., *Incidents of the War*, January 1, 1865, 246.

57. Maroney, ed., "Civil War Journal of Octavia Wyche Otey," September 10, 1864, 3.

58. Maroney, ed., "Civil War Journal of Octavia Wyche Otey," October 4, 1864, 13.

59. Maroney, ed., "Civil War Journal of Octavia Wyche Otey," October 5, 1864, 13. North Alabama Confederates were also enduring confiscation raids from Confederate soldiers. Governor Thomas Hill Watts told Confederate General R. Taylor to stop foraging in North Alabama. If they needed provisions, Watts suggested they head to "some rich prairie [counties] in South or Central Alabama." The governor told Taylor that "The cries of the starving people are coming up to me, almost every day, from counties in that section of Ala" (Thomas Hill Watts to R. Taylor, December 9, 1864, Governor Thomas Hill Watts Correspondence, 1863–1865, ADAH).

60. Rohr, ed., *Incidents of the War*, February 12, 1865, 260. High-ranking Union officers supported Union soldiers' conduct. In Athens, William Titze noted that as his comrades dragged a hog to their camp "Gen. Dodge and Col. Fuller . . . walked directly behind us & only smiled" (March 9, 1865, William Titze Diary, Lincoln Library).

61. Axford, ed., Mary Fielding Diary, January 7, 1865, 152–153.

62. Axford, ed., Mary Fielding Diary, January 15, 1865, 154.

63. Rohr, ed., *Incidents of the War*, February 12, 1865, 260.

64. Elisha A. Peterson to Parents, February 28, 1865, Elisha A. Peterson Papers, Duke University.

65. *Cincinnati Gazette*, February 21, 1865.

66. *Cincinnati Gazette*, February 25, 1865.

67. *Louisville Daily Journal*, February 12, 1865.

68. March 31, 1865, William Titze Diary, Lincoln Library.

69. *Cincinnati Gazette*, March 29, 1865.

70. March 27, 1865, S. V. Shipman Diary, ADAH.

71. Julius C. Greene Reminiscences, ADAH.

72. Rogers, Sr., et al., *Alabama: History of a Deep South State*, 220–221; Grimsley, *Hard Hand of War*, 170.

73. Rubin, *A Shattered Nation*, 117; Faust, *Mothers of Invention*, 238.

74. Rohr, ed., *Incidents of the War*, April 4, 1865.

75. Axford, ed., Mary Fielding Diary, February 1, 1865, 155.

76. Axford, ed., Mary Fielding Diary, August 8, 1865, 159.

77. May 13, 1865, Catherine Fennell Diary, HMCPL.

78. March 20, 1865, Sarah Rousseau Espy Diary, ADAH.

79. May 6, 1865, Sarah Rousseau Espy Diary, ADAH.

80. Scott, ed., "Marshall C. Wilson's Memories of the Civil War," 36.

81. "Unnamed Diary of a Young Man, donated by Mr. John M. Doyle from Huntsville," no date, Uncatalogued Manuscript Collection, ADAH.

82. Ibid.

83. Alonzo B. Palmer Diary, April 29, 1865, Alonzo B. Palmer Collection, Hoole Library.

84. Alonzo B. Palmer Diary, May 13, 1865, Alonzo B. Palmer Collection, Hoole Library.

85. April 21, 1865, James B. Irvine Diary, ADAH.

86. Axford, ed., Mary Fielding Diary, August 8, 1865, 159.

87. April 24, 1865, Joshua Burns Moore Diary, ADAH.

88. April 22, 1865, Joshua Burns Moore Diary, ADAH.

89. Donald, *Lincoln*, 596; *New York Herald*, April 15, 1865.

90. Donald, *Lincoln*, 597–599.

91. Plummer, *My Life during the Civil War*, RBD. When Catherine Fennell and Mary Field-

ing learned of Lincoln's death, their comments were nearly devoid of emotion. Fielding succinctly wrote she had heard "that Abe Lincoln has been murdered," while Fennell stated "Old Abe Lincoln was shot by an actor by the name of Booth. . . . So Andy Johnson is president of the United States" (Axford, ed., Mary Fielding Diary, April 15, 1865, 158; May 5, 1865, Catherine Fennell Diary, HMCPL).

92. Rohr, ed., *Incidents of the War*, April 16, 1865, 288.

93. Rohr, ed., *Incidents of the War*, April 17, 1865, 289.

94. Carolyn L. Harrell, *When the Bells Tolled for Lincoln: Southern Reaction to the Assassination* (Macon, Ga.: Mercer University Press, 1997), ix. For Lincoln's views on Reconstruction immediately before his death, see Donald, *Lincoln*, 583, 591–592.

95. Andrew Johnson to Edwin Stanton, July 26, 1862, *OR*, ser. I, vol. XVI/II, 216.

96. Charles Sumner to Francis Lieber, April 17, 1865, Beverly Wilson Palmer, ed., *The Selected Letters of Charles Sumner,* volume II (Boston: Northeastern University Press, 1990), 294. The senator assumed that even though Johnson was not a Radical Republican, he would support the Radical's agenda to achieve black equality in the South and punish aristocratic whites (Trefousse, *Radical Republicans*), 311, 313.

97. Rohr, ed., *Incidents of the War*, April 15, 1865, 287.

98. April 15, 1865, April 16, 1865, James B. Irvine Diary, ADAH.

99. April 22, 1865, Joshua Burns Moore Diary, ADAH.

100. May 10, 1865, Sarah Rousseau Espy Diary, ADAH.

Epilogue: "It Is All Nonsense to Talk about Equalizing a Negro with a White Man"

1. See Michael Perman, *Reunion Without Compromise: The South and Reconstruction, 1865–1868* (New York: Cambridge University Press, 1973).

2. *Cincinnati Gazette*, May 26, 1865.

3. Ben C. Truman to Andrew Johnson, October 13, 1865, Niven, ed., *Salmon P. Chase Papers*, vol. IV, 185.

4. May 23, 1865, Joshua Burns Moore Diary, ADAH.

5. *Cincinnati Gazette*, May 27, 1865.

6. Storey, *Loyalty and Loss*, 188.

7. Testimony of General Clinton B. Fisk, January 30, 1866, *Report of the Joint Committee on Reconstruction, at the 1st Session, Thirty-Ninth Congress* (Washington: Government Printing Office, 1866), 29.

8. Testimony of D. C. Humphreys, February 7, 1866, *Report of the Joint Committee on Reconstruction*, 64.

9. Testimony of General Edward Hatch, January 25, 1866, *Report of the Joint Committee on Reconstruction*, 7.

10. *Cincinnati Gazette*, July 22, 1865.

11. Alonzo B. Palmer Diary, May 10, 1865, Alonzo B. Palmer Collection, Hoole Library.

12. *Cincinnati Gazette*, July 22, 1865.

13. May 10, 1865, Catherine Fennell Diary, HMCPL.

14. Zillah Haynie Brandon Diary, July 6, 1865, Zillah Haynie Brandon Diaries, ADAH.

15. *Cincinnati Gazette*, July 22, 1865.

16. For months after Appomattox, civilians had difficulty planting and harvesting their crops.

According to one correspondent, "Famine seems ready to follow in the footsteps of war in its desolating march over this fair land. . . . The people, already many times devastated by armies and marauding bands, have now to mourn over the poverty of their thinly planted fields" (*Cincinnati Gazette*, September 4, 1865); William Warren Rogers, Sr., *The One-Gallused Rebellion: Agrarianism in Alabama, 1865–1896* (Tuscaloosa: University of Alabama Press, 2001), 4.

17. May 17, 1865, Catherine Fennell Diary, HMCPL.

18. April 24, 1865, Joshua Burns Moore Diary, ADAH.

19. *Cincinnati Gazette*, May 30, 1865.

20. April 24, 1865, Joshua Burns Moore Diary, ADAH.

21. Testimony of D. C. Humphreys, February 7, 1866, *Report of the Joint Committee on Reconstruction*, 66.

22. Wilmer Walton to J. Miller M'Kim, May 15, 1865, *The Pennsylvania Freedmen's Bulletin*, August 1, 1865.

23. Testimony of General Clinton B. Fisk, January 30, 1866, *Report of the Joint Committee on Reconstruction*, 29. The Freedmen's Bureau achieved some success in the region by establishing black schools, but these limited accomplishments nearly always faced considerable white hostility (Foner, *Reconstruction*), 144–146.

24. General Clinton B. Fisk, January 30, 1866, *Report of the Joint Committee on Reconstruction*, 30; Testimony of D. C. Humphreys, February 7, 1866, *Report of the Joint Committee on Reconstruction*, 66.

25. William B. Holberton, *Homeward Bound: The Demobilization of the Union and Confederate Armies, 1865–1866* (Mechanicsburg, Pennsylvania: Stackpole Books, 2001), 8; Storey, *Loyalty and Loss*, 171. If Holberton's figure of eighty-percent demobilization rate is applied to Storey's figure of 35,000, there would have been roughly 7,000 Union soldiers stationed throughout Alabama by November 1865 (calculations done by author).

26. Foner, *Reconstruction*, 143, 176–182, 190.

27. Harold M. Hyman and William M. Wiecek, *Equal Justice under the Law: Constitutional Developments, 1835–1875* (New York: Harper and Row, 1982), 304.

28. *Louisville Daily Journal*, June 8, 1865; Foner, *Reconstruction*, 187. In a congratulatory letter to then Vice President–elect Johnson, Jeremiah Clemens stated that "Mr. Lincoln's proclamation emancipating the slaves is not enough to insure its eradication—to be effectively done it must be done by the people. . . . But to do this you must have *men* in the Governorship, not seekers of popularity among the Slave holders." Leroy P. Graft, ed., *The Papers of Andrew Johnson, volume 7, 1864–1865* (Knoxville: University of Tennessee Press, 1986), November 19, 1864, 303. A few months later, Clemens urged Lincoln to appoint a unionist who would "make no compromises" with former wealthy Confederate slaveholders as provisional governor (Jeremiah Clemens to Abraham Lincoln, January 21, 1865, Abraham Lincoln Papers, American Memory, www.loc.gov). Aside from Parsons, there were three other main candidates, two of which, D. W. Benham of Limestone and D. C. Humphreys of Madison, were from North Alabama (*Louisville Daily Journal*, June 22, 1865).

29. David Warren Bowen, *Andrew Johnson and the Negro* (Knoxville: University of Tennessee Press, 1989), 124; Hans L. Trefousse, *Andrew Johnson: A Biography* (New York: W. W. Norton & Company, 1989), 223.

30. June 3, 1865, Joshua Burns Moore Diary, ADAH.

31. Testimony of J. J. Giers, January 26, 1866, *Report of the Joint Committee on Reconstruction*, 15.

32. Testimony of J. J. Giers, January 26, 1866, *Report of the Joint Committee on Reconstruction*, 15.

33. Testimony of General Edward Hatch, January 25, 1866, *Report of the Joint Committee on Reconstruction*, 7.

34. Ash, *When the Yankees Came*, 231; Foner, *Reconstruction*, 188.

35. Rohr, ed., *Incidents of the War*, 308. When outraged Union officers learned Gurley had been elected sheriff, they received permission to re-arrest Gurley and again sentence him to die for killing McCook. However, he was eventually released and lived until 1920 (see Frank Gurley Diary, November 30, 1865, Frank Gurley Papers, HMCPL).

36. Storey, *Loyalty and Loss*, 175; Rogers, Sr., et al., *Alabama: History of a Deep South State*, 231.

37. June 3, 1865, Joshua Burns Moore Diary, ADAH.

38. June 3, 1865, Joshua Burns Moore Diary, ADAH.

39. Rogers, Sr., et al., *Alabama: History of a Deep South State*, 238; J. W. Shepard, ed., *The Constitution, and Ordinances, Adopted by the State Convention of Alabama, which Assembled at Montgomery, on the Twelfth Day of September, A.D. 1865, with Index, Analysis, and Table of Titles* (Montgomery: Gibson and Whitfield, 1865), 15, 20, 42, 45.

40. *Acts of the Session of 1865–6, of the General Assembly of Alabama, Held in the City of Montgomery, Commencing on the 3rd Monday in November, 1865* (Montgomery: Reid and Screws, 1866), Act 112, Approved December 15, 1865, 119. Also see Theodore Brantner Wilson, *The Black Codes of the South*, (Tuscaloosa: University of Alabama Press, 1965).

41. *Acts of the Session of 1865–6*, Act 112, Approved December 15, 1865, 119.

42. Storey, *Loyalty and Loss*, 179.

43. Testimony of Colonel Milton M. Bane, February 19, 1866, *Report of the Joint Committee on Reconstruction*, 76–77.

44. Testimony of General George E. Spencer, January 26, 1866, *Report of the Joint Committee on Reconstruction*, 10.

45. Testimony of J. J. Giers, January 26, 1866, *Report of the Joint Committee on Reconstruction*, 15.

46. Testimony of General Edward Hatch, January 25, 1866, *Report of the Joint Committee on Reconstruction*, 7.

47. Testimony of D. C. Humphreys, February 7, 1866, *Report of the Joint Committee on Reconstruction*, 65.

Bibliography

Primary Sources

Manuscript Collections

Abraham Lincoln Presidential Library, Springfield, Illinois
    William M. Austin Diary
    Abiel Barker Letters
    Charles Dahlmer Letters
    James Fenton Diary
    Adolph and Robert Gaes Letters
    Andrew W. Johnson Papers
    Geza Mihalotzy Papers
    John C. Norton Diary
    Henry Nurse Letters
    William Pepper Papers
    William Titze Diary

Alabama Department of Archives and History
    Robert Bliss Papers
    Zillah Haynie Brandon Diaries
    Edward Norphlet Brown, Sr. Letters
    James S. Clark Speech, 1861
    Sarah Rousseau Espy Diary
    Julius C. Greene Reminiscences
    John W. Inzer Recollections
    James B. Irvine Diary
    Kinnion S. Lee Civil War Letters
    Journal of Miss Sarah Lowe
    Thomas J. McClellan Letters
    William McDowellin Civil War Letters
    The Late Reverend James Monroe Mason, DD: An Account of Some of the Activities of Confederate Forces in and around Huntsville, Alabama
    Robert S. Merrill Papers
    William Henry Mitchell Papers
    Joshua Burns Moore Diary
    L. J. Morgan Letter
    H. C. Reynolds Papers

S. V. Shipman Diary
John Gill Shorter Papers
Unnamed Diary of a Young Man, donated by Mr. John M. Doyle from Huntsville
Alonzo A. Van Vlack Letters
Governor Thomas Hill Watts Correspondence, 1863–1865
S. A. M. Wood Papers

Auburn University, Ralph Brown Draughon Library
Laura Wharton Plummer, *Memoirs of Laura Wharton Plummer: A Brief Sketch of My Life during the Civil War; Written Exclusively for and Dedicated to her Children and Grandchildren* (unknown publisher, 1910)

Duke University, William R. Perkins Library
Clay Collection
Robert Anderson McClellan Papers
Eugene Marshall Papers
Elisha A. Peterson Papers
Henry Ackerman Smith Papers
Samuel Styre Papers
Rebecca Vasser Journal

Emory University, Robert W. Woodruff Library
Nimrod William Ezekiel Long Letters

Huntsville/Madison County Public Library
Catherine Fennell Diary
Clay Collection
General Orders 13a, February 26, 1862
General Orders 81, March 15, 1862
General Orders 85, March 23, 1862
Lillie Bibb Greet, "Personal Reminiscences of Civil War Times in Huntsville"
Frank Gurley Diary
Journal of Miss Sarah Lowe
Ormsby M. Mitchel, "Proclamation to the Citizens of Alabama North of the Tennessee River"
Edward F. Reid Papers
Rowena Webster Memoir

Indiana Historical Society
Hugh Gaston Civil War Letters
Martin Moor Diaries
Edward F. Reid Papers
Thomas M. Small Diary

State Historical Society of Iowa
Diary of E. P. Burton

Grenville M. Dodge Papers: Secret Service Records
Thomas Hoffman Diaries

University of Alabama, W. S. Hoole Special Collections Library
Manly Family Papers
John S. McGraw Letters
Civil War Letters of William Nazareth Mitchell, Hoole Archives
Alonzo B. Palmer Collection
Autobiography of Rev. F. A. Ross, D. D. in Letters to a Lady of Knoxville, Tennessee, (no publication date), 1, 9.

University of North Carolina, Southern Historical Collection, Chapel Hill
Buchanan-McClellan Family Papers
George Hovey Cadman Papers
D. Coleman Diary
William Cooper Diaries
Henry C. Lay Papers
Edward Asbury O'Neal Papers
Wyche-Otey Papers

Electronic Census Material
Historical Census Browser, the University of Virginia, Geospatial and Statistical Data Center: http//fisher.lib.virginia.edu.

Electronic Collections
The Avalon Project at Yale Law School: www.yale.edu/lawweb/avalon.
Abraham Lincoln Papers at the Library of Congress, American Memory: www.loc.gov.
Center for Archival Collections, Bowling Green University: www.bgsu.edu/colleges/library/cac/civilwar.html
Robert H. Caldwell Papers
James Wilson Davison Papers
Robert S. Dilworth Papers
Hill/Morgan Family Collection
Rachel Stanton/Searles Family Papers
Liberty Warner Papers

Newspapers
Agitator (Wellsboro, Penn.)
Beaver Dam Argus (Wisc.)
Boston Daily Advertiser
Charleston Courier, Tri-Weekly
Charleston Mercury
Chicago Times
Christian Recorder (Philadelphia)
Cincinnati Gazette
Columbus Daily Enquirer (Ga.)

Coshocton County Democrat (Ohio)
Council Bluffs Bugle
Daily Cleveland Herald
Daily Morning News (Savannah, Ga.)
Daily National Intelligencer (Washington, D. C.)
Daily Picayune (New Orleans)
Daily South Carolinian (Columbia)
Daily Southern Crisis (Jackson, Miss.)
Dakotian (Yankton, S. D.)
Fayetteville Observer (N. C.)
Frank Leslie's Illustrated Newspaper (New York)
Huntsville Confederate
Jacksonville Republican (Ala.)
Liberator (Boston)
Louisville Daily Journal
Memphis Daily Appeal
Milwaukee Daily Sentinel
Mobile Register
Newark Advocate (Ohio)
New Hampshire Statesman (Concord)
New York Evening Post
New York Herald
New York Times
Pennsylvania Freedmen's Bulletin (Philadelphia)
Ripley Bee (Ohio)
Ripon Weekly Times, (Ripon, Wisc.)
Semi-Weekly Mississippian (Jackson, Miss.)
Southern Confederacy (Atlanta)
Vermont Chronicle (Bellow Falls, Vt.)
Weekly Mississippian (Jackson, Miss.)
Wisconsin State Register (Portage, Wis.)

Government Documents

General Oeders No. 100, Instructions for the Government Armies of the United States in the Field. Washington, C. D.: Government Printing Office, 1863.

Report of the Joint Committee on Reconstruction, at the 1st Secession, Thirty-Ninth Congress. Washington D.C.: Government Printing Office, 1866.

War of the Rebellion: A Compilation of the Official Records of the Union and Confederate Armies, 127 volumes. Washington D.C.: Government Printing Office, 1880–1901.

Proceedings

Proceedings of the Cincinnati Astronomical Society in Commemoration of Prof. Ormsby M. Mitchel, Late Director of the Cincinnati Observatory. Cincinnati: Bradley & Webb, Steam Printers and Stationers, 1862.

Ambrose, D. Lieb. *From Shiloh to Savannah: The Seventh Illinois Infantry in the Civil War*. De Kalb, Illinois: Northern Illinois University Press, 2003.

Athearn, Robert G., ed. *Soldiers in the West: The Civil War Letters of Alfred Lacey Hough*. Philadelphia: University of Pennsylvania Press, 1957.

Axford, Faye Acton, ed. *"To Lochaber Na Mair": Southerners View the War*. Athens, Ala.: Athens Publishing Company, 1986.

Bancroft, Frederic, ed. *Speeches, Correspondence, and Political Papers of Carl Schurz*. New York: G. P. Putnam's Sons, 1913.

Basler, Roy P., ed. *The Collected Works of Abraham Lincoln*. New Brunswick: Rutgers University Press, 1953.

Beatty, John. *The Citizen-Soldier: The Memoirs of a Civil War Volunteer*. Lincoln: University of Nebraska Press, 1998.

Berlin, Ira, Steven F. Miller, Joseph P. Reidy, and Leslie S. Rowland, eds. *Freedom: A Documentary History of Emancipation, 1861–1867*, series I, volume II. New York: Cambridge University Press, 1993.

Blegen, Theodore C., ed. *The Civil War Letters of Colonel Hans Christian Heg*. Northfield, Minnesota: Norwegian-American Historical Association, 1936.

Burlingame, Michael, ed. *Lincoln's Journalist: John Hay's Anonymous Writings for the Press, 1860–1864*. Carbondale: Southern Illinois University Press, 1998.

Burnett, Edmund Cody, ed. *Letters of Three Lightfoot Brothers, 1861–1865*. Savannah, Ga.: privately published, 1942.

Cooke, Chauncey Herbert. *Soldier Boy's Letters to His Father and Mother, 1861–5*. New York: News Office, 1915.

Eddy, T. M. *The Patriotism of Illinois: A Record of the Civil and Military History of the State in the War for the Union, with a History of the Campaigns in Which Illinois Soldiers Have Been Conspicuous, Sketches of Distinguished Officers, the Roll of the Illustrious Dead, Movements of the Sanitary and Christian Commissions*. Chicago: Clarke & Co., 1865.

Fehrenbacher, Don E., and Virginia Fehrenbacher, eds. *Recollected Words of Abraham Lincoln*. Palo Alto: Stanford University Press, 1996.

Franklin, John Hope, ed. *The Diary of James T. Ayers, Civil War Recruiter*. Springfield: Illinois State Historical Society, 1947.

Fremantle, Sir Arthur James Lyon. *Three Months in the Southern States: April–June, 1863*. Edinburgh: William Blackwood & Son, 1863.

Fry, James B. *Operations of the Army under Buell from June 10th to October 20th, 1862*. New York: D. Van Nostrand, 1884.

Gaughan, Helen Bragg, ed. *Letters of a Confederate Surgeon, 1861–1865*. Camden, Ark.: The Hurley Company, 1960.

Graft, Leroy P., ed. *The Papers of Andrew Johnson, Volume 7, 1864–1865*. Knoxville: University of Tennessee Press, 1986.

Grimsley, Mark, and Todd D. Miller, eds. *Union Must Stand: The Civil War Diary of John Quincy Adams Campbell, Fifth Iowa Volunteer Infantry*. Knoxville: University of Tennessee Press, 2000.

Hackemer, Kurt H., ed. *To Rescue My Native Land: The Civil War Letters of William T. Shepherd, First Illinois Light Artillery*. Knoxville: University of Tennessee Press, 2005.

Hodgson, Joseph. *Cradle of the Confederacy, or the Times of Troup, Quitman and Yancey: A Sketch of Southwestern Political History from the Formation of the Federal Government to A.D. 1861*. Spartanburg, South Carolina: The Reprint Company, 1876.

Hogan, Brian, ed. "My Very Dear Wife: The Letters of a Union Corporal, Part I," *The Huntsville Historical Review*, 28 (summer–fall 2002): 16–67.

Horrall, Spillard F. *History of the 42nd Indiana Volunteer Infantry.* Chicago: Donohue, Henneberry Printers, 1892.

Johnson, Michael P., ed. *Abraham Lincoln, Slavery, and the Civil War: Selected Writings and Speeches.* Boston: Bedford/St. Martin's, 2001.

Jones, Jenkins Lloyd. *An Artilleryman's Diary.* Madison: Wisconsin History Commission, 1914.

Kellogg, Mary E., ed. *Army Life of an Illinois Soldier: Including a Day by Day Record of Sherman's March to the Sea: Letters and Diary of the Late Charles W. Willis, Private and Sergeant 8th Illinois Infantry, Lieutenant and Battalion Adjutant 7th Illinois Cavalry, Captain, Major, and Lieutenant Colonel 103rd Illinois Infantry.* Washington D.C.: Globe Print Company, 1906.

Kirkpatrick, George Morgan. *The Experiences of a Private Soldier of the Civil War.* Indianapolis: The Hoosier Bookshop, 1973.

Lewis, D. P., to Confederate Attorney General Thomas Hill Watts, February 9, 1863, *Old Lawrence Reminiscences* 8 (1994): 20.

Lyon, William Penn. *Reminiscences of the Civil War.* San Jose: Press of Muirsen and Wright, 1907.

Maroney, Mickey, ed. "Civil War Journal of Octavia Wyche Otey." *Huntsville Historical Review* 1 (1991): 1–30.

McDaniel, Mary Jane, ed. "Reminiscences of Mrs. N. C. Cunningham." *Journal of Muscle Shoals History* 6 (1978): 72–76.

———. "Civil War Memories of Mrs. Josephine Thompson Bryan." *The Journal of Muscle Shoals History* 7 (1979): 65–73.

Nicolay, John, and John Hay. *Abraham Lincoln: A History.* New York: Century, 1886.

Niven, John, ed. *The Salmon P. Chase Papers: Volume I, Journals, 1829–1872.* Kent, Ohio: Kent State University Press, 1993.

Otto, John. *History of the 11th Indiana Battery; Connected with an Outline History of the Army of the Cumberland during the War of the Rebellion, 1861–1865.* Auburn, Ind.: unknown publisher, 1891.

Palmer, Beverly Wilson, ed. *The Selected Letters of Charles Sumner,* volume II. Boston: Northeastern University Press, 1990.

Rawick, George P., ed. *The American Slave: A Composite Autobiography;* volume 6, *Alabama and Indiana Narratives.* Westport, Conn.: Greenwood Publishing Company, 1941.

Rohr, Nancy M, ed. *Incidents of the War: The Civil War Journal of Mary Jane Chadick.* Huntsville, Ala.: Silver Threads Publishing, 2005.

Roth, Margaret Brobst, ed. *Well Mary, Civil War Letters of a Wisconsin Volunteer.* Madison: University of Wisconsin Press, 1960.

Saunders, Ella Virginia. "War Time Journal of a Little Rebel." *Old Lawrence Reminiscences* 1 (March, 2006): 12–14.

Scott, William C., Jr., ed. "Marshall C. Wilson's Memories of the Civil War." *Journal of Muscle Shoals History* 9 (1981): 30–42.

Shepard, J. W., ed. *The Constitution, and Ordinances, Adopted by the State Convention of Alabama, which Assembled at Montgomery, on the Twelfth Day of September, A.D. 1865, with Index, Analysis, and Table of Titles.* Montgomery: Gibson and Whitfield, 1865.

Simpson, Brooks D., and Jean V. Berlin, eds. *Sherman's Civil War: Selected Correspondence of William T. Sherman, 1860–1865.* Chapel Hill: University of North Carolina Press, 1999.

Smith, William R. *The History and Debates of the Convention of the People of Alabama, Begun and Held in the City of Montgomery, on the Seventh Day of January, 1861.* Spartanburg, South Carolina: The Reprint Company, 1975.

Sterling, Ada, ed. *A Belle of the Fifties; Memoirs of Mrs. Clay of Alabama, Covering Social and Political Life in Washington and the South, 1853–1866. Put into Narrative Form by Ada Sterling.* New York: Da Capo Press, 1969.

Thomson, James. "Letters from a Union Soldier." *Limestone Legacy* 10 (1988): 20–22.

———. "Letters from a Union Soldier." *Limestone Legacy* 11 (1989): 93–94.

———. "Letters from a Union Soldier." *Limestone Legacy* 12 (1989): 19–24.

———. "Letters from a Union Soldier." *Limestone Legacy* 12 (1990): 55–58.

Thorndike, Rachel Sherman, ed. *The Sherman Letters: Correspondence Between General and Senator Sherman, 1837–1891.* New York: De Capo Press, 1969.

Watts, C. Wilder, ed. "Civil War Journal of Thomas Washington Peebles." *Journal of Muscle Shoals History* 6 (1978): 64–71.

Williams, Frederick D., ed. *The Wild Life of the Army: Civil War Letters of James A. Garfield.* East Lansing: Michigan State University Press, 1964.

Secondary Sources

Ash, Stephen V. *When the Yankees Came: Conflict and Chaos in the Occupied South, 1861–1865.* Chapel Hill: University of North Carolina Press, 1995.

Barney, William L. *The Secessionist Impulse: Alabama and Mississippi in 1860.* Tuscaloosa: University of Alabama Press, 1974.

Belz, Herman. *Abraham Lincoln, Constitutionalism, and Equal Rights in the Civil War Era.* New York: Fordham University Press, 1998.

Benedict, Michael Les. *A Compromise of Principle: Congressional Republicans and Reconstruction, 1863–1869.* New York: W. W. Norton and Company, 1974.

Bowen, David Warren. *Andrew Johnson and the Negro.* Knoxville: University of Tennessee Press, 1989.

Bradley, George C., and Richard L. Dahlen. *From Conciliation to Conquest: The Sack of Athens and the Court-Martial of Colonel John B. Turchin.* Tuscaloosa: University of Alabama Press, 2006.

Burton, Orville Vernon. *The Age of Lincoln.* New York: Hill and Wang, 2008.

Carnahan, Burrus M. *Act of Justice: Lincoln's Emancipation Proclamation and the Law of War.* Lexington: The University Press of Kentucky, 2007.

Danielson, Joseph W. "'Twill be Done Again': Union Occupation of North Alabama, April through August, 1862." (M.A. thesis: University of Alabama, 2004).

Donald, David Herbert. *Lincoln.* New York: Simon & Schuster, 1995.

Ely, Melvin Patrick. *Israel on the Appomattox: A Southern Experiment in Black Freedom from the 1790s through the Civil War.* New York: Alfred A. Knopf, 2004.

Engle, Stephen D. *Don Carlos Buell: Most Promising of All.* Chapel Hill: University of North Carolina Press, 1999.

Faust, Drew Gilpin. *The Creation of Confederate Nationalism: Ideology and Identity in the Civil War South.* Baton Rouge: Louisiana State University Press, 1988.

———. *Mothers of Invention: Women of the Slaveholding South in the American Civil War.* New York: Vintage Books, 1996.

Foner, Eric. *Reconstruction: America's Unfinished Revolution, 1863–1877*. New York: Perennial Classics, 2002.

Fredrickson, George M. *The Black Image in the White Mind: The Debate on Afro-American Character and Destiny, 1817–1914*. Hanover: Wesleyan University Press, 1971.

Gallagher, Gary W. *The Confederate War: How Popular Will, Nationalism, and Military Strategy Could not Stave off Defeat*. Cambridge, Mass.: Harvard University Press, 1997.

Glatthaar, Joseph T. *Forged in Battle: The Civil War Alliance of Black Soldiers and White Officers*. New York: The Free Press, 1990.

Grimsley, Mark. *The Hard Hand of War: Union Military Policy toward Southern Civilians, 1861–1865*. New York: Cambridge University Press, 1995.

Harrell, Carolyn L. *When the Bells Tolled for Lincoln: Southern Reaction to the Assassination*. Macon, Ga.: Mercer University Press, 1997.

Hettle, Wallace. *The Peculiar Democracy: Southern Democrats in Peace and Civil War*. Athens: University of Georgia Press, 2001.

Holberton, William B. *Homeward Bound: The Demobilization of the Union and Confederate Armies, 1865–1866*. Mechanicsburg, Penn.: Stackpole Books, 2001.

Hogue, L. Lynn. "Lieber's Military Code and Its Legacy," in Charles R. Mack and Henry H. Lesesne, eds. *Francis Lieber and the Culture of the Mind*. Columbia: University of South Carolina Press, 2005.

Holt, Michael F. *The Fate of Their Country: Politicians, Slavery Extension, and the Coming of the Civil War*. New York: Hill and Wang, 2004.

Hyman, Harold M. *Era of the Oath: Northern Loyalty Tests during the Civil War and Reconstruction*. Philadelphia: University of Pennsylvania Press, 1954.

Hyman, Harold M., and William M. Wiecek. *Equal Justice under the Law: Constitutional Developments, 1835–1875*. New York: Harper and Row, 1982.

Jordan, Winthrop. *White over Black: American Attitudes toward the Negro, 1550–1812*. Chapel Hill: University of North Carolina Press, 1968.

Mack, Charles R., and Henry H. Lesesne, eds. *Francis Lieber and the Culture of the Mind*. Columbia: University of South Carolina Press, 2005.

Manning, Chandra. *What This Cruel War Was Over: Soldiers, Slavery, and the Civil War*. New York: Alfred A. Knopf, 2007.

Martin, Bessie. *A Rich Man's War, a Poor Man's Fight: Desertion of Alabama Troops from the Confederate Army*. Tuscaloosa: University of Alabama Press, 2003.

McMillan, Malcolm. *Constitutional Development in Alabama, 1798–1901: A Study in Politics, the Negro, and Sectionalism*. Chapel Hill: University of North Carolina Press, 1955.

———. *The Disintegration of a Confederate State: Three Governors and Alabama's Wartime Home Front, 1861–1865*. Macon, Ga.: Mercer University Press, 1986.

McPherson, James M. *Battle Cry of Freedom: The Civil War Era*. New York: Oxford University Press, 1988.

———. *For Cause and Comrades: Why Men Fought in the Civil War*. New York: Oxford University Press, 1997.

Mitchel, Frederick A. *Ormsby MacKnight Mitchel: Astronomer and General*. New York: Houghton, Mifflin, and Company, 1887.

Morgan, Edmund S. *American Slavery, American Freedom: The Ordeal of Colonial Virginia*. New York: W. W. Norton & Company, 1975.

Morris, Thomas D. *Southern Slavery and the Law, 1619–1860*. Chapel Hill: University of North Carolina Press, 1996.

Morrison, Michael A. *Slavery and the American West: The Eclipse of Manifest Destiny and the Coming of the Civil War*. Chapel Hill: University of North Carolina Press, 1997.

Neely, Mark E. *The Fate of Liberty: Abraham Lincoln and Civil Liberties*. New York: Oxford University Press, 1991.

Paludan, Phillip Shaw. *The Presidency of Abraham Lincoln*. Lawrence: University Press of Kansas, 1994.

Perman, Michael. *Reunion without Compromise: The South and Reconstruction, 1865–1868*. New York: Cambridge University Press, 1973.

Prokopowicz, Gerald J. *All for the Regiment: The Army of the Ohio, 1861–1862*. Chapel Hill: University of North Carolina Press, 2001.

Rable, George C. *Civil Wars: Women and the Crisis of Southern Nationalism*. Urbana: University of Illinois Press, 1991.

———. *The Confederate Republic: A Revolution against Politics*. Chapel Hill: University of North Carolina Press, 1994.

———. *God's Almost Chosen Peoples: A Religious History of the American Civil War*. Chapel Hill: University of North Carolina Press, 2010.

Raymond, Gregory A. "Lieber and the International Laws of War," in Mack et al., *Francis Lieber and the Culture of the Mind*. Columbia: University of South Carolina Press, 2005.

Rogers, Sr., William Warren. *The One-Gallused Rebellion: Agrarianism in Alabama, 1865–1896*. Tuscaloosa: University of Alabama Press, 2001.

Rogers, Sr., William Warren, Robert David Ward, Leah Rawls Atkins, Wayne Flynt. *Alabama: The History of a Deep South State*. Tuscaloosa: University of Alabama Press, 1994.

Royster, Charles. *The Destructive War: William Tecumseh Sherman, Stonewall Jackson, and the Americans*. New York: Random House, 1993.

Rubin, Anne Sarah. *A Shattered Nation: The Rise and Fall of the Confederacy, 1861–1868*. Chapel Hill: University of North Carolina Press, 2005.

Siddali, Sivana R. *From Property to Person: Slavery and the Confiscation Acts, 1861–1862*. Baton Rouge: Louisiana State University Press, 2005.

Storey, Margaret M. *Loyalty and Loss: Alabama's Unionists in the Civil War and Reconstruction*. Baton Rouge: Louisiana State University Press, 2004.

Sutherland, Daniel E. *A Savage Conflict: The Decisive Role of Guerrillas in the American Civil War*. Chapel Hill: University of North Carolina Press, 2009.

Thornton, J. Mills. *Politics and Power in a Slave Society: Alabama, 1800–1860*. Baton Rouge: Louisiana State University Press, 1978.

Trefousse, Hans L. *Andrew Johnson: A Biography*. New York: W. W. Norton & Company, 1989.

———. *The Radical Republicans: Lincoln's Vanguard for Racial Justice*. New York: Alfred A. Knopf, 1969.

Varon, Elizabeth R. *Disunion! The Coming of the American Civil War, 1789–1859*. Chapel Hill: University of North Carolina Press, 2008.

Wilson, Theodore Brantner. *The Black Codes of the South*. Tuscaloosa: University of Alabama Press, 1965.

Index